Studies in African American History and Culture

Edited by
Graham Hodges
Colgate University

A Routledge Series

Studies in African American History and Culture

Graham Hodges, *General Editor*

The Mysterious Voodoo Queen, Marie Laveaux
A Study of Powerful Female Leadership in Nineteenth-Century New Orleans
Ina Johanna Fandrich

Race and Masculinity in Contemporary American Prison Narratives
Auli Ek

Swinging the Vernacular
Jazz and African American Modernist Literature
Michael Borshuk

Boys, Boyz, Bois
An Ethics of Black Masculinity in Film and Popular Media
Keith M. Harris

Movement Matters
American Antiapartheid Activism and the Rise of Multicultural Politics
David L. Hostetter

Slavery, Southern Culture, and Education in Little Dixie, Missouri, 1820–1860
Jeffrey C. Stone

Courting Communities
Black Female Nationalism and "Syncre-Nationalism" in the Nineteenth-Century North
Kathy L. Glass

The Selling of Civil Rights
The Student Nonviolent Coordinating Committee and the Use of Public Relations
Vanessa Murphree

Black Liberation in the Midwest
The Struggle in St. Louis, Missouri, 1964–1970
Kenneth S. Jolly

When to Stop the Cheering?
The Black Press, the Black Community, and the Integration of Professional Baseball
Brian Carroll

The Rise and Fall of the Garvey Movement in the Urban South, 1918–1942
Claudrena N. Harold

The Black Panthers in the Midwest
The Community Programs and Services of the Black Panther Party in Milwaukee, 1966–1977
Andrew Witt

Words and Songs of Bessie Smith, Billie Holiday, and Nina Simone
Sound Motion, Blues Spirit, and African Memory
Melanie E. Bratcher

Blaxploitation Films of the 1970s
Blackness and Genre
Novotny Lawrence

Womanism, Literature, and the Transformation of the Black Community, 1965–1980
Kalenda Eaton

Racial Discourse and Cosmopolitanism in Twentieth-Century African American Writing
Tania Friedel

Racial Discourse and Cosmopolitanism in Twentieth-Century African American Writing

Tania Friedel

Routledge
Taylor & Francis Group
New York London

First published 2008
by Routledge
711 Third Avenue, New York, NY 10017

Simultaneously published in the UK
by Routledge
2 Park Square, Milton Park, Abingdon, Oxfordshire OX14 4RN

Routledge is an imprint of the Taylor & Francis Group, an informa business

First issued in paperback 2012

Typeset in Sabon by IBT Global

Library of Congress Cataloging-in-Publication Data

Friedel, Tania, 1973–
Racial discourse and cosmopolitanism in twentieth-century African American writing / by Tania Friedel.
p. cm. — (Studies in African American history and culture)
Includes bibliographical references and index.
ISBN 978-0-415-96355-8
1. American literature—African American authors—History and criticism. 2. American literature—20th century—History and criticism. 3. Cosmopolitanism in literature. 4. Race in literature. 5. African Americans—Intellectual life—20th century. 6. African Americans in literature. I. Title.

PS153.N5F75 2007
810.9'355--dc22 2007036116

ISBN13: 978-0-415-96355-8 (hbk)
ISBN13: 978-0-415-54308-8 (pbk)
ISBN13: 978-0-203-93038-0 (ebk)

To my parents, whose love is the strongest encouragement.
And to Jack, who never ceases to bring me joy.

The story of the Negro in America
is the story of America—or more precisely,
it is the story of Americans.

—James Baldwin, "Many Thousands Gone"

Contents

Credit Lines

Selections from the correspondence of Jean Toomer and manuscript materials from the Jean Toomer Papers are quoted by permission of the Yale Collection of American Literature, Beinecke Rare Book and Manuscript Library, Yale University.

Selections from CANE by Jean Toomer. Copyright 1923 by Boni & Liveright, renewed 1951 by Jean Toomer. Used by permission of Liveright Publishing Corporation.

Selections from THERE IS CONFUSION by Jessie Redmon Fauset. Copyright 1924 by Boni & Liveright, Inc., renewed 1951 by Jessie Redmon Fauset. Used by permission of Liveright Publishing Corporation.

Selections from COMEDY: AMERICAN STYLE, (African-American Women Writers, 1910–1940) by Fauset, Jessie Redmon (Author). 1995. Reprinted with permission of Gale, a division of Thomson Learning: www.thomsonrights.com. Fax 800–730–2215.

Selections from THE WAYS OF WHITE FOLKS by Langston Hughes, copyright 1934 and renewed 1962 by Langston Hughes. Used by permission of Alfred A. Knopf, a division of Random House, Inc.

Selections from "Good Morning Revolution," "Negro," "Goodbye Christ," "Peace Conference in an American Town," "Evenin' Air Blues," "Merry-Go-Round," "Graduation," "Ballad of the Seven Songs," "Second Generation: New York," "The Kids in School with Me," "We're All In the Telephone Book," from THE COLLECTED POEMS OF LANGSTON HUGHES by Langston Hughes, edited by Arnold Rampersad with David Roessel, Associate Editor, copyright © 1994 by The Estate of Langston Hughes. Used by permission of Alfred A. Knopf, a division of Random House, Inc.

Selections from the correspondence of Langston Hughes are quoted by permission of Harold Ober Associates.

Selections from the correspondence of Mrs. Charlotte Osgood Mason are quoted on behalf of Prof. Edmund R. Biddle (son of Katherine Garrison Chapin Biddle).

Acknowledgments

I wish to thank Elizabeth McHenry, for her words of encouragement and criticism; without her guidance and support this book would not have come to fruition. I am also indebted to Ross Posnock who inspired this project and whose intellectual example continues to guide my work. I would like to thank George Shulman, Cyrus Patell, Megan Obourn and the other participants in the 20th Century American Literature and Political Theory seminar for their inspiring conversation and lively debate; this group's ongoing dedication to exploring the intersections of aesthetics and politics has been an indispensable source of insight and reflection. Thanks are also in order to the participants and organizers of the Critical Race Analysis and Literary Studies group and the Modern Colloquium at New York University. These diverse and rigorous intellectual circles have provided a critical space for discussion and debate, as well as a sense of intellectual community amidst what is often the solitary work of researching, writing and revising.

In addition, I wish to thank Harold Ober Associates for permission to quote from Langston Hughes' letters, the Carl Van Vechten Trust for permission to quote from Carl Van Vechten's letters, Frances E. D. Biddle (Mrs. E. R. Biddle) for permission to quote from Mrs. Charlotte Osgood Mason's letters, and the Beinecke Library of Yale University for permission to quote from the Jean Toomer Papers.

Introduction

Racial Discourse and Cosmopolitanism

This book grows out of my desire to recuperate "cosmopolitanism" as a critical term in order to identify a particular intellectual stance regarding racial discourse in the United States and to illustrate this position through several African American writers who have not only been integral figures in a larger tradition of cosmopolitan thought but have also advanced this critical mode to meet its own theoretical principals in the contested arena of racial discourse. W. E. B. Du Bois is the seminal figure for this study because he is both part of an existing tradition of cosmopolitan thought in the United States and distinct from that tradition in important ways. Du Bois's distinction stems from his subverting the idea that African American culture is marginal to mainstream America, a revaluation that precedes and influences cultural modes and critical practices that did not gain currency until the late twentieth century—such as his theorization of double consciousness and his arguing from a platform of race while arguing against essentializing race, or any identity category, for that matter. The cosmopolitanism of Du Bois influenced and inspired the writers I examine in this study—Jean Toomer, Jessie Fauset, Langston Hughes and Albert Murray—and it provides a useful model for like-minded critics and intellectuals today who struggle to find a way out of the unproductive double binds of multiculturalism and an unreflective hegemonic universalism. I argue that a careful analysis of these writers' work is appropriate for reconsideration in our time as we grapple with contemporary debates regarding multiculturalism and universalism in a rapidly, yet unevenly, globalizing world.

My central theoretical concern is to recognize the differences between ethnic groups in the racial hierarchy of the United States but also to emphasize and value, for the sake of a working democratic ideal, the interrelations, influences and blurred boundary distinctions that occur among different groups. Rather than become mired in fixed categorical distinctions between ethnic groups, a cosmopolitan position begins with and values the pluralist belief in the distinctiveness of different cultural groups, supporting and promoting their continuation and inclusion in a larger cultural sphere, yet this is not an endpoint. Cosmopolitanism moves beyond cultural pluralism by thinking, at one and the same time, about difference *and* a democratic common ground and cultural field of mutual influence and growth. Cosmopolitanism allows for the possibility of inter-ethnic subjectivities, intercultural affiliations, and change in any given mode of identification. It also recognizes democratic common ground as an imagined or theoretical space, one that requires active, willed participation for its very existence.

To this end, I will first outline how I arrived at this project before moving on to an elucidation of the elements of cosmopolitanism, its current critical usefulness, its history and its limitations. I will then engage the tradition of cosmopolitan intellectuals in the United States and their links to pragmatism and pluralism in order to set up Du Bois as the prototypical figure for what I argue is a more fully realized version of these cosmopolitan theories—one that exposes the shortcomings of some of his contemporaries and predecessors, as well as contributes to the current debates regarding multiculturalism, race and democracy in the United States and this rapidly globalizing era.[1] Finally, I will delineate the chapters of this book and the role of the writers whose literary creations provide a productive testing ground for the cosmopolitan ideals that, to paraphrase Kwame Anthony Appiah, do not require that we come to agreement but that ask us to take up the hard yet interesting work of trying to understand one another.[2]

In re-traveling the circuitous pathways of my journey to this book, I can see how the lens of cosmopolitanism became so indispensable to my literary interests, scholarly pursuits, and ideological concerns. While exploring the intersection of my interests in modernism, postmodernism, racial discourse, and the politics of representation in American culture, I began to focus specifically on twentieth-century African American literature: writing that explicitly encounters what is often hidden beneath the surface or repressed in mainstream America, what "l[ies] buried" in "the strange meaning of being black," as W. E. B. Du Bois wrote in his 1903 *The Souls of Black Folk,* while introducing his "Gentle Reader" to "the problem of the Twentieth-Century . . . the problem of the color-line."[3] Also of interest to me was the realization that this literature never fit neatly into the categories of modernism and post-modernism, but rather most intriguingly upset and called into question the very ground of those distinctions. As a result, African American literature is often doubly marginalized: both in terms of the modernist canon and in terms of ethnic and racial distinctions that create sub-groups of study in American literature. Yet my larger sense of American culture told me that African American art is nothing if not quintessentially American, often on the cutting edge of the next dominant cultural form in the ever-shifting landscape of American art. Once I began researching these ideas and encountering like-minded critics, my commitment to and excitement in this course of inquiry only further intensified. One such critic, who reveals a similar sense of dissatisfaction regarding the categorical breakdown between modern and post modern, is Mary Louise Pratt. In her essay "Modernity and Periphery: Towards a Global and Relational Analysis," she argues that what we designate as "post" is rather a "rethinking of modernity" from a much more "global and relational" perspective, one that results in a "decolonization of knowledge" and puts "an end to the center's self-interested and deluded understanding of modernity."[4]

My questioning the relationship between modernism and postmodernism is also deeply informed by Phillip Brian Harper's *Framing the Margins: The Social Logic of Postmodern Culture.* Harper configures postmodernism as "both a break from and a continuation of the modernist undertaking." While a preoccupation with and representation of the disintegration and fragmentation of modern human existence marks a line of continuity, Harper identifies a fine distinction in postmodernism's break from modernism's "aestheticist endeavors that counterbalance" the "discontinuity and disorder" of modern existence.[5] Most important for my thinking, though, are Harper's claims for what he calls the "literature of marginality," which finds itself strangely ahead of its time in its ability to foreground and highlight the psychic decenteredness that "derives specifically from the socially marginalized and politically disenfranchised status of the populations treated in the works."[6] Harper's ideas about a "literature of marginality" prompted me to think further about twentieth-century African American texts, which seem so centrally bound to grappling with the conditions of modernity yet are often relegated to the peripheries of the modernist canon.

As a brief example, I will compare the critical frameworks surrounding two contemporaneous books that illustrate this central problematic, as I encountered it: namely, W. E. B. Du Bois's *The Souls of Black Folk,* published in 1903, and Gertrude Stein's *Three Lives,* published six years later in 1909. Stein's unconventional narrative, marked most explicitly by her use of repetition with subtle variation in order to attempt to represent the way in which the mind and emotion change with barely perceptible movement, consists of three stories that explore the inner lives and relationships of three women of various ethnic descent: Anna, a "solid lower middle-class [woman of] south german stock"; Melanctha, "a graceful, pale yellow, intelligent, attractive negress"; and Lena, "simple and human, with the earth patience of the working, gentle, german woman."[7] This book is widely accepted as a modernist classic, one that, in the words of Malcolm Cowley, "marks an era in our literature," and according to the 1990 Penguin edition's introduction, it "ushered in the modern period in American prose . . . of bold experimentation with literary form and language."[8] The 1989 introduction to the Penguin edition of Du Bois's *The Souls of Black Folk,* however, makes no such claims. Its focus is on the book's political implications in the context of U. S. history and race relations and an explication of the personal life and work of its author. In striking contrast to the Stein introduction, Donald Gibson writes in his introduction to Du Bois's text, "*Souls* is not a *literary* text per se, though it has literary qualities. It is a text of some formal interest, but it would be something of a perversion to pursue its formal qualities alone."[9] While it might be perverse to pursue any text for its formal qualities alone, Du Bois's text is no less experimental and unconventional than Stein's in its mix of genres, styles and narrative forms; its slippery use of pronouns in order to subtly shift the speaker's relation to the reader and to unsettle the (implicitly white) reader's relation to the text's (explicitly black) subjects; its formal representation of and variations on double consciousness, one of the central ideas of the text; and its active re-envisioning of the "kingdom of culture" with the juxtaposition, in each chapter's epigraph, of canonical lyric poetry (with authors duly mentioned) and bars of notated music (with no identificatory marks) from the "Sorrow Songs" or Negro spirituals.

Du Bois's literary techniques are not the only indication of his modernity, however. The idea of "double consciousness," which Du Bois introduces in this text and which will become a central thematic in African American letters, places his representation of (African) American experience at the center of the interwoven discourses of modernity and debates about American identity, particularly in the discourse of critical cultural nationalism that will be a focus of this project. The apparent contradiction that is the double self of "one dark body" is nothing if not an unsettled and unsettling experience. Du Bois writes, "One ever feels his two-ness,—an American, a Negro; two souls, two thoughts, two unreconciled strivings; two warring ideals in one dark body."[10] The difficulties entailed in representing such subjective complexity (the words "vague," "uncertain," "strange" and "peculiar" reoccur throughout *The Souls of Black Folk*) resemble Stein's project for depicting the subtleties of consciousness and require a literary language of indirection. It is no coincidence, moreover, that both Stein and Du Bois studied under William James at Harvard and were deeply influenced by his idea that consciousness is not a fixed or stable entity but a process or "affair of relations."[11] My ultimate point here is that if doubleness, fragmentation, uncertainty, marginality, and hybridity define the very nature of modernity, then Du Bois is certainly no less a modernist than Stein.

It is with my interest in Du Bois, then, that I became familiar with a book that has been indispensable for the early stages of this project: Ross Posnock's *Color and Culture: Black Writers and the Making of the Modern Intellectual.*[12] Posnock's work introduced me to a conceptual tool, a critical lens and vocabulary to begin articulating some of my hunches regarding the primary literature towards which I had turned my attention. "Cosmopolitanism," the central term of *Color and Culture,* was first given expression in the West by the Greek Cynic Diogenes in the fourth century and the Cynic-influenced Stoics of the third century. It meant seeing oneself as "a citizen of the world," connected in a fundamental way to those outside family groups and conventional polities, yet without precluding the possibility of local connections. In *Perpetual Peace* (1795) Kant, along with many other Enlightenment thinkers, adopts a cosmopolitan perspective when he argues that individuals have rights as "citizens of the earth" rather than as citizens of particular states. In addition to these moral and political forms of cosmopolitanism, the focus of Posnock's study is *cultural* cosmopolitanism.[13] Reiterating the cosmopolitan position as one that "tak[es] individuals—not nations, tribes or 'peoples'—as the proper object of moral concern," Appiah explains, "Cosmopolitans take cultural difference seriously, because they take the choices individual people make seriously."[14]

Like Posnock, the form of cosmopolitanism I adopt in this project is primarily cultural yet with moral and political implications. Most importantly, I use the term to identify a mode of critical thinking that is committed to struggling with the paradoxes and contradictions of cultural identity and discourse. In particular, it helps me take into account those texts that are centrally bound to grappling with the processes of modernity but that reside at the periphery of the modernist canon because the politics of representation focus attention on racial identity and social content and away from literary technique and formal innovation.[15] For example, Du Bois sounds a modernist chord by depicting fragmentation while desiring wholeness when he claims that the American Negro wishes "to merge his double self into a better and truer self." Yet Du Bois also writes that "[i]n this merging he wishes neither of the older selves to be lost," and he repeatedly employs the language of "strivings" and "strife," complicating what might otherwise be interpreted as an unreflective desire for synthesis.[16] The paradox of double consciousness is parallel to the paradoxical merging in Du Bois's two-fold project of racial uplift and resistance to the essentializing and narrowing effects of racial identity, "for he both works within the 'Veil of black America and seeks to move beyond it to what he called 'the kingdom of culture.'"[17] By "insisting on a dialectic that preserves the interplay of universal and particular," Du Bois rethinks the burden of double consciousness and its attendant conflicts and contradictions as a potential gift, a source of great creative energy and critical insight.[18] It is the dialectical nature of Du Bois's literary and sociological project, the way in which he both "celebrates and contests racial identity,"[19] which inspires the cosmopolitan perspective I adopt in this study, and it is this particular form of cosmopolitan thought that I wish to extend in my readings and examination of Toomer, Fauset, Hughes and Murray.

Before I proceed, however, let me pause to further elucidate some key elements of cosmopolitanism, some current critics' use of it, and the ideals and potential pitfalls that thinkers in this vein strive to address so that I might better explain my particular use of it for thinking about the racial formation process in America. A cosmopolitan position implies an overarching concern for humanity that requires an acknowledgement of the important particularities of local identity claims. Grounded in cultural multiplicity and democratic principles, cosmopolitanism respects difference while asserting a common ground of equality that mediates between the particular and the universal. In "Cosmopolitanism, Universalism, and the Divided Legacies of Modernity," Amanda Anderson describes cosmopolitanism as "endors[ing] reflective distance from one's cultural affiliations, a broad understanding of other cultures and customs and a belief in universal humanity."[20] It will become more apparent, however, especially as we look at Jean Toomer's writing, that the idea of a "universal" is deeply problematic and so contested that many critics, if they would not abandon the term "cosmopolitanism" entirely, would at least agree to disagree on certain uses of it. "[C]osmopolitanism is a flexible term," explains Anderson, "whose forms of detachment and multiple affiliation can be variously articulated and variously motivated."[21] I argue that it is useful to recuperate cosmopolitanism in part because it is a term that in the history of ideas emerges particularly in times of rapid growth and "radical destabilization."[22] In my use of the term, cosmopolitanism has been and still can be integral to what I consider progressive racial discourse, or discourse that takes part in the racial formation process by rearticulating the meaning of the category of race itself in America.[23] This is because it names the central paradox with which one must necessarily struggle when considering the historical and socio-political realities of racial particulars while *at the same time* acknowledging the equally important possibility of non-essentialized being, or identity that is grounded in practice and fluid enough to incorporate new experience. In my understanding, the term "cosmopolitanism" makes this point.

A cosmopolitan perspective understands that subject positions and identities do not neatly fit into categorical distinctions. Even the most seemingly conventional identity categories bear internal conflicts. The self is informed "from here, there, and everywhere," as Jeremy Waldron describes Salman Rushdie's notion of personal identity: "Bits of cultures come into our lives from different sources, and there is no guarantee that they will all fit together. . . . [E]ach person has or can have a variety, a multiplicity of different and perhaps disparate communal allegiances."[24] "The internal politics of the self" necessarily entail conflicts and antagonisms; it is precisely this friction which defines life in a modern world full of discontinuity.[25] Acknowledging and valuing the centrality of conflict within our own selves helps us think about other identities, particularly those that have historically relegated people to subordinate subject positions, and to extend that thinking into the realm of democratic government and its attendant conflicts in a pluralistic society, as well as our relationships with people of other nations in a radically destabilized era of globalization.[26]

While we might claim that cultural pluralism is a dominant mode of discourse in the United States today, we overlook subtle tensions and ignore important debates in assuming agreement within pluralist discourse. This is especially the case when we consider what David Hollinger identifies as "an increasingly acute but rarely acknowledged tension [within the multiculturalism of our own time] between cosmopolitan and pluralist programs for the defense of cultural diversity."[27] Given that "identity politics [is] the dominant form of multiculturalism," we must examine "the grid of identity and difference (which is built into the logic of identity)."[28] The logic of identity is circular, notes Posnock, because in being unable to refuse "the paradigm of identity/difference," it risks "becoming a mirror image of what it sets out to repudiate—racialist, nativist thinking."[29] Posnock follows Walter Benn Michaels, who notes that "the commitment to pluralism requires in fact that the question of who we are continue to be understood as prior to questions about what we do."[30] Another way of putting this is that "pluralist commitment to difference" makes difference essential.[31] Although controversial on the surface, the theoretical point is well made: the identity politics/cultural pluralist strain of multiculturalism today "make[s] culture a matter of blood inheritance or ownership ('ours'), rather than something achieved, such as citizenship."[32] Cosmopolitanism, then, can be a tool for carving out a space within pluralist discourse that resists the essentializing drive of the logic of identity/difference.

In addition to resisting multiculturalism's identity politics, a cosmopolitan perspective refuses to accept liberalism's call to transcend "racial and sexual difference in the name of the universal rights of human beings."[33] Both the authenticity of particularity and the absolute transcendence of universality are denied so that difference, in the words of Michel Feher, "neither . . . define[s] an inviolable territory nor [is] reduced to a secondary particularity." While cosmopolitanism values the democratic protection of both liberalism's "individual rights" and multiculturalism's "cultural specificity," it also would insure that people "of all backgrounds . . . have the liberty to question the way in which society identifies them, and thus to invent their own relations to themselves and to other people," writes Feher.[34]

Fixed identity and cultural specificity, however, determine much of human existence, and they cannot be so easily dispensed. Indeed, those who have been in a position to seriously question and invent new relations to their cultural identities and values attest to the painfulness of such disruption. Tzvetan Todorov argues that cultural specificity is what makes us human and that our humanity is the only materially universal criteria to which we all fit. "There is no path toward the universal," Todorov reminds us, "except the path that traverses the particular, and whoever masters one specific culture has a chance of being heard throughout the world." Thus, our "attachment to a language, a landscape, a custom . . . is what makes us human," and in fact, such attachment to a specific culture "is indispensable to the full development of each individual."[35] A cosmopolitan perspective understands our common humanity as a result of our various particularities. This understanding ensures that any return to universalism—a concept that has been intensely criticized, in the words of Seyla Benhabib, for its "metaphysical props and historical conceits"—will not be a simple one. For this reason, many theorists who would recuperate "universalism" qualify the term first. Benhabib, for instance, argues for a post-Enlightenment universalism that is interactive and knowingly contingent rather than legislative and supposedly timeless, one that is "cognizant of gender difference not gender blind, contextually sensitive and not situation indifferent."[36] Although Benhabib's main concern is gender, her comments are just as relevant for discussions of race, ethnicity and color differences. She carefully qualifies the term "universalism" in order to counteract the metaphysical illusions of the Enlightenment: "the illusions of a self-transparent and self-grounding reason, the illusion of a disembedded and disembodied subject, and the illusion of having found an Archimedean standpoint, situated beyond historical and cultural contingency."[37] The importance of understanding the situatedness of any attempt towards universalism, which both Todorov and Benhabib stress in their defense of a *new* universalism, resembles the emphasis that each writer considered herein—Jean Toomer, Jessie Fauset, Langston Hughes and Albert Murray—places on the necessary contextualization of the particular when striving for universal implications.

Parallel to this dialectic between the particular and the universal and building from a conception of the self as unsettled and process-oriented is another key element of cosmopolitanism: the merging of aesthetic ways of thinking with political ways of being in the world. Such a notion of "aesthetic politics" is grounded in the pragmatist thought of William James and John Dewey, contemporaries and direct influences on Du Bois. In a discussion of Du Bois's aesthetic politics, Posnock investigates the ways in which the aesthetic and the political intersect as "experimental modes of conduct" that "thriv[e] on risk" and respect the "unclassified residuum" of experience.[38] Du Bois displays a pragmatist understanding of politics as "a mode of conduct that requires immersion in unsettled, shifting matters" as opposed to a rationalist approach to politics which refuses the contingency of experience by grounding its practice in already established truths.[39] Likewise, the aesthetic unsettles or, as Du Bois says, "The truth of Art tampers."[40] Quoting John Dewey, Posnock writes, "Rather than subordinate experience to 'something beyond itself' such as 'systematic thought,' the aesthetic is 'experience directly had.'"[41] While not explicitly linked with politics, pragmatism's refusal of absolutes and emphasis on the open-endedness of experience holds possibilities for our political lives and is ground a cosmopolitan perspective eagerly explores.

According to Hannah Arendt, the very nature of politics is grounded in opinion rather than truth, and it is in "matters of opinion, but not in matters of truth [that] our thinking is truly discursive, running, as it were, from place to place, from one part of the world to another, through all kinds of conflicting views, until it finally ascends from these particularities to impartial generality."[42] This impartiality, however, "is not the result of some higher standpoint," but as Arendt makes clear, "is obtained by taking the viewpoints of others into account."[43] Hence, the aesthetic and its exercising of the imaginative faculty can enlarge our thinking and result in a richer political life, informed by the ability to imagine and critically engage other positions than our own.[44] In fact, Arendt explains, "train[ing] one's imagination to go visiting" is what it means to adopt the position of Kant's world citizen.[45]

In the United States, the cosmopolitan practice of aesthetic politics has been associated with a creative and critical cultural nationalism, exemplified by a group of New York intellectuals, who called themselves the "Young Americans" and began publishing their ideas and views in the mid-1910s. This interethnic group (half Jewish, half WASP), which included Lewis Mumford, Waldo Frank, James Oppenheim, Van Wyck Brooks, Randolph Bourne and Paul Rosenfeld, published their writing in *The Seven Arts,* a magazine deeply invested in the relation of art and politics and the promotion of a new American cosmopolitanism. Many of the Young Americans had studied at Harvard or Columbia under the influence of American pragmatists, like William James, John Dewey, and George Santayana, and other left-leaning academics, like Josiah Royce and Joel Spingarn. These intellectual influences are the link between the cosmopolitanism of the Young Americans and that of Du Bois, who also studied at Harvard, digested the ideas of Josiah Royce and was a friend of Spingarn, the man who became chairman of the NAACP after teaching literature and literary criticism at Columbia. The most important difference between Du Bois and the Young Americans, however, and what makes them appear less related on the surface of their writings, is the fact that the Young Americans mainly framed their ideas in terms of (white) ethnic groups, while Du Bois, and other black intellectuals who followed his lead, took on the even more difficult problem of the color line and its connection to the very formations of a powerful discourse of race in America. Before moving in for a closer look at Du Bois and other black cosmopolitan intellectuals influenced by him, a brief overview of his academic mentors, philosophical influences and like-minded contemporaries is in order.[46]

Most foundational to the critical cultural nationalism and cosmopolitan stance of these early twentieth-century critics and intellectuals was the pragmatism of William James and John Dewey. America's major contribution to philosophy, pragmatism places the highest value on the open-ended, process-oriented nature of experience and the self, hence the ultimate revisability of our constructed "truths." Pragmatism shuns absolutes in its emphasis on individual experience, multiple perspectives and interpretation; however, this does not mean we are isolated and alone in our individuality. Rather, our perspectives and experiences are enlarged and enriched as we come into contact with one another, and this reciprocity can occur on the level of culture, as well as amongst individual people.

In conjunction with James's and Dewey's pragmatism is Josiah Royce's notion of "wholesome provincialism," which argues that local (or provincial) loyalties would actually deepen American cultural nationalism because they can mediate between the individual and the nation.[47] Royce, a faculty member at Harvard, taught both Du Bois and Horace Kallen. Kallen would extend Royce's teachings into the key concept of "cultural pluralism," a term he coined in 1924, in turn influencing the next generation of Harvard students, including several members of *The Seven Arts* group and the future editor of *The New Negro,* Alain Locke. Thus, we find Locke echoing Royce's ideas about "the principle of loyalty" mediating between the individual and the nation and binding various communities to one another, "which is nothing less than a vindication of the principle of unity in diversity carried out to a practical degree of spiritual reciprocity."[48] Notably, such a willingness to incorporate discussions of the human spirit or inner being with social, political, and national identity was a defining feature of the pragmatist's refusal to abide by the separation of various spheres of knowledge and ways of experiencing the world.

Although both Kallen and Du Bois build upon Royce's teaching, Kallen's cultural pluralism differs significantly from that of Du Bois. The latter focuses on the dialectical relationship between different localized communities and a common national striving and, in true pragmatist form, values that productively unsettling tension. On the other hand, Kallen, a Zionist, tends to reify ethnic identity in a way that made Dewey, for one, cringe because he thought such reification neglected "the profound and complex interrelations between different cultural groups" that were necessary in a democratic society.[49] Some critics, like George Hutchinson, name the subtle yet important differences between Kallen's and Du Bois's positions as the difference between "hard" and "soft" cultural pluralists. Instead of Kallen's reification of ethnic identity and belief in the fixity of difference, a "soft" cultural pluralist would emphasize and value, for the sake of democracy, the interrelations, influences and blurred boundary distinctions that occur among different groups. I choose to name such an emphasis on the impossibility of fixed or "hard" categorical distinctions between ethnic groups "cosmopolitanism." This makes the most sense to me because the difference is more important than simply "hard" or "soft" beliefs regarding ethnic purity. Cosmopolitan thinkers like Du Bois incorporate and value the cultural pluralist emphasis on the distinctiveness of different cultural groups. However, a cosmopolitan position demands that one take into consideration simultaneously both difference *and* the possibility of a democratic common ground and cultural field of mutual influence and growth. Such a position is more sophisticated, albeit more difficult to maintain, because it acknowledges the contradictory nature of inter-ethnic subjectivities and intercultural affiliations, the possibility of change in any given mode of identification, and the coexistence of conflictual elements in any one self.

Like Du Bois, Randolph Bourne, one of the key figures of *The Seven Arts* group, was inspired by Kallen's cultural pluralism yet differed from his ideas in ways that more closely align him with cosmopolitanism. In *Our America,* Waldo Frank celebrates Bourne, a cripple and a hunchback, who died in 1918 at the age of thirty-two in the flu epidemic. Frank writes of Bourne's aesthetic politics: "More than any of our fellows, he pointed the path of fusion which American leadership must take. His political discussions were actually lit by a spiritual viewpoint."[50] While a student of Dewey at Columbia, Bourne also studied Royce's work and borrowed his phrase "Beloved Community" to express his ideal for an American democratic society that is both rationally shaped and loving, a community informed by the traditional bonds of ethnic communities. Moreover, Bourne's concept of "trans-nationalism," which "urge[s] us to an investigation of what Americanism may rightly mean," was inspired by Kallen's ideas in its "assert[ion of] a higher ideal than the 'melting-pot,'" but he also importantly diverges from Kallen's pluralism.[51] Bourne's "federated ideal" includes an America made up of the people of many nations, "inextricably mingled, yet not homogeneous," "merged[d] but . . . not fuse[d]."[52] "Colonialism has grown into cosmopolitanism," which, for Bourne, means that America can no longer be defined and dominated by Anglo-Saxons but by "all who have anything life-enhancing to offer to the spirit [of the nation]."[53] Consider the slight but important difference between these statements by Bourne and Kallen's similar claims: "What do Americans *will* to make of the United States—a unison, singing the old British theme 'America,' the America of the New England School? Or a harmony, in which that theme shall be dominant, perhaps, among others, but one among many, not the only one?"[54] The parts, while harmonious, maintain "the distinctive individuality of each nation" in Kallen's version, rather than change their very substance and form in the influences and appropriations of cultural exchange.[55] Bourne's cosmopolitanism, on the other hand, requires a dialectical mode of thought that resides somewhere between fusion and separation: a merging that is much more interesting, complex and difficult to name than fusion because it retains the tension between differences and remains unsettled.

Bourne's aesthetic politics were also influenced by Columbia literature professor, Joel Spingarn, who espoused an Emersonian ideal of scholarship as creative activity, claiming, in true cosmopolitan spirit, that American criticism which followed this ideal "will give us at one and the same time a wider international outlook and a deeper national insight." Spingarn continues, "One will spring from the other, for the timid Colonial spirit finds no place in the heart of the citizen of the world; and respect for native talent, born of a surer knowledge, will prevent us alike from overrating its merits and from holding it too cheap."[56] Spingarn, who would become chairman of the NAACP in 1914, was a friend of Du Bois,

Van Wyck Brooks and Lewis Mumford and became closely involved with *The Seven Arts* in the late 1910s. He was a vocal opponent of the cultural elitism of New Humanists, like Irving Babbitt, and their adherence to the Anglo-Saxon domination and Victorian ethos of Matthew Arnold's "Cult of the Best." Rather than an intellectual realm sequestered away from public life and practice, Spingarn's creative scholarship is an active force, capable of unsettling accepted truths and transgressing boundaries. This creative activity follows Emerson's idea of "The American Scholar" as "*Man Thinking,*" not "the victim of society . . . a mere thinker, or still worse, the parrot of other men's thinking."[57] Randolph Bourne puts it another way when he states that the intellectual's "task will be to divide, confuse, disturb, keep the intellectual waters constantly in motion to prevent any such ice [as a result of blind conformity] from ever forming."[58] Van Wyck Brooks, in an essay entitled "The Critics and Young America," which was originally published in 1917 in *The Seven Arts,* concurs when he recognizes Whitman as "the representative poet of America" because he "release[s] the creative faculties of the American mind" and "turn[s] democracy from a fact into a spiritual principle."[59] The cultural nationalism of the Young Americans, following in the tradition of Emerson and Whitman, is both critical and creative, joining the political and the cultural in a "spiritual democracy" and calling for a vital new American culture made from a "national fabric of spiritual experience."[60]

Tracing this particular strain of American cultural nationalism takes us through Walt Whitman's poetics and an Emersonian tradition in American art and letters to philosophical pragmatism and its version of aesthetic politics in the ongoing pursuit of democracy, to the creative intellectual work of the Young Americans. W. E. B. Du Bois and other black intellectuals associated with the New Negro movement, like Jessie Fauset, Alain Locke and Jean Toomer, who studied the same books with the same professors often in the same classrooms, fit firmly within this tradition; however, as George Hutchinson's brilliant study, *The Harlem Renaissance in Black and White,* laments, this is too often overlooked or ignored. In keeping with Hutchinson's call that literary scholars discover and give shape to the cultural and intellectual connections between black and white Americans in the early twentieth century, I want to emphasize that this battle for a new definition of American culture was an interracial endeavor of like-minded people. This book focuses on African American writers, however, because there is often a gap in the thinking of the white intellectuals I outlined above regarding the centrality of race in America. While many address ethnicity in their debates about pluralism, nativism, universalism and nationalism, there is often a strange silence regarding racial difference and the color line.

Du Bois's work fills out these discussions, and for this reason, it is more theoretically savvy and politically complex; one might even say it is ahead of its time. In a sense, then, many intellectuals have not lived up to their cosmopolitan theories or have stopped short of fully exploring a cosmopolitan perspective. While these shortcomings might be used as arguments against cosmopolitanism, it would be more accurate to say that these problems stem from too little, rather than too much, cosmopolitanism. In this context, Du Bois's cosmopolitan arguments and his theorization of double consciousness become all the more important in their laying the groundwork for a tradition of intellectual thought, which many African American writers have engaged and extended. Their work illuminates a position that mainstream American culture has indeed moved closer to but has yet to entirely embrace. I hope to illustrate and highlight this particular strain of African American cosmopolitanism as a living legacy for cosmopolitan thinkers today.[61]

For the most part, the primary literature I examine falls into two broad generic categories: the essay and prose fiction (both the novel and short story forms). The predominance of the essay form in cosmopolitan intellectual traditions is both culturally and politically significant. Moreover, I have purposefully chosen writers who utilize prose fiction to enact, illustrate and contextualize their cosmopolitan theories in a complementary way with their essayistic writing. When we consider its mixed-genre form, Du Bois's *The Souls of Black Folk* appears as a particularly seminal text in the cosmopolitan tradition. On the surface, it is simply a collection of essays, yet it incorporates fiction in "Of the Coming of John" and narrative technique in "Of the Passing of the First-Born" and "Of Alexander Crummell"; it is deeply personal yet at the same time broadly historical and sociological; it is both political and spiritual, rationally grounded in the principles of democracy yet based on a faith in Christian teachings.

The essay form was also the favored genre of the Young Americans, and as Ellery Sedgwick, editor of the *Atlantic*, noted, regarding Randolph Bourne's employment of the essay style, it combined "a philosophical breadth of view with a deep note of personal conviction."[62] That the essay form lends itself so well to a blending of the particular and the general is in keeping with Du Bois's and Bourne's aesthetic politics, their "seeking in each work to 'supply interpretation of things larger' than the work itself, illuminating in the process 'the course of individual lives and the great tides of society.'"[63] In "The Essay as Form," Adorno explains this interesting mixture of the universal and the particular as essential to the essay itself: "the essay has to cause the totality to be illuminated in a partial feature. . . .

It corrects what is contingent and isolated in its insights in that they multiply, confirm, and qualify themselves, whether in the further course of the essay itself or in a mosaiclike relationship to other essays."[64] Thus, the essay is provisional and experimental: "It thinks in fragments, just as reality is fragmentary, and finds its unity in and through the breaks and not by glossing them over."[65] Adorno adds, "Discontinuity is essential to the essay; its subject matter is always a conflict brought to a standstill."[66] Hence, it is particularly appropriate for a cosmopolitan project of thinking contradictory positions at one at the same time, of mediating between the universal and the particular, and of unsettling totalizing and abstract truths. Adorno writes of the essay's ability to resist identity, or the fixing of essential characteristics, and its valuing of contingency and the unclassifiable. "The essay," he states, "does not try to seek the eternal in the transient and distill it out; it tries to render the transient eternal. Its weakness bears witness to the very nonidentity it had to express."[67] The essay's weakness, the fact that it "remains vulnerable to error," that "it has to pay for its affinity with open intellectual experience with a lack of security that the norm of established thought fears like death," is also its strength.[68] In attempting, or essaying, to think through the contradictions and paradoxes of race in American society, the cosmopolitan intellectual finds the essay form particularly congenial to uniting "thought's utopian vision of hitting the bullseye" with "the consciousness of its own fallibility and provisional character." Such a project does not take place "systematically but rather as a characteristic of an intention groping its way."[69] Moreover, as we note in the most powerfully poetic and intellectually dense passages in Du Bois's writing, "emancipation from the compulsion of identity gives the essay something that eludes official thought—a moment of something inextinguishable, of indelible color."[70]

The writers I examine—Jean Toomer, Jessie Fauset, Langston Hughes, and Albert Murray—not only make extensive use of the essay form but, like Du Bois, also find prose fiction a productive testing ground for their cosmopolitan theorizing. As Barbara Christian suggests in "The Race for Theory" (1987), many African American intellectuals recognize that "literature is, of necessity, political" and that its particular kind of political engagement promotes "dynamic rather than fixed ideas" because "in having to embody ideas and recreate the world, writers cannot merely produce 'one way.'"[71] In other words, Christian attests, creative literature "seemed to me to have the possibilities of rendering the world as large and as complicated as I experienced it, as sensual as I knew it was. In literature I sensed the possibility of the integration of feeling/knowledge, rather than the split between the abstract and emotional in which

Western philosophy inevitably indulged."[72] Literary narrative, then, can become "a place where theory takes place," as Judith Butler phrases it, through a dynamic and sensual play with language, which enables a kind of complexity that is often undermined in the abstract and fixed language of theory.[73] My analysis of the prose fiction of the four writers presented here attempts to answer a call like Seyla Benhabib's in *Situating the Self* to "move beyond the metaphysical assumptions of Enlightenment universalism" by addressing "the narrative structure of action and personal identity."[74] Similarly, Shamoon Zamir regards Du Bois's ability to "[resist] essentializing both epistemology and self-consciousness" as the result of his struggle "to describe the shape of a life's imaginative investigations of its own context." Zamir adds, "Only such description can be simultaneously open to the unique and the universal, which together constitute the imaginative life."[75] It is the interplay of particular and universal in the imaginative lives of Toomer, Fauset, Hughes and Murray that we find illuminated in their personal essays and political fiction, and it is my concern to access their critical cosmopolitanism through a careful unpacking of this literature.[76]

Chapter One situates Jean Toomer's mixed-genre *Cane* amongst his early essays, which celebrate miscegenation as a wellspring of possibility in his life and as a tool for opening up racial discourse in the United States. The representation of miscegenation in *Cane*, however, is far more problematic and complex in the deep anxieties it reveals, anxieties that are inseparable from its potential in Toomer's other life writing. *Cane* embodies this tension and, in so doing, becomes a testing ground for Toomer's cosmopolitanism, a critical stance that both celebrates black cultural distinctiveness and at the same time refuses fixed racial boundaries and essentialized racial identities. The fact that the success of this work became the very catalyst for publicly fixing Toomer's own racial identity is one of the great ironies of his literary career and one from which he would never fully recover. As a result, his later writing suffers from a potential pitfall of a cosmopolitan position, an impossibly abstract universalism. In order to avoid this pitfall, cosmopolitan thinkers must maintain a difficult balance between the interrelated tensions of the particular identity categories we inhabit as part of our lived experience and the limits of those categorical distinctions in accounting for the unclassifiable residuum of our lives. Toomer, however, in failing to maintain this dialectic, falls into a dangerously untethered universalism that is too abstract and cosmically transcendent to do any real work in unsettling the very discursive and social structures he sought to affect.

Chapter Two takes a close look at the cosmopolitan strategies Jessie Redmon Fauset employs in her novels to maintain a difficult balance between the virtues of racial identification and its costs, as well as the values of individualization and its pitfalls. I argue that applying a cosmopolitan framework to Fauset's critical engagement with the complex intersections of race, gender, class and nationalism enables a close examination of what is too often ignored or misunderstood in critical readings of her texts, namely the productive tension between the private, the domestic, and personal desire—typically aligned with sentimental, middle-brow or women's literature and the protocols of public racial identification more often aligned with modernist conceptions of black identity and a male-dominated literary field of black writing. Fauset's cosmopolitan position mediates seemingly contradictory aspects of experience, from the universal to the particular, from group identity and community to an individuated sense of self and personal longing. Identifying and emphasizing cosmopolitan textual strategies in her writing enables a more complex reading of her negotiation between public racial identification and private subjectivity, an aspect of her work that has been given too little attention in past literary critical and historical treatments.

Chapter Three seeks to describe the link between the modernist aesthetic practice of Langston Hughes's black vernacular or blues poetry of the 1920s and the more overtly political engagement of his socially radical writing of the 1930s in terms of an ongoing cosmopolitan project which he continued to refine throughout his life as a writer. I read his 1934 short story collection, *The Ways of White Folks,* as a pivotal moment in his coming to terms with some of the more trying aspects of his early career, such as the frustrating lack of artistic control that often accompanied white patronage and publishing options. In coming to terms with and moving beyond these early frustrations, Hughes developed a more sophisticated aesthetic politics and literary practice. I argue that Hughes's literary cosmopolitanism, a seamless blending of his aesthetics and his politics, culminates in the black vernacular and critical cultural nationalism of his writing in the 1940s, a representative sampling of which appeared in *Common Ground,* a little magazine that published more of his writing than any other magazine of the decade.

Chapter Four examines Albert Murray's fiction and essay writing in conjunction with the myriad literary figures and cultural forms on which he riffs and signifies. Murray's work is an appropriate conclusion to this project because he so artfully and explicitly brings together and illuminates the tradition of black cosmopolitan intellectuals and artists that I have been tracing throughout this study. His writing, moreover, underscores an important and frequently criticized aspect of the discourse of cosmopolitanism: elitism. Like the requisite dialectic between universalism and particularity, the elitism which often accompanies a cosmopolitan perspective must be tempered by a rootedness in the everyday and a deep devotion to democratic ideals. Murray recalls Du Bois's notion of a Talented Tenth, which while unarguably elitist is also equally focused on bringing as many others along with it as possible. The only way this becomes viable is to remain firmly planted in the everyday life of the "so-called common people," as Murray phrases it. For this reason, Murray draws extensively on a black tragicomic sensibility and participates in a blues idiom as well as a high art tradition, blending and blurring the distinctions between them, reveling in the tensions and contradictions that result, and continuing the line of an intellectual cosmopolitanism that remains rooted in everyday life.[77]

I hope my work, too, inspires the continuation of a cosmopolitan perspective as we rethink our approach to contemporary debates about racial discourse in the United States and democracy in a rapidly, yet unevenly, globalizing world. The writers and thinkers considered herein point the way, but because of its unsettling refusal of dichotomous and systematic ways of knowing, the cosmopolitan position requires constant re-articulation. What is at stake is not just the important work of rethinking modernism from the literature of marginality but the possibility of shaping the discourse that takes part in the racial formation process by rearticulating the meaning of the category of race and identity itself. What is possible is a richer political life, informed and enlarged by the aesthetic and its aid in exercising our ability to imagine other positions than our own—not to come to agreement but to try to understand one another.

Chapter One

Cane's Betrayal and Jean Toomer's Untethered Universalism

In a very truthful way it is a fact that we are not only what we think of ourselves but equally what others think of us.

—Jean Toomer[1]

In Jean Toomer's essayistic writing on race, most of which remained unpublished during his life, miscegenation is a highly valued and celebrated aspect of American culture.[2] Toomer knew, however, that due to the insufficiency of contemporary race categories based on the either-or logic of a color line, he could not simply celebrate miscegenation without introducing the demand for a new discourse that would sufficiently represent people, like himself, of mixed race and ethnicity.[3] Toomer called this new racial category the "American race" and fashioned himself one of its first articulate members. One of Toomer's aims in these essays, then, is to take part in the process of racial formation, defined by Michael Omi and Howard Winant, as "the sociohistorical process by which racial categories are created, inhabited, transformed, and destroyed."[4] If we consider Toomer's essays on race in light of Omi and Winant's racial formation theory, Toomer's project to discursively create a new racial subject is also an attempt to "*redefin[e] the meaning of racial identity,* and consequently of race *itself,* in American society."[5]

While Toomer represents miscegenation in his essays as a tool for opening up racial discourse and, by extension, transforming actual social structures, it figures much more problematically in the work for which he is best known, the mixed-genre *Cane*. Instead of being cause for celebration, miscegenation, particularly in the first section of *Cane,* is often a point of anxiety and even terror. This is, in part, because the aesthetic realm of fiction provided a different space for Toomer to confront, albeit indirectly, the deep anxieties which were inseparable from his celebration of being racially mixed in America. *Cane*'s embodiment of this tension between anxiety and celebration is partly what makes it the most sophisticated of Toomer's work and why I read it as his greatest success in achieving the difficult balance of related tensions required by a cosmopolitan ideal. Because literature, as Barbara Christian notes, has "the possibilities of rendering the world as large and as complicated as [we experience] it," because it holds "the possibility of the integration of feeling/knowledge, rather than the split between the abstract and the emotional," Toomer avoids in *Cane* the more simplistic single-mindedness of some of the essays I examine later in this chapter.[6] I ultimately argue, however, that *Cane* (which in later years Toomer sometimes spelled as *Cain*) betrayed Toomer by becoming the catalyst that publicly fixed his racial identity as black, counteracting the racial project of re-articulation he struggled to enact in his essays.

In this chapter, I recuperate much of Toomer's unpublished writing[7] in order first to trace Toomer's movement from an openness to a variety of identity choices to a growing concern with taking part in the racial formation process, and finally, as a result of the limiting responses to *Cane,* to a more defensive stance regarding his own identity. In the aftermath of *Cane*'s publication, Toomer increasingly distanced himself from African American culture and eventually attempted to withdraw from racial issues entirely in his life and writing. This gradual movement was at first accompanied by his assertion of a cosmopolitan ideal, stressing universalism and commonality amongst all human beings without erasing the differences of particular or local identities. Strongly linked to the intellectual cosmopolitanism of contemporary thinkers such as W. E. B. Du Bois, John Dewey and Randolph Bourne, Toomer's unpublished papers include many compelling treatises on art, democracy, Americanization, and individuality, revealing their analogous nature as ongoing processes that are inextricably linked. In much of this writing, he values the intellectual activity of thinking across ostensibly distinct categories and discourses, such as the particular and the universal, the humanities and science, aesthetics and politics, the spiritual and the material, in order to enrich discourse and representation, and by extension, ways of being in the world. This chapter argues, however, that while Toomer's understanding of particular identities as the result of action rather than an antecedent essence remains especially valuable, his version of universalism eventually became too detached from the particularities of lived experience, too abstract and cosmically transcendent to remain relevant to his initial attempts to affect racial discourse and, by extension, actual social structures in America.

The first section begins with an examination of Toomer's challenge to the pre-existing racial order in his creation of a new discursive category, an "American race," that defies rigid boundaries in setting up miscegenation as its standard. Toomer's use of the word "American," moreover, signifies beyond national identity towards a cosmopolitan ideal of universality. Some of the problems that inhere in Toomer's articulation of the universal are already recognizable in this early stage of his life writing, yet I suspend a critique of his weaknesses in favor of first examining his strengths. Toomer's most celebrated work, the mixed-genre *Cane,* is central to this examination because the conditions of its creation and reception contextualize the problematic aspects of Toomer's writing. I read *Cane* as Toomer's most successful achievement of a cosmopolitan stance because it is here that he artfully maintains that delicate and balanced tension between the particulars of a black cultural distinctiveness and the more universal concerns of a critical American cultural nationalism. This latter aspect of Toomer's project, supported and informed by like-minded contemporaries, can be described as a commitment to the transformation of American culture in general and the redefinition of the "literary" in particular. Pivotal in this cultural shift and essential to Toomer's success at this point in is career are the strong interracial ties, both institutional and personal, between the New Negro movement, the Harlem Renaissance and the Young Intellectuals associated with *Seven Arts, The Freeman* and *Dial* as well as publishers such as Boni & Liveright, Knopf, and Harcourt, Brace, who nourished the Little Renaissance of New York.[8] That these cultural alliances were not drawn along racial lines but rather formed around a common vision and commitment to critical American nationalism, cultural pluralism and literary modernism is, I argue, in direct relation to Toomer's achievement of a cosmopolitan stance. Yet Toomer was ultimately unable to maintain that stance given that his deep anxieties were inseparable from his celebration of a black cultural distinctiveness. The final section of this chapter, then, examines the failure of Toomer's attempts to completely withdraw from racial discourse, an impossibility in a country whose very foundations rest on the fraught notion of a color line. The bitter irony of his attempted withdrawal is that it was triggered, in part, by the very limits placed on his identity as a result of *Cane*'s publication. In the aftermath of his greatest success, Toomer slipped further and further away from the difficult probing of racial identity which a truly cosmopolitan stance would require, as he sought refuge in notions of a problematically untethered universalism.

"THIS NEW AMERICAN RACE": MISCEGENATION AS SOLUTION

To begin with Toomer's challenge to racial discourse, we might turn to a privately printed and circulated pamphlet, titled *A Fiction and Some Facts.*

Toomer writes, "In biological fact I am, as are all Americans, a member of a new people that is forming in this country. If we call this people the Americans, then biologically and racially I am an American."[9] The "biological fact" to which Toomer refers is the various strains that compose his ethnic and racial background: "French, Dutch, Welsh, Negro, German, Jewish, and Indian."[10] This varied ancestry, Toomer argues, results in the necessity for a new discourse that more adequately represents a racial identity that is both "interracial and unique."[11]

As Toomer introduces this new discursive category, he simultaneously challenges the validity of categorical distinctions, hence the very ground upon which the current racial order rests. In his essay "The Crock of Problems," Toomer emphasizes the insufficiency of the current race categories based upon color. "It is evident that in point of fact none of the standard color labels fit me," he explains. "I am not white. I am not black. I am not red. I am not yellow. I am not brown. Yes, any one of these can be made to fit me; I can be tagged with anything."[12] The point, however, is that a new discursive category is required to adequately describe his elusive racial identity. Toomer continues,

> I am at once no one of the races and I am all of them. I belong to no one of them and I belong to all. I am, in a strict racial sense, a member of a new race. This new race, of which I happen to be one of the first articulate members, is now forming perhaps everywhere on Earth, but its formation is more rapid and marked in certain countries, one of which is America. The individual members of it are not and will not necessarily be composed of as many racial strains as I am composed of. But there will be a sufficient number of these strains to produce a type of man who is structurally distinguishable from the heretofore existing types.[13]

Pre-existing racial discourse is unable to account for this structurally distinct type. Toomer, therefore, attempts to instate a new discursive category, grounded in the fact of miscegenation, which simultaneously points out the insufficiency of current race categories. Toomer's "challenge to the dominant racial ideology," in the words of Omi and Winant, is "not only [a] reconceptualiz[ation of his] own racial identity, but a reformulation of the meaning of race in general."[14]

Significantly, Toomer's challenge to the racial order occurred at a time when race categories were becoming even more narrow and rigid in the United States due, in part, to immigration, the migration of rural black agricultural workers to northern cities, and a growing trend of nativism.[15]

Thus, George Hutchinson claims, "the great irony of Toomer's career is that modern American racial discourse—with an absolute polarity between 'white' and 'black' at its center—took its most definite shape precisely during the course of his life."[16] Toomer, moreover, was particularly situated at the center of this challenge, given his family background and their physical location in Washington, D. C., where being a member of a long established upper class black community or "mulatto elite" meant the intersection of race and class figured prominently.[17]

While Toomer's assertion of an "American race" may at first seem simply to replace identity categories based on race with one based on nationality, his purpose was to use Americans both as symbols of the possibility and evidence of the already existent reality of this new racial identity that opened up the way old identity categories were defined. In an unfinished draft titled "Member of Man," his stress is, as always, upon the miscegenated roots that "in the case of Americans" are "undoubtedly a new unity in the making."[18] Toomer explains,

> These various strains in my body and in your body, whatever they may be, do not exist as separate and distinct strains. They can, as it were, be separated verbally. They are not separate in reality. In reality they have been blended to form one blood, a new unity. This new unity cannot be either defined or understood in terms of even all the elements that have entered into its make-up. Confronted with the reality, the idea of strains proves inadequate and breaks down, and the impartial mind comes to recognize that the large truth is the only truth: each and all of us are members of mankind.

This passage illustrates Toomer's shift from the various and particular racial and ethnic backgrounds of Americans to the commonality of "one blood" that unifies the miscegenated American. Toomer further stresses that the "new unity" of Americans should not serve to fix a national identity that separates Americans from other nationalities but to exemplify the possibility and reality of the unity of all humans: "the function of our people is not to hold fast to the things that make us different from other peoples but is to stress and realize the things that make us similar to all peoples. In fine, our function in reality and in symbol is to become and represent Universal Man."

Toomer's shift from describing Americans as representative of a radically inclusive racial type to describing Americans as representative of the universality of all humans is clearly a move in the direction of a mode of thinking that I identify as cosmopolitan. When he proposes a

"Universal Man" or claims, "the large truth is the only truth: each and all of us are members of mankind," he employs the language of cosmopolitanism. Martha Nussbaum, in her recent defense of cosmopolitanism, says, "[W]e should not allow differences of nationality or class or ethnic membership or even gender to erect barriers between us and our fellow human beings. We should recognize humanity wherever it occurs, and give its fundamental ingredients, reason and moral capacity, our first allegiance and respect."[19] Like Nussbaum, Toomer articulates the ideology of cosmopolitanism, but upon closer examination some of his ideas should give us pause. For example, in the passage quoted above from "A Member of Man," Toomer suggests that the reality of miscegenation points to the illusoriness of the concept of race. He argues that once we allow for the reality of miscegenation the notion of "separate and distinct strains . . . proves inadequate and breaks down." Toomer dismissively mentions that the "various strains" can then only "be separated verbally." But Toomer, who has already placed importance on the realm of discourse in remaking racial identity, and by extension, the structure of a racially stratified society, should know better than most the weightiness of discourse. Instead, he wants to gloss over this fact in arguing that because the "reality [of miscegenation] exists" all "we need do is to make it real to ourselves . . . to change our consciousness, so that our consciousness keeps pace and expands with the unfolding reality [which] was, is and always will be—Mankind Is One."[20]

Toomer's abrupt leap from stressing the inadequacy of understanding race as essence or something fixed in biology to arguing its polar opposite, that race is merely an illusion, or in the words of Omi and Winant, "a purely ideological construct which some ideal non-racist social order would eliminate," is highly problematic.[21] The concept of race continues to signify regardless of its status as reality; in fact, the concept itself orders reality and informs our perceptions of others as well as ourselves. Needless to say, when Toomer wrote in his journal circa 1912, "In a very truthful way it is a fact that we are not only what we think of ourselves but equally what others think of us," he implicitly recognized the power of the concept of race to inform the way our lives and identities take shape around us. "[T]he concept of race continues to play a fundamental role in structuring and representing the social world," argue Omi and Winant. "The task for theory is to explain this situation. It is to avoid both the utopian framework which sees race as an illusion we can somehow 'get beyond,' and also the essentialist formulation which sees race as something objective and fixed, a biological datum."[22] Although Toomer, on some levels, does challenge the pre-existing racial order through both highlighting the reality of miscegenation and introducing a new discursive category to more adequately represent this reality, his claims for the universal tend to ignore actually existing structures and representations with an impractical desire to transcend socio-historical realities.

"FACING" THE SOUTH: MISCEGENATION AS DIFFICULT YET CREATIVE TENSION

The assertion that American consciousness has not kept pace with the unfolding reality of miscegenation is a point upon which Toomer also dwells in his essay "Race Problems and Modern Society." He states that "the consciousness of most so-called Americans lags for [*sic*] behind the organic process" and that "it is rare indeed to find anyone who is genuinely conscious of being an American."[23] What Toomer does not stress in his essayistic writing on race but which seeps into his fictional book *Cane* is that this lack of consciousness is *willed* on the part of many Americans whose anxieties over miscegenation resulted in another new and what became a more widespread racial discourse in the 1920s and 1930s. A discursive practice such as the "one-drop rule" reinterpreted racial categories along a rigid color line and reorganized social structures, for example, by the removal of the term "mulatto" from census forms.[24] Walter Benn Michaels argues, "mulattoes vanish by being made black. Thus the desire not to produce mulattoes is fulfilled by the assertion that there are no such things as mulattoes. And the discovery that there are no mulattoes marks the literally definitive defeat of the melting pot."[25] With this historical context in mind, then, we might better be able to address the discrepancy between Toomer's contradictory treatment of miscegenation as cause for celebration in his essayistic writing and point of anxiety and even terror in *Cane*.[26]

In this section of the chapter I begin with a detailed reading of the ghost tale, "Becky," from Part One of *Cane* in order to illustrate how miscegenation operates and is figured as the cause of terror, horror and monstrosity. I argue that miscegenation, while left unnamed, lies behind what is often the seemingly inexplicable sense of horror infusing the first part of *Cane*. I then address the discrepancy between the representations of miscegenation in the essays and in *Cane* by considering Toomer's confrontation through fictional representation of his anxieties concerning his own position within the dominant racial order in America. This discussion is informed by a glimpse at Toomer's biography and the way it is reflected and expressed through the terror of "Kabnis," the third and final section of *Cane*.

The ghost tale, "Becky," begins and ends with the same few lines: "Becky was the white woman who had two Negro sons. She's dead; they've gone away. The pines whisper to Jesus. The Bible flaps its leaves with an aimless rustle on her mound."[27] The birth of her first son, whose appearance is evidence of miscegenation, prompts her ostracism by both the white and black folks of the community: "the white folks said they'd have no more to do with her. And black folks, they too joined hands to cast her out" (7). In a sense, the people pronounce Becky dead to them when they cast her out of their community, making her a ghost while she is yet alive. But this ghost haunts them as individuals, separate from the will of the community, in that they are forever secretly caring for her by providing her with shelter, food and supplies, and even "crumpled slips of paper scribbled with prayers" (7). This fugitive care, however, abruptly stops when it is clear that she has born a second son: "'Becky has another son,' was what the whole town knew. But nothing was said, for the part of man that says things to the likes of that had told itself that if there was a Becky, that Becky now was dead" (8). Now her status as dead to the community is no longer a mere public pronouncement amongst the people. This second son disproves any lingering notion the townspeople might have had about the first being an accident (i.e. the possibility for the white folk that she was raped by a "Damn buck nigger," even though "She wouldn't tell," or the black folk who want to dismiss her as just "poor-white crazy"). Before they discredited her existence to each other, but now their disavowal of the possibility of a white woman's desire for a black man is so strong that it is directed inward.

Becky, however, still haunts "[t]he part [of the townspeople] that prayed"; they "wondered if perhaps she'd really died, and they [the sons] had buried her" (8). As Becky's sons, the visual reminder of her act of miscegenation, grow and take jobs amongst the townspeople, they become another, more pressing, cause of fear in the tale: "White or colored? No one knew, and least of all themselves. . . . We, who had cast out their mother because of them, could we take them in? They answered black and white folks by shooting up two men and leaving town. 'Godam the white folk; godam the niggers,' they shouted as they left town" (8). After this the townspeople begin to realize, however vaguely, their role in having made the two boys into the "sullen and cunning" men they have become, and even more so, when they still see smoke rising from the chimney after her two boys leave town, a dim vision of their own responsibility for the horror that is Becky's death-in-life begins to dawn upon them. They are not entirely cognizant of nor do they fully understand the implication of their actions, but the "creepy feeling [that] came over all who saw that thin wraith of smoke" registers a sense of terror they cannot shake: "Becky if dead might be a hant, and if alive—it took some nerve even to mention it . . . O pines, whisper to Jesus . . ." (8, ellipses in original). Why is the fact of Becky's life more unspeakably terrifying to the townspeople than the possibility of her ghost haunting the cabin? What does the invocation of the pines signify, and what are they called upon to say? Perhaps the pines whisper to Jesus for Becky's salvation because, having been cast out of the society of men, the natural world is her last place of comfort and friendship. Perhaps the townspeople's terror stems from their inability to believe that God would not have already stricken Becky down for her sins.[28] Even more important, however, is that their terror results from a growing awareness of the responsibility they bear for this act of human cruelty. They have alienated Becky from all fellow society and support in the name of their religion and the Bible, which is left flapping aimlessly on her poor excuse for a grave in the final image of this tale. The pines, then, which alone stand apart from the cruelty of humans, are all that remain for Becky of kindness, warmth and salvation in this world.

The voice that invokes the pines, however, is distinct from the tone of the rest of the narration. Here the narrator turns aside from standard third-person narration to directly express emotion as regards the tale being told. This expression registers as a lament, even, oddly enough, as regret, and this may be accounted for if we examine the narrator's position within the tale. An odd shift occurs in the passage quoted above: "White or colored? No one knew, and least of all themselves. . . . We, who had cast out their mother because of them, could we take them in?" (8). The narrator, who was seemingly positioned outside the events of the tale, occasionally relating the townspeople's speech indirectly or their thoughts through free indirect discourse, suddenly erupts into the tale with the pronoun "we" as a member of the community, fully implicated in bearing responsibility for having ostracized Becky and alienated her sons from the community. This eruption, in turn, affects the way in which the lines of invocation are read and prepares us, however slightly, for the dramatic ending to this pathetic tale.

The narrator is physically present at the events of the final scene; in fact, he is a member of the church congregation who has, with silent but deadly force, shaken its head in condemnation at Becky all these years. The narrator sets the scene: "It was Sunday. Our congregation had been visiting at Pulverton, and were coming home" (8). The atmosphere is nothing if not oppressive: "There was no wind. The autumn sun, the bell from Ebenezer Church, listless and heavy. Even the pines were stale, sticky, like the smell of food that makes you sick" (8). As the narrator's buggy approaches Becky's cabin, which is yet out of sight, the horses begin to act strangely, not wanting to go any further. As he spots the "thin smoke curl[ing] up from the leaning chimney" in the distance, the narrator relates, "Goose-flesh came on my skin. . . . Eyes left their sockets for the cabin. Ears burned and throbbed. Uncanny eclipse! fear closed my mind" (8). How might we account for the terror the narrator experiences *before* the chimney falls into the cabin, *before* the narrator thinks he hears a groan from underneath the mound of bricks that had been the chimney? Another piece of information, introduced at this point, is that the narrator is riding with another man, Barlo, who is a more prominent character in the story "Esther," later in the book. We know from this story that Barlo is "a clean-muscled, magnificent, black-skinned Negro," somewhat of a mystic and a ladies' man (22). Could it be that Barlo is the father of Becky's children, and the narrator has some knowledge of this? Barlo is the one who "mumbl[es] something" and "thr[ows] his Bible on the pile" (9). Could it be that the narrator himself has had relations with Becky? While we are not meant to answer these questions conclusively, we are to understand that the element of terror in this tale has its roots in the fact of miscegenation, evidenced in the color of Becky's sons and, even more, her abandonment and exile by the impotent judgment of the people of the community. The tale ends as it begins with the narrator returned to town and "folks crowded round to get the true word of it": "Becky was the white woman who had two Negro sons. She's dead; they've gone away. The pines whisper to Jesus. The Bible flaps its leaves with an aimless rustle on her mound" (9).

Although it is never explicitly acknowledged, reference to and images of miscegenation abound in the first section of *Cane*. More often than not, its presence invokes insanity, crime, and violent death—a double gesture that attempts to erase even as it advances this presence. For example, Becky's introduction as "the white woman who had two Negro sons" is immediately followed by an announcement of her death—"She's dead; they've gone away"—that also functions for the town folk of the tale as a kind of erasure of evidence of miscegenation (7). Similarly, but on a more metaphorical level, "Blood-Burning Moon" ends with a lynching that is the result of a sort of mental miscegenation or the "jumble" in Louisa's mind of the black Tom Burwell and the white Bob Stone (30). On nearly every page of *Cane*, people (mostly women)[29] of mixed race and the mixture of colors, in general, register anywhere on a scale from uncanny and weird to horrific and terrifying. Carma's "mangrove-gloomed, yellow flower face," coupled with her desire, sends her jealous husband to the chain gang (12). Fern's "creamy brown color," "the soft suggestion of down slightly darkened," and her Semitic features (her surname is Rosen) seem to cast a spell upon the narrator (16). She falls into a convulsive trance, "her body . . .

tortured with something it could not let out," until "it found her throat, and spattered inarticulately in plaintive, convulsive sounds" like "a Jewish cantor singing with a broken voice" (19). Esther, who "looks like a little white child" with "her high-cheek-boned chalk-white face" and who desires the "clean-muscled, magnificent, black-skinned" Barlo (24), ends up "a little crazy," "her mind . . . a pink meshbag filled with baby toes" (26). The devastating poem, "Portrait in Georgia" combines, on the level of imagery, the body of a lynched black man with the stylized description of a white woman's body, "white as the ash of black flesh after flame" (29).[30] In each of these examples, miscegenation is publicly hidden or silenced but privately manifests itself through people's inner lives in the forms of desire, insanity, and murderous rage.

The narrator's role and his position in relation to the people, situations, and settings of the first section of *Cane* is also a key to understanding the terror that hovers around the issue of miscegenation and Toomer's ability to confront and represent his anxieties about being a person of mixed race in the South. In some pieces, such as "Karintha," "Carma" and "Esther," the narrator seems at a remove from the events narrated. In other pieces, such as "Becky," the narrator appears as a member of the community. More often than not, however, the reader gathers a general sense that, as in "Fern," the narrator is both an outsider yet a sometimes-participant in the people's lives he narrates. On one level, this positioning parallels Toomer's experience: he was born and raised as a member of the mulatto elite in Washington, D.C., but traveled to the deep South in 1921 to spend two brief, yet intense, months in Georgia as a substitute principal. On another level, however, Toomer's elusive narrator enables him not only to keep an aesthetic distance from the social structures of the South but to harness the possibilities fiction writing affords for slipping between subject positions. George Hutchinson concurs when he writes that it "was precisely the liminal potential of literary expression, in other words, its ability to mediate between realms of possible experience, that appealed to Toomer."[31]

Toomer's life story shows him constantly trying on new roles and avoiding the limitations of a particular identity.[32] Between the years of 1915 and 1920, he moved back and forth between Washington, D. C., Wisconsin, New York City and Chicago, and during this time he enrolled in six different colleges, majoring in various subjects from agriculture to sociology, before his sojourn to Georgia and return to Washington, D.C. After deciding to become a writer, he moved to New York City and joined with the Greenwich Village *Seven Arts* group, which included such New York intellectuals as James Oppenheim, Waldo Frank, Randolph Bourne, Paul Rosenfeld and Van Wyck Brooks. In 1923, Toomer turned to spiritualism and joined G. Gurdjieff's Institute for the Harmonious Development of Man, and around 1940, his spiritual pursuits led him to Quakerism and the Society of Friends. This kind of possibility and openness to experience is related to Toomer's high valuation of his varied racial and ethnic background. But to say that he saw the fact of miscegenation in his life as nothing more than a cause for celebration because it gave him more ground to explore would be far too simple. One could also interpret his incessant moving about and change of occupation and identity as desperation, and placed in the context of American civil rights history, his constant movement begins to look like repeated attempts to flee not just any identity but specifically an African-American one.

Toomer's experience in Georgia as a person of mixed race was particularly frightening for him. This is written into the pages of *Cane,* perhaps most intensely in the third section, "Kabnis," a play about a lemon-colored northerner who has taken a job in Georgia as a teacher but is cracking up due to his terror of being in the South. Yet Toomer was peculiarly reticence about addressing his time in Georgia directly.[33] In a letter to Waldo Frank, his friend and mentor throughout the writing of *Cane,* Toomer states, "When they, in all good faith have advised me, as Sherwood Anderson did, to keep close to the conditions which produced Cane, I have denied them. Never again in life do I want a repetition of those conditions."[34] Toomer does not go into detail about "those conditions" in any of his correspondence or autobiographical writing, but fiction writing seems to have offered him a safer space for exploration, evidenced in another letter to Frank which reveals, "Kabnis is *Me.*"[35]

In trying to piece together, then, the cause of Toomer's terror in Georgia we can turn to "Kabnis" for clues. Near the opening of the play, Kabnis says, "If I could feel that I came to the South to face it. If I . . . could become the face of the South. How my lips would sing for it, my songs being the lips of its soul" (83–84).[36] Here we have the artist, who would, as in the poem "Song of the Son" that appears earlier in *Cane,* sing "an everlasting song" about the "souls of slavery, / What they were, and what they are to me" (14).[37] It would seem that Toomer's confrontation of the history of slavery and the way a person of mixed race is positioned in the South ("to face it") is made possible through the narrative agency of representation (to "become the face of"). The power of representation and the aesthetic distance of fiction enable Toomer to confront and complicate what he often overlooks or willfully ignores in his essays.

But there is also anxiety expressed in the conditional status of the sentences, the sense that the fear of "facing" the history of slavery and its implications for a person of mixed race in both the past and present of the

South will suffocate all creative impulses and maybe even life itself. Kabnis is haunted by visions of lynching: "He sees himself yanked beneath that tower. He sees white minds, with indolent assumption, juggle justice and a nigger" (85–86). And he also feels, as Toomer must have felt, as if the North were a lifetime away. Kabnis says of New York: "Impossible. It was a fiction. He had dreamed it" (86). Toomer's return north, then, might have seemed like an escape of sorts, an escape from the South, its history and the way that history positioned him as a subject. But the history of the South is also the history of America, and even in New York, Toomer would have to face the manifestation of his fears when others tried to narrow and limit his identity. In the next section I look at what became just as devastating and frightening for Toomer as his experience in Georgia—the way readers and publishers responded to *Cane* in fixing its identity as an African-American text and by extension, Toomer's identity as an African American.

THE BETRAYAL OF *CANE*: FROM HARMONY TO DISSONANCE

"It is a sign of the fundamentally segregated nature of American society," writes George Hutchinson, "that *Cane* could only be understood as a 'black' text and in relation to African American identity."[38] While Hutchinson finds it "entirely fitting to read *Cane* in the context of African American literary tradition," he emphasizes Toomer's ambivalence in relation to that tradition. Central to my thinking in this chapter is his subsequent point: "Indeed, it is precisely the ambiguity—and mobility—of Toomer's 'identity' in a society obsessed with clarity on this score that motivated the restless searching through which *Cane* came about, through which Toomer left it behind, and without which there could be no book like it."[39] In this section, I explore the shifts in Toomer's attitude toward his racial identity as responses to the fear and anxiety written into and issuing from the publication of *Cane*. Tracing the biographical provides a context for the emergence and steadily increasing assertion, in Toomer's writing, of a universal humanism and a conception of identity as deriving from action rather than a fixed essence. I argue that while Toomer values a process of becoming, or "individualization," which remains open to experience, over the stasis of identity, he also recognizes the necessity of living within social groups, which necessarily entails subscribing to particular group identities.

While Toomer was still writing *Cane* and publishing completed pieces of it in magazines, he expressed to interested parties the inspirational and creative effects of his having embraced and explored an African-American identity. Importantly, and too often overlooked by his contemporaries,

Toomer saw his identification with African Americans as one among many possible identity choices for himself. In a 1922 letter to *The Liberator,* to which he had submitted material from *Cane,* he writes of the way his status as a mulatto elite has granted him a certain mobility but that, ultimately, he identifies as an American: "I have lived equally amid the two race groups. Now white, now colored. From my own point of view I am naturally and inevitably an American." He then writes of his attempt to attain a spiritual state that parallels the biological fact of miscegenation: "I have striven for a spiritual fusion analogous to the fact of racial intermingling. Without denying a single element in me, with no desire to subdue, one to the other, I have sought to let them function as complements. I have tried to let them live in harmony." The letter concludes, however, with a discussion of his having focused on a particular identity over the past few years and the powerful connection he felt once he opened himself to its gifts: "Within the last two or three years, however, my growing need for artistic expression has pulled me deeper and deeper into the Negro group. And as my powers of receptivity increased, I found myself loving it in a way that I could never love the other. It has stimulated and fertilized whatever creative talent I may contain within me."[40]

When Toomer made similar statements to Sherwood Anderson, however, about the creative powers he drew from his connection with an African-American identity, Anderson's subsequent responses both proved his inability to separate an active choice from a static identity category and alarmed Toomer. On separate occasions between 1922 and 1924, Anderson wrote to Toomer, "Your work is of special significance to me because it is the first negro [*sic*] work I have seen that strikes me as being really negro"; "you are the only negro . . . who seems really to have consciously the artist's impulse"; and "When I saw your stuff first I was thrilled to the toes. Then I thought 'he may let the intense white man get him. They are going to color his style, spoil him.' I guess that isn't true. You'll stay with your own, wont you."[41] Toomer objected to Anderson's narrow vision of both *Cane* and his racial identity. In a draft of a letter to Waldo Frank in 1923, Toomer expresses dissatisfaction with Anderson, who, he writes, "'limits me to Negro.'"[42]

Due to such limiting responses, Toomer developed a more defensive, less open stance regarding his identity. In a 1923 letter to his publishers, Boni & Liveright, he writes,

> As a B and L author, I make the distinction between my fundamental position and the position which your publicity department may wish to establish for me in order that *Cane* reach as large a public as possible.

> In this connection I have told you . . . to make use of whatever racial factors you wish. Feature Negro if you wish, but do not expect me to feature it in advertisements for you. For myself, I have sufficiently featured Negro in *Cane*. Whatever statements I give will inevitably come from a synthetic human and art point of view; not from a racial one.[43]

Toomer asserts that he had merely been exploring an African-American subject position but had not intended to limit himself to it. His final point about "a synthetic human and art point of view" is one he will continue to shape throughout the 1920s into a cosmopolitan ideal that highlights the universality of humans, aesthetics and, eventually, spirituality. By 1930, however, he still felt the need "to clear up a misunderstanding of [his] position which has existed to some extent ever since the publishing of CANE."[44] In reply to James Weldon Johnson's request for permission to include four poems from *Cane* in the revised anthology, *The Book of American Negro Poetry,* Toomer declines, saying "I do not see things in terms of Negro, Anglo-Saxon, Jewish, and so on. As for me personally, I see myself an American, simply an American." Here we have Toomer's familiar articulation of an American race, a formulation that downplays "the matter of descent, and of divisions presumably based on descent" which he believed had been given "over-emphasis"; instead he "aim[s] to stress the fact that we all are Americans." In order for him to carry through this plan, then, he tells Johnson, "I must withdraw from all things which emphasize or tend to emphasize racial or cultural division. I must align myself with things which stress the experiences, forms, and spirit we have in common."

Toomer's stress on commonality and experience aligns him with pragmatist thinkers, such as William James and John Dewey, who conceived of identity not as an inherent or static essence but rather what one makes of oneself. In a draft of an essay called "World America," Toomer explores the way "racial obsession," in general, "makes us focus, not on functions, but on appearances."[45] And in another draft titled "Thus May It Be Said," he writes, "the important thing about any individual man or woman is not his color or features, not his nationality, not his class, not his money, not his external identities and affiliations. . . . [T]hese are given: he finds himself with them. The main question is, given these, *what does he make of himself*."[46] Practice and function, then, rather than essence or appearance, inform Toomer's thinking about identity.

Keeping this pragmatist view of identity in mind and thinking ahead to writers such as Ralph Ellison and James Baldwin, Toomer's uncertainty and anxiety about African-American identity come into focus. In preliminary notes for an essay to be titled "The Individual in America," Toomer writes, "The Negro, a dark, different, unknown, portentious [*sic*] man, is a symbol of the white American's subconscious, which is dark, different, unknown, portentious [*sic*]. Etc."[47] This quote prefigures Baldwin's later and more eloquent articulation of what he calls "the story of Americans," which is "the story of the Negro in America . . . a series of shadows, self-created, intertwining, which now we helplessly battle" and which "does not really exist except in the darkness of our minds." This story, Baldwin writes, is "told, compulsively, in symbols and signs, in hieroglyphics" and reveals not only how deeply "the Negro has affected the American psychology" but the ways in which "our estrangement from him is the depth of our estrangement from ourselves."[48] Likewise, Toomer's resistance to a particular racial identity stems from this sense that, at its very roots, "the Negro" is a fiction created by the fears of white Americans, who in turn construct their own group identity upon this limiting fiction.

To subscribe to a particular identity, whether one thinks that identity is limiting or beneficial, is, for Toomer, *not* to be an individual. In "The Individual and Democracy," he describes his conception of the individual and the reasons for his investment in this concept: "I should say at once that what I have in mind is a *process,* and would therefore better be expressed by *individualization*—the process of becoming an individual, the kind of life in general that would produce men and women capable of doing their own thinking, feeling, and acting."[49] To be an individual, then, is to be in a constant state of becoming; it is more about process itself than a fixed end point to be reached. Toomer sets up individuality as an ongoing process of self-realization necessarily open to the constant flux of experience in contrast to identity as that which arrests movement and the possibility of change. In "Values and Fictions," a book-length manuscript he sent to Boni & Liveright in January 1926, Toomer stresses how unaware most people are of the extreme complexity of their being. He describes a person as "a compound of impressions, actions, habits, feelings, traits, words, names, ideas, thoughts, attitudes, qualities, and attributes which, if it were possible to count them, would total many millions." This being the case, he continues, "you merely assume yourself to be an identity." Although these assumptions "collapse at the first serious challenge" he says that we, being "wholly given to them," are "effectively sealed . . . from the slightest contact with whatever reality there is within [ourselves] and in the world around [us]."[50] Identity, then, shuts down the possibility of play and, what is worse, closes one off from being significantly affected by experience with "the world around you." In other words, too great an attachment to a particular identity is not only developmentally stunting but bars one from the process of becoming that is, for Toomer, what it means to be an individual.

In a draft from 1935, titled "A Preface to a Place and Function in Society," Toomer elaborates his conception of the individual in relation to the social systems and institutions through which people function in the world. In addressing his anti-capitalist leanings, he explains that he is not a "collectivist" because "this term means regimentation and rule by herd psychology. I believe in human individualization, in rule by wisdom, in the voluntary reasoned and spontaneous cooperation of responsible human beings who have individualized themselves and at the same time realize that all are interdependent." This point about interdependency is crucial because it shows that Toomer sees the individual in society as necessarily situated within a group or groups. Toomer believes in the "reciprocality" of the individual and the group: "Not this or that," he writes, "but this *and* that since in the nature of reality there are both individuals and groups and neither can exist without the other."[51] For Toomer, then, it is precisely as a member of a group that identity comes into play. In other words, identity is, necessarily, *group* identity, while individual identity is oxymoronic. If the individual and the group are in a reciprocal relation, one need not choose between identity with a group or the process of individualization but instead must not lose sight of either in an ongoing struggle to balance the two.

In regards to group identity, however, Toomer is always in alignment with pragmatist belief, which derives identity from action rather than essence. Toomer is less interested, borrowing Ross Posnock's formulation, in "national [or racial] consciousness (preoccupied with who people are)" than he is with "political and social consciousness (focused on people acting in relation to others)."[52] In "A Preface to a Place and Function in Society," Toomer makes it clear that he wants to perform the work of reconciling "warring factions" (of different racial or class-based groups) over simply subscribing to one or another group. Another way to think of this is through David Hollinger's distinction between "[c]osmopolitanism [which] is more oriented to the individual, whom it is likely to understand as a member of a number of different communities simultaneously," and "[p]luralism [which] is more oriented to the group, and . . . likely to identify each individual with reference to a single, primary community."[53] Toomer's desire to unite "warring factions . . . not on the basis of compromises but on the basis of their common humanity" requires a kind of intellectual work that I identify with a cosmopolitan cultural project of affecting social structures rather than merely working within them. Toomer, then, aligns himself with intellectuals, who "must teach rather than be given instructions." He says, "it is our duty to remake the world, transforming and expanding it into a phase beyond the present clash of limitations."[54]

"THE WHOLE THING LINKED AND ORGANIC": MODERNITY, FRAGMENTATION AND THE DESIRE FOR WHOLENESS

Toomer understands social inequalities between and among race and class groups as intricately linked to economics and the growth of capitalism, which he identifies with a far-reaching process of modernization. Toomer believes, however, that a strict reliance on economic terms for explaining social ills cannot sufficiently address the depth and complexity of modernization. In this section, I focus on Toomer's concern with modernization; in so doing, I hope to bring together the various strains of Toomer's work in aesthetics, sociology, psychology and spirituality by showing how they are linked through Toomer's overarching concern with creating unity and wholeness in order to combat the effects of modernity's fragmentation and mechanization. I argue that this concern is centered in the realm of discourse itself and, moreover, is directly related to a dialectical mode of thinking across different spheres of knowledge and experience, which I have identified with cosmopolitanism.

In "Race Problems and Modern Society," as in most of his analyses of social ills, Toomer grounds his discussion in economic foundations. "There is no need to present new facts to support the statement that race problems are closely associated with our economic and polticial [*sic*] systems," he asserts. "[W]henever two or more races (or nationalities) meet in conditions which are mainly determined by acquisitive interests, race problems arise as by-products of economic issues."[55] In his line of argument, Toomer also implies that there is parallel growth with the system of capitalism and "the 'acquisitive urge' for land, natural resources, and cheap labor."[56] The "acquisitive urge," in turn, heightens class- and race-based oppression and exploitation so that modernization, or the rise of capitalism, and the escalation of racial problems become intricately linked in a circular logic: "[T]he sharp sociological divisions between the white and colored people . . . have steadily become more and more fixed and crystallized. They have grown up, so to speak, with the growth of our economic, political, and social systems. And the probability is that they will continue to increase with the increase of these systems."[57] "Socially constructive forms of activity" are also present with modernization; however, "being less powerful and in the minority," they can do little to stop the crystallization of racial division that occurs with the rise of capitalism and its stimulation of "acquisitive urges."[58]

While Toomer relies on Marxist theory for understanding class- and race-based oppression and exploitation, he is also dissatisfied with explanations that use the growth of capitalism as *the* fundamental reason for all social ills. In a 1937 typescript of "Psychologic Papers,"[59] Toomer writes,

> Thus in Marxism the cause of evil is seen in the predatory and profit motives. But Marxism . . . though having a true (if partial) perception of the evil, fails to see its roots, because instead of looking for them *in man,* it assumes to see them clearly in the system of bourejoise [*sic*] capitalism. . . . Instead of realizing that the cause is that *all* men in their false natures are stuck to things and are thus committed to an evil feeding and warfare, it claims the cause to be only that the capitalists are stuck to profits.

Toomer's concern in this passage is that while Marxism is a valuable discourse for understanding social ills, it is also somehow insufficient: "Even should the socialists succeed in establishing a world-wide socialistic state, there would still remain the fundamental task of *uprooting* the inner cause of our obsession with things." This "inner cause," which he accuses "the generality of present day socialists and communists" of deliberately overlooking "out of an ignorance of man as dark as that which benights the worst capitalists," is spiritual in nature.

Toomer's elaboration of one of his main aims in writing, to "spiritualize experience," may help us understand just how the spiritual functions for him. "To spiritualize," he writes, "is to have one's psyche or spirit engage in a *process* similar to that of the body when it digests and assimilates food. To spiritualize is to digest, assimilate, upgrade, and form the materials of experience—in fine, *to form oneself.* It is the direct opposite of sensualization, and of mechanization."[60] By "sensualization" and "mechanization," I understand Toomer to mean something like the abstraction and compartmentalization often closely associated with a fragmented modern existence. Toomer expressed concern for "the fragmented lives to which we are committed," evidenced in the way businessmen, artists, and scientists reduce all things to their particular sphere of knowledge or practice.[61] The spiritual and, by extension, the aesthetic, in their assimilative functions, would seem to enable the reintegration of fragmented modern life.

Modernization, according to Toomer, experienced in "the financial and commercial interdependence of nations . . . the congestion of population in great cities, the mechanization of life, the automatism of the individual . . . tend[s] to obliterate . . . individuality."[62] Counteracting this tendency is the spiritual, which plays an important role in the process of "individualization," discussed earlier in this chapter and evident in the quote above where "to spiritualize" is described as a "process" of assimilating experience in order "to form oneself." In this light, then, Toomer's work with Gurdjieff, which he began after the publication of *Cane,* and his eventual gravitation towards Quakerism, were continuous with his early attempts to individualize himself and to help guide others through the process.[63]

In his notes to "The Individual in America," Toomer marks a particularly powerful "anti-individualistic" trend in America: "There is an increasing body of opinion to the effect that America is the last place in which you would expect to find conditions favorable for the development of individuals, that it is the first place in which you would expect to find a mechanized mass-psychology. We are told, 'In America the herd rules—rules out—the individual, and the machine rules the herd.'"[64] In another piece, however, Toomer notices that this "anti-individualistic" trend creates an equally strong desire for its opposite: "On the other hand, the very strength of this tendency gives rise to a proportionally urgent need to develop individuality."[65] Toomer senses a struggle between the opposing forces of mechanization and creative energy in a rapidly changing modern world. The question, then, is how to link the creative potential of modernity with a spiritual vitality that, according to Toomer, is dying out with the process of modernization. Before turning to the discourses of psychology and spirituality, Toomer explored the consequences of fragmentation and mechanization, as well as the possibilities for reintegration and wholeness, in the aesthetic realm of *Cane* to which I now turn for illustration.[66]

Images and instances of modernity lend a feeling of incongruity to the rural setting in the first section of *Cane* and, in some respects, the presence of modernization contributes to the terror already noted in relation to miscegenation.[67] In "Becky," for instance, the "eye-shaped piece of sandy ground . . . islandized between the road and railroad track" where Becky lives is passed six times each day by "a blue-sheen God" which portentously shakes the ground under her cabin (7). The "trembling of the ground" adds to the "creepy feeling" that comes over people when they see the "thin wraith of smoke" curling up from her cabin. And because the leaning chimney falls as a result of "the ground trembl[ing] as a ghost train rumbled by" Becky's death is, in part, the result of this symbol of modernity rushing by one side of her cabin as the congregation passes on the other side in the horses and buggies which still travel the road (8).

The disjunction of elements of modernity with those of a largely agricultural and pre-modern, rural South connotes a period of transition that is anything but smooth as time and again it registers some kind of violence. The poem "Reapers" juxtaposes "black reapers" sharpening their scythes with "black horses driv[ing] a mower through the weeds." The image of the reapers is serene, their motion a "silent swinging." The mower, on the other hand, which represents an element of modernity, unwittingly startles and kills a field rat. The closing image of the poem is "the blade, / Blood-stained" as it "continue[s] cutting weeds and shade" (5). While the violence of this image is apparently the work of a machine, the ambiguity of the poem lends itself to an additional and darker reading—that modernity will also displace the seemingly peaceful "black reapers," and in that displacement, a long pent-up violence will be released.

In the second section of *Cane*, which takes place in the already modernized northern cities of Washington, D. C. and Chicago, images of modernity have an even more ambiguous status as Toomer recreates the tension between both the positive energy of modernity and its negative effects. "Her Lips Are Copper Wire" turns the gleam of city lights into the breath and whisper of a lover whose kiss will make the poet "incandescent" (57). The urban street life depicted in "Seventh Street" pulses with the energy of "jazz songs and love, thrusting unconscious rhythms, black reddish blood into the white and whitewashed wood of Washington" (41). This mixture of vitality and violence is due to Seventh Street's status as "a bastard of Prohibition and the War." The war was one of the factors that brought many African Americans from the rural South to the northern cities, and Prohibition opened up jobs for "Bootleggers in silken shirts / Ballooned, zooming Cadillacs." However, the bootleggers' money, which "burns the pocket," has been procured through illegal means so that the question of this piece, "Black reddish blood. . . . Who set you flowing?" is eerily related to this illegal occupation (41). Toomer frequently links the frenzy of life in northern cities to "bootleg licker" (57), so that the incessant movement of "zooming," "whizzing," "thrusting," "swirling" (41) is in part due to drunkenness, which again renders this ecstatic energy ambiguous. In "Beehive," the city is a "black hive . . . [with] a million bees . . . intently buzzing, / Silver honey dripping from the swarm of bees." The speaker, "a drone, / Lying on my back, / Lipping honey, / Getting drunk with silver honey," wishes for escape, to "fly out past the moon / And curl forever in some far-off farmyard flower" (50). Although the city is teeming with life, that life is somehow artificial, forced, infertile, so that in the short story "Avey," for instance, the narrator continuously dreams of "the South" and its soil "fall[ing] like a fertile shower upon the lean streets of the city" (48). This "memory" of the South as fertile and connected runs through the second section of *Cane* in contrast to life in the northern city which is infertile and disconnected.

Toomer registers the deadening effects of middle class city life in "Rhobert," where the protagonist "wears a house, like monstrous diver's helmet, on his head. . . . His house is a dead thing that weights him down. . . . Like most men who wear monstrous helmets, the pressure it exerts is enough to convince him of its practical infinity" (42). Rhobert's house, symbolizing the increasing obsession for material things that Toomer theorizes with the growth of capitalism, is slowly cutting him off from the vital forces of life: "life is water that is being drawn off" (42). In such cases, when the inner life is starved for lasting nourishment, the speaker/narrator calls upon elements of the folk-life, as in "Avey" when the narrator "hum[s] a folk-tune" or imagines a wind blowing from the South, bringing with it a breath of a more essential life than the city can offer (48). In "Calling Jesus" the female protagonist's "soul is like a little thrust-tailed dog that follows her, whimpering. . . . [E]ach night when she comes home and closes the big outside storm door, the little dog is left in the vestibule, filled with chills till morning" (58). The narrator suggests, however, that the protagonist's loneliness and alienation could be alleviated in dreams of the rural South, "where she sleeps upon clean hay cut in her dreams" and is "cradled in dream-fluted cane," which brings warmth and comfort to her soul (58).

The South, for Toomer, is intricately linked to a vital spiritual force, but if we think back to the analysis of miscegenation in the first section of *Cane,* the South is also a site of anxiety and terror, resulting from a history of slavery and its contemporary repercussions. The North, intricately linked to the ecstatic energy and possibility of modernization, is, at the same time, futile and infertile in its chaos, cut off from a spiritual vitality in its obsession with things. These contradictions, which draw Toomer towards and away from each region, inevitably result, then, in a perpetual back and forth movement, which enables an integration, assimilation and adjustment of elements and impulses. In a letter to Margaret Naumberg, Waldo Frank's wife and Toomer's short-term lover, in which Toomer outlines an early idea for what would eventually become *Cane,* he expresses this sense of productive movement between the two regions of North and South:

> It will attempt to organically relate and create an America of at least the eastern seaboard. Beginning with a New York of scattered brilliant surfaces, or up-rooted industrialism, business, machines, thoughts, art,—of these things stray, futile, neurotic, tortured, clogging a deep spiritual heave,—external movement converges to an inner intensity that shoots a central character to the soil of Georgia, and plants him there. For months he is submerged and germinal. He soaks in the deep rich beauty-in-adjustment of Southern Negroes. And then he stirs, is stirred, rather, first by the now quickening migratory impulse of the

> blacks, then by the invasion of pioneer, commercial rhythms (and consequent rivalries and prejudices), till he, sufficiently healed and nourished, commences his pull upward from this peasant base. Washington is the next phase. Here the commercial pulse beats louder. But not so strong yet as to drown the soil rhythms. New notes enter. Jazz. Spiritual complications. Georgia is partially digested and related. New York prepared for. Intellectual and spiritual lines distend, expand, belly, a second phase of chaotic impulses and perception. These finally swing together and drive the character to New York. *Birth in New York*. And the final expansion, inclusion, digestion, adjustment, integration. The whole thing linked and organic.[68]

I quote this letter at length to give the full effect of its movement and a sense of Toomer's desire to accumulate and assimilate the different energies and spirits of place toward the ongoing project of "individualization," or the integration of experience in the formation of oneself. Toomer would also have this process of assimilation occur on the level of culture itself. According to George Hutchinson, "Seventh Street" is representative of a "stage in the ultimate 'absorption' of the folk spirit into the modern 'chaos,' [which] at the same time transform[s] the dominant culture itself."[69] The letter to Naumberg illustrates a dialectical movement between inside and outside, surface and depth, material and spiritual, which in turn mirrors the movement between North and South and the final synthesis that is, at this early stage in the development of *Cane*, the "birth in New York." Moreover, Toomer's preoccupation with a "linked and organic" synthesis in both the form of the work itself and the central identity with which it is concerned exhibits a typically modernist desire for the aesthetic creation of unified wholes out of the fragmented and chaotic experience of modernity.

For Toomer, however, the desire for wholeness and unity is not confined to the realm of aesthetic creation but is also a matter of great personal and cultural consequence. In a 1925 issue of *Opportunity*, Gorham Munson explains Toomer's interest in psychology and his work with the Gurdjieff Institute as the outcome of two convictions: "One was that the modern world is a veritable chaos and the other was that in a disrupted age the first duty of the artist is to unify himself."[70] While it may seem apt to associate the concept of a unified self with a fixed and stable identity, we know from previous discussions that Toomer means something else entirely, namely, that to unify the self is to integrate and assimilate seemingly discordant elements in the ongoing *process* of individualization. This process can, in turn, be transformed to operate as an assimilative force for conflicting elements on the level of culture itself. Thus, Munson goes on to clarify, "Having achieved personal wholeness, then perhaps he would possess an attitude that would not be merely a reaction to the circumstances of modernity, merely a reflection of the life about him, but would be an attitude that could act upon modernity."[71] Although his use of the word "achieved" is misleading given Toomer's conception of the integration of conflicting forces in the self as a never-ending process, Munson correctly recognizes the way in which assimilative activity at the personal level, in turn, enables one to act in a similar manner upon the fragmented modern world.

Toomer's search for wholeness, then, is a search for a way to think and live across different spheres of knowledge and experience that are, in a specialized modern world, often perceived as in conflict with one another, hence kept separate and distinct. P. D. Ouspenski, a Russian philosopher who was also a member and teacher in the Gurdjieff group, wrote that "in order to comprehend the world of many dimensions, [we] must renounce the idol of duality. . . . We must train our thought to the ideas that separateness and inclusiveness are not opposed in the real world, but exist simultaneously without contradicting each other."[72] Toomer understands, then, that while our minds and social order separate the world into easily digestible dualities, we are also capable of rethinking conflicting categorizations in a simultaneous and inclusive way that results in a more complex perception of the world. This coincides with Josiah Royce's interpretation of Hegel in his book *The Spirit of Modern Philosophy* (1892): "Consciousness . . . differentiates itself into various, into contrasted, forms and lives in their relationships, their conflicts, their contradictions, and in the triumph over these. . . . So, in short, everywhere in conscious life, consciousness is a union, an organization, of conflicting aims, purposes, thoughts, strivings."[73] Royce's articulation of "dialectical negativity," or "the process by which a higher harmonization and unity are achieved"[74] is similar to, if slightly more sophisticated than, Toomer's explanation, in "Values and Fictions," of the way in which

> the processes of our consciousness . . . are sequential: they are concerned with parts, and only parts in sequence are recorded by them. But it is evident that, in order to apprehend a totality, these processes must be simultaneous. . . . The effort to make sequential processes (sequential impressions) simultaneous, is an effort to apprehend the whole. The effort to apprehend the whole is an effort towards reality.[75]

Toomer's explanation of a consciousness that separates life into sequential parts corresponds to Royce's description of a consciousness that "differentiates . . . into various, into contrasted forms." The forms into which consciousness breaks down reality become the "relationships, their conflicts, their contradictions" in which we then live. Just as "separateness and inclusiveness" exist simultaneously and "without contradicting each other" "in the real world" (Ouspenski), so too is consciousness capable of simultaneously processing differentiation and unity in the world.

But what are the conflicting forms that Toomer struggles to unite? This question leads us back to Toomer's interest in spirituality and social theories, his work with Gurdjieff which combined the study of psychology and Eastern mysticism, and his sense that, however much scientific discourse could aid him in understanding and articulating the functions of society and the mind, certain experiences still could not be accounted for in the terms of this discourse. Toomer writes in "Values and Fictions,"

> There was a time when you, completely given to the attitude of material determinism, sought to rule out certain exceptional experiences on the grounds that, should you include them, your integrity and your (then) sense of reality would be impaired. . . . At the time, you said that they were blind spots in your sense of reality. Indeed you did have blind spots, but these related not to the experiences, but to your denials of them.[76]

Because science "works to free itself from sentimentality," human emotions and spiritual values are bracketed out of scientific discourse and its explanations of how humans function in the world.[77] Toomer, however, sees the metaphysical and the material as organically related; hence, it is his desire to create new forms of discourse that would be capable of combining scientific and rational thought with human feelings and spirituality.

In his article "We Still Have Hearts,"[78] Toomer laments the fact that "much of our thinking occurs without feeling," which results in thought that is "dry," "sterile," "partial" and "lopsided." He explains, "This has come about because of rationalists, in ruling out emotional coloring *of* thought, have also ruled out emotional cooperation *with* thought. They know a lot but understand little." "Understanding," which Toomer describes as "that which happens in us when thinking and feeling coordinate," should be highly valued, but instead we are taught to "develop a factual mind" and to "dismiss or discredit all other types, particularly the imaginative types—and the mystical type fills us with righteous abhorrence." He claims that we undervalue discourse that is not strictly rational or factual because "our feeling and emotional life" and especially our sense of spirituality are "not a means either of mercenary or of egotistical gain."

Like his concept of "understanding" that combines thought and feeling, which are usually kept separate and distinct in modern spheres of discourse, Toomer also develops a theory of "The Third View of Man" which combines the opposing views of materialists and metaphysicians. In "Psychologic Papers," he explains, "[I]n order to have a complete and truly representative view of a human being, one must remove the dividing line between the two mentioned views and regard man, not as this *or* that, but as this *and* that." Toomer calls this third view "the psychologic view." In anticipation of objection, he denies that this view is akin to "riding the fence"; rather, "it is doing what Francis Bacon, among others, would have had us do, namely, found our views on experience of all kinds."[79]

Toomer was not alone in his thinking that one of the most formidable problems of modernity is precisely a problem of the specialization, hence fragmentation, of fields of knowledge, a problem that registers itself on the level of discourse and in the human consciousness. Toomer kept newspaper clippings of reviews of books by people and about subjects that were of particular interest to him. These clippings, which span the years 1923 to 1951, are arranged in subject files under such headings as "Psychology and religion" and "Social history." Many authors, such as J. Huizinga, who wrote *In the Shadow of Tomorrow* (1936), identify the root of most problems specific to modernity in the loss of a culture that "require[s] a certain balance of material and spiritual values."[80] According to one reviewer, Harvey Fergusson, author of *Modern Man: His Belief and Behavior,* "tackles the puzzlements of the individual," even while most of "his contemporaries among the intelligentsia" do not "dare discuss human problems except as group problems."[81] A *New York Times* article of September 14, 1936, with the lengthy title, "Scholars Favor 'Court of Wisdom' to Guide World; Plan Would Develop Harvard 'Macroscope' of Science into Permanent Idea; Anti-War Influence Seen; Dewey and Others Say America Must Lead in Move to Free All Men's Minds," Bronislaw Malinowski calls for a new discourse that would, like Toomer's "psychologic view," bridge the fields of science and the humanities: "In my opinion, it is the recognition of the structurally scientific character of social and psychological sciences on the one hand, and the humanizing of the theoretical and applied exact sciences which is the most needed development."[82] And in the same article, John Dewey calls for a broadening of scientific method and discourse so that "scientific thought could be applied to practical human affairs." He implies that it is deeply problematic for a society to rely on mutually exclusive spheres of knowledge, for example, the belief that science is strictly concerned with material "facts" and not at all with ethical and philosophical questions. Dewey argues, "the scientific man . . . should realize his responsibility toward the wider range of human affairs. . . . English scientists seem to be further along than we are in this country in feeling on this subject.

They are giving serious thought, for instance, to the question whether science is simply to be used to promote war and ultra-nationalism."[83]

To some extent, then, all these writers are concerned, as is Toomer, with the real world consequences of a split in discourse between science and the humanities. Another important model for Toomer was the intellectual cosmopolitanism of Randolph Bourne who also wanted to "fuse humanism and science."[84] In his writing on the First World War and the role intellectuals played in it, Bourne criticized intellectuals who cared about "the technical side of the war . . . not the interpretive or political side."[85] Toomer had noted, "Bourne . . . carried an intellect that . . . joined logic to feeling."[86] He understood "that the intellect is not (need not be) a solvent of sensibility; but that the intellect is the only adequate precipitant of it, in a critical form."[87] Such a realization "cut [the] false rationalization" that could justify, in the name of democracy, the use of the technological advances of science for the material advantages of war, a justification that could only be made if it were kept separate from questions of ethical responsibility. Aldous Huxley, another of Toomer's foremost role models,[88] had noted in *Ends and Means* (1937),

> the means employed inevitably determine the nature of the ends produced. . . . In increasing their armaments to take a "firm stand" against fascist aggression, the democratic countries are gradually but systematically being transformed into the likeness of the fascist States they so much detest. "Those who prepare for war start up an armament race and, in due course, get the war they prepare for."[89]

Huxley's fear echoes Bourne's theory that "economies depend on war, and the people depend on the economy. Once weapons are designed and built—in the name of peace, of course—they must be deployed."[90] Bruce Clayton, Bourne's biographer, says, "This line of reasoning . . . brought Bourne to write the most chillingly ironic line of his life: 'War is the health of the State.'"[91]

Bourne's opinions about the First World War, moreover, had a profound influence on many of his contemporaries, most notably the *Seven Arts* group of which he was a member with Waldo Frank and with which Toomer was closely associated. In *Our America* (1919), Frank commemorates Bourne who died in the influenza epidemic of 1918. Bourne had studied under Dewey at Columbia University, but Frank notes, "the war, which drove all the world including Dewey mad, drove Bourne sane. The crisis which set and fixed the master [Dewey], freed Bourne and made him fluent."[92]

More important for my discussion of Toomer, however, is Frank's claim that Bourne's significance "lies in the joining, through his work, of the political and the cultural currents of advance."[93] Bourne's ability to bridge the realms of thought and feeling made him the prime exemplar for cultural critics who cared to listen. Toomer must have been all ears, given the striking resemblance between Frank's description of Bourne and Toomer's own rhetoric: "His political discussions were actually lit by a spiritual viewpoint. They took into account the content of the human soul, the individual soul, the values of *being*."[94] This desire to link the political to the spiritual or cultural is one of the main features of a cosmopolitan project of "aesthetic politics." Even though there is a shift in Toomer's rhetoric from early discussions of art to later discussions of spirituality, the aesthetic and the spiritual function in similar ways in relation to the political. "The aesthetic and the political," for such figures as Toomer, Bourne, Dewey and Du Bois, "are experimental modes of conduct that delve into 'gross experience' . . . [and suggest] 'possibilities of human relations not to be found in rule and precept.'"[95] In addition, the aesthetic can serve, as Marxist theorists such as Benjamin, Adorno and Lukács, have noted as "a paradigm of ethical behavior and cultural critique."[96] It is my argument, then, that the mode or structure of dialectical thought Toomer exhibits in his writing is part of a tradition of cosmopolitanism in which it is understood that to think across ostensibly separate discourses or contradictory categories, such as the humanities and science, aesthetics and politics, the spiritual and the material, the particular and the universal, is also to enrich each of those discourses in its ability not only to address but to affect ways of knowing and being in the world.

Like Du Bois, who "instead of segregating culture from politics" sought "to develop a 'higher and broader and more varied human culture,' a project he described as the 'main end of democracy,'" Toomer conceived of the aesthetic, the individual, and the democratic as intricately linked through their status as ongoing processes of becoming rather than fixed endpoints to be reached.[97] In a journal entry from 1923, Toomer writes, "Nothing is. All life is becoming. Art is the highest expression, manifestation, of this process."[98] And in "The Individual and Democracy," which we looked at earlier for his discussion of the assimilative process of becoming an individual, Toomer states, "In brief, my thesis is that the process of individualisation and the process of genuine democratisation are practically one and the same thing."[99] Toomer's desire to replace the idea of fixed identity with an assimilative act of individuality that remains open to experience is analogous, then, to the process of democratization. In "Trans-National America," Bourne also writes about this process, which he variously calls democratization or "Americanization," when he urges us to re-examine and, in fact, to make a "general readjustment of our attitude and our ideal" in "assert[ing] a higher ideal than the 'melting-pot'":

> Surely we cannot be certain of our spiritual democracy when, claiming to melt the nations within us to a comprehension of our free and democratic institutions, we fly into panic at the first sign of their own will and tendency. We act as if we wanted Americanization to take place only on our own terms, and not by the consent of the governed . . . neglect[ing] to take into account this strong and virile insistence that America shall be what the immigrant will have a hand in making it, and not what a ruling class, descendant of those British stocks which were the first permanent immigrants, decide that America shall be made.[100]

Similarly, Toomer understands that the process of democratization, like the process of individualization, must remain open to new elements and experience in order to assimilate them, not by making the new elements conform to a static idea but in reciprocally changing the idea itself. In his examination of Dewey's response to the march of fascism in 1939, Posnock writes that democracy, like individuality, is a process of becoming, not "a stable entity engraved in a constitution and guaranteeing us immunity from the disease of totalitarianism." What is most important about culture, politics and individuality, and what Toomer, too, would have us realize, is their status as "perpetual pursuits" in "the deferral of identity."[101]

As Posnock illustrates through the language of Du Bois and Dewey, "democracy and art" are "strenuous ways of being in the world," such that "to achieve the ideal of equality and to achieve art require forsaking the comforts of the already given . . . for the risks of improvisatory, that is, political, conduct."[102] If democracy is an ongoing process like Americanization, then we can begin to see how, in Toomer's cosmopolitan project, art, democracy and individuality are analogous to each other. Recalling Bourne's words quoted above, Posnock writes, "'Americanness' defies exactitude because its identity is not preordained (something to which one measures up) but rather is the very process of playing 'the appropriation game.'" In a way that corresponds with Toomer's description of an "American race," he continues, "it seems reasonable to infer that cosmopolitan and American are synonymous."[103]

"MANKIND UNITED": TOOMER'S FLIGHTS OF UNIVERSALIST FANCY

Toomer's writing should be valued for its emphasis on experience, practice and process rather than fixed identity categories, as should his capacity to think across ostensibly discrete discourses and categorical distinctions, such as the humanities and science, aesthetics and politics, the spiritual and the material, the particular and the universal. I identify this rigorous mode of thinking as cosmopolitan and argue for its importance as a kind of intellectual action that enriches discourse and representation, and by extension, actual social structures and ways of being in the world. In the concluding section to this chapter, however, I argue that Toomer's cosmopolitan project ultimately fails to make a lasting effect on a realm of discourse that deeply affects social structures in American society, namely, racial discourse. Rather than sustain the tension between particular and universal in matters of race, a tension that is required for the kind of cosmopolitanism I promote in this project, Toomer takes off on flights of cosmic universalism with a problematic and impractical will to transcend the socio-historical and political realities of particular racial identities and local experiences.

We have already noted Toomer's attempt to affect racial discourse in theorizing an "American race" with miscegenation as its standard. In *A Fiction and Some Facts* he clarifies this position as not preoccupied with national identity but with a cosmopolitan ideal of "develop[ing] beyond national moulds and becom[ing] a citizen of the world in the Socratic sense."[104] Martha Nussbaum, in her defense of cosmopolitanism, argues:

> [T]o be a citizen of the world one does not need to give up local identifications, which can be a source of great richness in life. . . . [W]e [should] think of ourselves not as devoid of local affiliations, but as surrounded by a series of concentric circles. . . . We need not give up our special affections and identifications, whether ethnic or gender-based or religious. We need not think of them as superficial, and we may think of our identity as constituted partly by them. . . . But we should also work to make all human beings part of our community of dialogue and concern, base our political deliberations on that interlocking commonality, and give the circle that defines our humanity special attention and respect.[105]

Cosmopolitanism is a valuable discourse because, like the "concentric circles" model, it mediates between the universal and the particular; it requires a rigorous mode of thinking structured around a dialectic of universal and particular. Within this dialectic, it might become possible to sponsor "a raceless society without erasing the historical experience of racism."[106]

It is in matters of race, however, that Toomer is most transcendent in his rhetoric, ignoring, disavowing and desperately trying to abolish the differences and particularities of racial identity and experience. His language belies a desire to "rise above," "extend beyond," and "overcome." It is as if the largest circle of universal humanity has disconnected from the other circles and is floating somewhere up in space like a flying saucer. In *A Fiction and Some Facts* Toomer states, "the only hope of mankind is to rise above egotism, extend beyond partisanship, overcome separatisms of all kinds and re-merge the now different and often antagonistic elements into a unified and harmonious whole." He ends the pamphlet with the dramatic claim, "In my thought, in my ideals, and in the very life I live from day to day I stand for Mankind United. This perhaps is the largest and the most significant single fact of my life."[107]

We might follow statements such as these with a question that should temper all gestures towards cosmopolitanism: "by whose standards do we define universalism?" Linda Zerilli, in "This Universalism Which Is Not One," points out that the question has arisen "as to whether the universal . . . is little more than an 'inflated particular.'"[108] Zerilli, following Ernesto Laclau, responds by asserting that the universal is actually an "empty place": "a site of multiple significations which concern . . . the irreducibly plural standpoints of democratic politics."[109] She explains, "There is nothing that we all share by virtue of being human or of living in a particular community that guarantees a common view of the world; there is nothing extralinguistic in the world that guarantees that we all share a common experience; there is no Archimedean place from which we could accede to a universal standpoint."[110] Yet this does not mean we must abandon the concept of universality; rather, we can reinterpret it to mean "not a preexisting something (essence or form) to which individuals accede but, rather, the fragile, shifting, and always incomplete achievement of political action; it is not the container of a presence but the placeholder of an absence, not a substantive content but an empty place."[111] Unlike Zerilli, who argues that the universal is not One, Toomer argues for "a unified and harmonious whole," a cosmically detached universal that most definitely is One.

Although Toomer does not sustain a dialectical mode of thought when it comes to matters of race, he continues to draw creative energy, throughout his life, from what he calls, in the title to a talk he gave to a Society of Friends school in 1939, "The Crucial Struggle" between individuality and group identity.[112] Too often, however, Toomer jettisons particulars, rather than living and writing within the antagonisms of difference or for a universal that is always incomplete, always requiring new forms of representation and political action. Although Toomer gave up writing about race specifically, his exemplary defiance of rigid categorization, his emphasis on experience and process, and his belief in the validity and importance of thinking and living the seemingly contradictory together are foundations that we can build upon and, hopefully, improve.

Chapter Two

The "Interminable Puzzles" of Race, Class and Gender in the Novels of Jessie Redmon Fauset

As Jessie Redmon Fauset's second novel, *Plum Bun,* approaches the neatly conventional dénouement of most sentimental fiction, its main character, Angela Murray, begins to admit her uncertainty regarding "'[j]ust what is or is not ethical in this matter of colour.'"[1] Although she had previously dismissed the difficulty of negotiating the gap between racial identity and color with a simple "when it seemed best to be coloured she would be coloured; when it was best to be white she would be that" (253), as the novel draws to a close, Angela's "head ached with the futility of trying to find a solution to these interminable puzzles" (337). In addition to the gap between racial identity and color, then, Angela's confusion reveals another disparity between the neatly wrapped forms of literary convention and the impossibility of reaching a satisfying solution in the complex tangle of race, gender and class that is Fauset's central concern.[2]

As I maneuver through such complex disparities in Fauset's four major works of fiction—*There Is Confusion* (1924), *Plum Bun* (1929), *The Chinaberry Tree* (1931), and *Comedy: American Style* (1934)—I hope to divulge two distinct yet interrelated movements. First, given that the first novel, *There Is Confusion,* introduces in some form all the major issues that Fauset would continue to explore in greater depth in her later novels, there is a progression or a pushing forward of sorts with each subsequent work of fiction to a greater sophistication in working through the "interminable puzzles" of race, gender and class in America. The second is more difficult to locate, yet for that reason more compelling, and it is what I will call Fauset's cosmopolitan complexity as she deftly shifts the emphasis from the virtues of a strong racial identification to its costs, from the values of personal growth and individualization to their pitfalls. Rather than cancel each other out, these careful and continuous shifts in emphasis between novels accomplish two things: first, they illustrate Fauset's refusal to simplify the central problematics of her work, and second, they require her audience to engage in the continuous struggle of thinking through the difficult contradictions and "interminable puzzles" in the intersections of race, gender, class and these United States.[3]

My reading of Fauset's novels follows, in part, Claudia Tate's study of black textuality, *Psychoanalysis and Black Novels: Desire and the Protocols of Race.* Tate posits the two terms of her subtitle, desire or "the individual and subjective experience of [the] personal" and the protocols of race or "explicit, public, racial identifications," as "two broad categories of experience" that are often in conflict both in the lives and the representations of black subjects.[4] Tate argues that literary critics who proceed from the demands of "modernist conventions of blackness" have tended to value representations with a racialist agenda over expressions of private longing.[5] Following this, she asks us to "examine novels written by African Americans that do not fit the typical racial paradigm because they did not conform to modern conceptions of black identity" or, in other words, because they accentuate the "expression of personal emotional meaning." Tate calls these "anomalous black novels" and wonders if "postmodern black criticism" might not be best suited for investigating them.[6]

Fauset's novels are perfectly suited for such an inquiry. In fact, while her novels were for the most part favorably received by her contemporaries, many of Fauset's early critics devalued her work in the very terms Tate employs, albeit with less sympathy or critical interest.[7] The folk has "been privileged as the 'authentic' African American voice and experience," writes Sharon L. Jones, which leaves fiction like Fauset's open to criticism for not being black enough, for uncritically representing bourgeois values, and for being removed from the lived reality of the black masses.[8] As for more current criticism, Cheryl Wall accuses Fauset's fiction of being "ultimately cripple[d]" by "the privileging of the private over the public, the retreat into domesticity, and the denial of difference."[9] And Hazel Carby claims that Fauset's "development of an ideology for an emerging black middle class" includes "the need for the protagonists to revise the irrelevant history of their parents, a history tied to the consequences of slavery."[10] I counter these critics by emphasizing rather than ignoring the tensions in Fauset's novels between the private, domesticity, and personal desire and the protocols of race or public, racial identifications that have been typically aligned with modern conceptions of black identity.

As I respond to Tate's call by examining Fauset's "anomalous black fiction" in this light, I also modify her idea that the postmodern is the term best suited to pursue an inquiry into works of literature that "make visible the ways in which we readers have circumscribed black subjectivity and black textuality by a reductive understanding of racial difference that has in turn made concepts of race and desire seem incompatible."[11] Instead, what I have been identifying as cosmopolitanism's ability to mediate seemingly contradictory aspects of experience, from the universal to the particular, from group identity and community to an individuated sense of self and personal longing, makes it the more appropriate term for exploring Fauset's fiction in all its complexity. Cosmopolitan textual strategies, then, aid the critic in identifying, describing, and making sense of "a process," to use Tate's words, "by which the respective author negotiates explicit, public, racial identifications . . . with the implicit, private psychological effects of narrative subjectivity."[12]

"LIFE AT ITS BEST IS A GRAND CORRECTIVE":[13] STRUGGLING FOR BALANCE

Fauset's first novel, *There Is Confusion* (1924) is primarily focused on the struggle to balance personal freedom and ambition with meaningful interpersonal relationships and self-sacrifice. While Fauset, through the structure of the bildungsroman, presses her characters towards lessons and choices that stand as "correctives" in their lives, she also introduces an underlying problematic which is developed more fully in her next novel, *Plum Bun:* the "interminable puzzle" of locating one's life between the often conflicted poles of racial identity and personal desire. In addition, *There Is Confusion* introduces several other issues through which Fauset will continue to work in subsequent novels, often with greater depth and complexity. Most important, and clearly aligned with Du Bois's notion of the "kingdom of culture" which he locates above the color line, are the main character Joanna Marshall's artistic aspirations and motivations, her independence, and her use of black culture to remake the idea of America. Another key problematic is centered on class boundaries and discrimination, most thoroughly examined with the working-class Maggie Ellersley and her various interactions with members of the bourgeois Marshall family.[14] Racial chauvinism is also explored through the character of Peter Bye and his complicated family history.

Starting with a discussion of Peter Bye's racial chauvinism will open up discussion for the other "confusions" of the text, so I begin with an early childhood scene from the novel between Peter at age twelve and Joanna at age ten on the day they first meet. Peter and Joanna are in the same classroom because Peter, having moved frequently with his father, is oddly "lacking and yet curiously in advance" (41). As he sits in class, Peter, who "wanted to shine, but did not realize that one shone only as a result of much mental polishing personally applied," admires Joanna, whose appearance is not only perfect but who has "assurance, [an] air of purposefulness, [and] . . . indifference" (42). As readers, we already recognize that Peter has a fairly large chip on his shoulder which he has inherited from his father, Meriwether, along with a family history that includes a slave master Joshua Bye, whose white son Meriwether, is the namesake of the black Isaiah Bye's son, Peter's father. Other characters talk about "the complex of color in Peter's life," a factor that they say is present at some point in every colored person's life; however, "Peter's got it worse than most of us because he's got such a terrible 'mad' on white people to start with" (179). With this information in mind, we must read the following passage closely, for Peter's first encounter with Joanna tells us more than we might at first assume:

> Peter had seen little girls with this perfection and assurance on Chestnut Street in Philadelphia and on Fifth Avenue in New York, but they had been white. He had not yet envisaged this sort of thing for his own. Perhaps he inherited his great-grandfather Joshua's spiritless acceptance of things as they are, and his belief that differences between people were not made, but had to be. (41–42)

The convoluted logic of this passage suggests that Peter's hatred of white people involves an insidious underside: an unacknowledged belief in white superiority which accompanies a belief in black inferiority. It also reveals a deeply rooted self-hatred.

Such a reading is supported by a passage that takes place slightly later in Joanna's and Peter's lives when she tells Peter that she wants to be a singer and he assumes she means in the town's choir. He is astonished when Joanna exclaims,

> "In my choir—I sing there already! No! Everywhere, anywhere, Carnegie Hall and in Boston and London. You see, I'm to be famous."
>
> "But," Peter objected, "colored people don't get any chance at that kind of thing."
>
> "Colored people," Joanna quoted from her extensive reading, "can do everything that anybody else can do. . . . I'm going to be the one colored person who sings best in these days, and I never, never, never mean to let color interfere with anything I *really* want to do."
>
> "I dance, too," she interrupted herself, "and I'll probably do that besides. Not ordinary dancing, you know, but queer beautiful things that are different from what we see around here; perhaps I'll make them

> up myself. You'll see! They'll have on the bill-board, 'Joanna Marshall, the famous artist,'—" (45)

Peter's doubt regarding colored people's opportunities blurs indistinguishably with his incredulity regarding Joanna's plans to reach as high as any other person who desires to use her abilities to do great things. Joanna, on the other hand, sees "the kingdom of culture," to borrow Du Bois's phrase, as a place where color does not matter: she will be billed as "the famous artist" who plays in the cosmopolitan capitals of the world, not the famous black artist who came up in the local town choir. Importantly, Joanna also associates this cultural realm above the color line with high art forms; thus, she will not dance "ordinarily" but will create "queer, beautiful things that are different from what we see around here." Nonetheless, Fauset builds an ironic twist into this passage, one that Joanna is typically responsible for voicing yet, just as typically, without awareness. Immediately before saying that she will never allow color to interfere with her dreams and ambitions, Joanna singles herself out as "the one colored person who sings best in these days." Peter might have asked, why only the "one," why not just *the* best singer in these days? That there can only be one who registers as an exception is a social reality of her day which Joanna mouths but does not contemplate. As we shall see, this is typical of Joanna until quite late in her development as a character.

Another typical trait of Joanna's that will stand corrected by the novel's end is her propensity for thoughtlessly declaring her independence and eschewing group identity, even if some group affiliations, while remaining unacknowledged, are clearly more important to her than others. For example, when Brian, Joanna's sister's fiancé, speaks to Joanna about her relationship and future with Peter, her career plans and determined independence, or in Brian's words, "your singing and dancing and your wildcat schemes of getting on the stage," he admonishes her to "stick to your own Janna, and build up colored art." But Joanna responds by crying with astonishment: "Why, I am. . . . You don't think I want to forsake—*us*. Not at all. But I want to show *us* to the world. I am colored, of course, but American first. Why shouldn't I speak to all America?" (76). Now, on the one hand, her declaration of a more general affiliation as "American" taking precedent over the particular affiliation, "colored," does not seem entirely problematic. As a matter of fact, Joanna's reasoning soundly implies the idea that Du Bois argues in *The Souls of Black Folk* and that is explicitly expressed later in the novel by Joanna's brother Philip when he starts an organization closely resembling the NAACP. In describing his vision to a group of both black and white enthusiasts, Philip says, "White and colored people alike may belong to it . . . but it is to favor primarily the interests of colored people. No, I'm wrong there. . . . It is to favor primarily the interests of the country" (129). Similar to the implications of Joanna's remarks, Philip's correction makes African-American-centered culture and politics not only representative of a minority position within the United States, a position which is somehow precluded from being representatively American; quite the contrary, African-American culture and politics are at the center of the country's ideals and visions.

On the other hand, and as Brian's response, "H'm, I suppose you're right," to Joanna's astonished cry belies, there is also cause for uncertainty about Joanna's remarks (76). Joanna's hesitation (marked by a dash in the text) in pronouncing "*us*" and the emphatic stress (marked by italics) on the word, reminds readers that something may be amiss. Joanna's frequent quips dismissing the "interminable puzzles" of the color line in America, her unexamined belief that, in the words of her French dance instructor, "if there's anything that will break down prejudice it will be equality or perhaps even superiority on the part of colored people in the arts" (97), and her oversimplification of matters of race, class, and gender, in general, make such a pronouncement cause for a certain amount of skepticism. It is not that Joanna is not partially right; however, her notions regarding race and art's ability to break down boundaries are always unsettlingly simplistic. Moreover, the transcending of color that occurs in the kingdom of culture apparently does not extend to class lines in Joanna's scheme of things. Again, she does not even see the hypocrisy in her inconsistent attitudes regarding race and class until much later in her development.

This is even more explicitly illustrated in another scene that takes place on a particularly hot night in Philadelphia between Joanna and Brian when they attend a concert together where "a gracious, mellow-voiced woman fill[s] a hall with sound that made them forget the heat" (77). Fauset structures the scene so that first we witness art's ability to break down boundaries in the ideal kingdom of culture. After the concert, Brian says, "'[M]y collar's wringing wet, and I never thought of it. Wonderful how music can make people forget.' 'Even color,' said Joanna thoughtfully. 'Did you see that white woman next to me edge away when I sat down? But when she heard me humming after it was over, she leaned over and asked me if I knew the words'" (77). This assertion, however, of art's ability to break down racial boundaries is immediately followed by the reinforcement of others on Joanna's part. She and Brian have been walking home from the concert when, in the same loaded sentence, Brian mentions Philip, Joanna's beloved older brother, and Maggie Ellersley, a friend of the family and the recipient of Philip's affections.

> Joanna, in the act of entering the door, stepped back and faced him sharply. "What's Maggie got to do with it?"
>
> "Well, she and Phil. They've always paired off together, haven't they? . . . ."
>
> "She wouldn't dare," said Joanna fiercely. "Why, Philip—he's going to be somebody great, wonderful, a Garibaldi, a Toussaint! And Maggie, Maggie's just nobody, Brian. Why, do you know what she's taking up? Hair work, straightening hair, salves and shampoos and curling-irons."
>
> "Joanna, you're an utter snob. I always knew you looked down on people unless they were following some mad will o' the wisp. Maggie's as good as any of us. Why look here, she graduated from high school with Sylvia. You can't look down on her."
>
> "Sylvia's my sister, thank you. She's Joel Marshall's daughter. She has background, she knows good music and pictures and worth while people."
>
> "You talk like a silly book. What's that got to do with it? . . . ." (77–78)

The irony of this passage is that Joanna upholds class boundaries like some uphold the color line, yet she remains unaware of the parallels between her prejudices and those which she refuses to let stand in her way. As a critique of exclusive bourgeois attitudes, this passage implies that not only are the highbrow intellectual and artistic endeavors associated with Du Bois and the Talented Tenth to be valued, but the business, trade and entrepreneurial skills associated with Booker T. Washington and the Tuskegee Institute are also necessary and important components of any solid community and should be valued on an equal basis. The narrator's positioning in this scene also implies a belief in education's yeast-like effect, enabling people to rise up, as opposed to a belief in fixed class lines. Moreover, there is the possibility that poverty might create not only a desire but a will to strive for greatness: "'What ambition has she?' Joanna asked herself fiercely, forgetting to measure the depth of the abyss of poverty and wretchedness from which Maggie had sprung. 'She shan't spoil my brother's chances'" (79). If for no other reason, such a lack of awareness and self-consciousness in Joanna's unwittingly hypocritical assertions problematizes the earlier ideals she expressed regarding the boundless kingdom of culture. It makes us reconsider how dangerous "forgetting" can be because, as with the white woman seated next to Joanna at the concert, it does not point to real social change, only moments and limited spaces of color blindness—and blindness and forgetting are anything but solutions to racial inequality in the United States. Her ideas of transcendence, then, are not the complex cosmopolitan stance to which Du Bois aspired where both racial particularity and universal connection can exist at one and the same time; rather Joanna's simplistic reading of the situation is, as Brian says regarding her class prejudices, just her "talking like a silly book."

Joanna does, at times, both talk and act like a silly book, putting into motion the pivotal plot developments in Fauset's parodic sentimental novel. Immediately following the above conversation with Brian, Joanna writes Maggie a cruel letter regarding her relationship with Philip, and the long-lasting effects of this letter bear out the rest of the story to its dénouement. According to Joanna's plan, Maggie and Philip are driven apart, yet the repercussions of this are not, on Joanna's part, as calculated or as desired: Maggie abruptly marries the gambler Henderson Neale, and this drives Peter away to teach school in the South. However, Joanna's meddling also highlights the ways in which both Maggie's and Joanna's lives stand in need of "correctives," and it points to a larger lesson beyond each character's personal development.

In regards to Maggie, Brian says that she "'doesn't see life in the large, she's too much taken up with getting what she wants out of her own life'" (180). This leads her to seek out a husband for safety, protection, stability, and reputation in order to attain the middle-class life of which she has always dreamed. Joanna, on the other hand, has one "persistent ambition" (267), an "inordinate craving for sheer success" (290), a "desire for greatness" (291) which takes precedent over all else in her life and permits her to carry out acts of cruelty and selfishness that ultimately leave her alone and grasping for meaning in her life. Although Maggie looks for security and protection in dependence on a man while Joanna's extreme independence in striving for her own career goals leads her to disregard the man she loves, the two are not entirely dissimilar. As a matter of fact, Maggie's dependence on men, her constant search for one that will satisfy her desire for middle-class respectability by marrying her, is described as "that old insistent ambition" (262), and herein lies the link between Maggie and Joanna. Both put a selfish ambition over everything else in their lives, never considering that there is also reward in self-sacrifice. Their development will then require a "corrective" to their respective ambitions. "Maggie's greatest secret triumph" is becoming "independent, self-reliant" (261) by first selflessly devoting her life to caring for wounded soldiers in the war, with "no impulse to attempt to realize that old insistent ambition," and then putting her energy into starting her own hair and beauty business (262). Joanna comes to understand that "the ordinary things of life," the very things on which Maggie had been so intently focused, are also "the essentials" while fame is just "the trimmings of existence" (290). Sacrificing some of her ambition to a life shared with Peter "left her her true self," and rather than creating a situation of dependence, we are told in a paragraph of only one sentence regarding her life changes, "Joanna was free" (291). Although no perfect and endlessly stable balance can be struck, Maggie learns to value independence while Joanna chooses to sacrifice some independence, and each finally learns that acting for a greater good rather than mere personal gain can also be ultimately rewarding.

Complicating this nicely balanced pair of lessons, however, is Philip, the self-sacrificing race man, whose "great obsession" has always been to go to "battle" for "the race." He tells Maggie that he "never consciously let any thought of self come to [him]" as he was growing up but instead "was always so sure that [he] was going to strike a blow at this great, towering monster" (266–67). Unlike either Joanna or Maggie, Philip's ambition has been entirely based on self-sacrifice and seeing "life in the large." He has been "so taken up with the business of being colored" that he has forgotten to look after his own "natural joys," love and his personal life (287, 266). Philip's great lesson, as he tells Joanna, is to "learn to look out for life first, then color and limitations" (287). Couching this lesson in the language of war, for which he ultimately sacrifices his life in defense of his country, he continues, "Our battle is a hard one and for a long time it will seem to be a losing one, but it will never really be that as long as we keep the power of being happy. And happiness has to be deliberately sought for, gained; even that doesn't solve the problem. . . . Happiness, love, contentment in our own midst, make it possible for us to face those foes without" (288). Philip makes clear the link between personal fulfillment and desire and the racial politics which inevitably entail some amount of personal sacrifice: rather than see them as opposed, he argues that one necessarily aids the other in a mutual striving. However, he does prioritize "life," or personal fulfillment and happiness, over devoting one's life to "this awful business of color in America" (266). This should give us pause, for it contradicts the lessons of self-sacrifice through which Joanna and Maggie have struggled. In addition, the underlying problematic of Fauset's text, and one that she develops with greater complexity in her next novel, *Plum Bun,* rests on this very contradiction.

All the "correctives" of characters' lives in *There Is Confusion* revolve around struggling for a balance between the personal and the public, between independence and sacrifice—a balance, albeit, that is never complete, never perfect, never entirely stable, but one that requires continual striving and constant struggle. This complicated solution, if one can even call it that, is further problematized by the implications of a conversation between Peter and his father's namesake, the white Meriwether Bye, who Peter meets in France as they both fight for their country in the First World War. Discussing white people's idealistic assumptions about America as a place of liberty and asylum for the oppressed, Meriwether admits his shame at having come to the realization that his perception of life as "beautiful and perfect" rested "quite specifically on the backs of broken, beaten slaves," a realization that gave him "a shock" which has "robbed [him] of happiness forever" (245–46). Peter responds frankly to the overly dramatic nature of this confession: "'I like to hear you acknowledge your indebtedness . . . but I don't think you should take on your shoulders the penitence of the whole white nation'" (246). Meriwether, maintaining his stance, explains:

> "No, I don't think I should, either . . . but that sort of extremeness seems to be inherent in the question of color. Either you concern yourself with it violently as the Southerner does and so let slip by all the other important issues of life; or you are indifferent and callous like the average Northerner and grow hardened to all sorts of atrocities; or you steep yourself in it like the sentimentalist—that's my class—and find yourself paralyzed by the vastness of the problem." (246)

Because "the question of color" in America is so complicated and fraught with inconsistencies and atrocities, it becomes nearly impossible to keep it in any sort of perspective or to struggle to balance it with the other confusions of life. If "extremeness" is "inherent in the question of color," then it seems to work as a counterforce to the moderation required in the other life lessons of the novel that stress an ongoing struggle for balance. To care deeply about the question of color, Fauset seems to suggest, will inevitably frustrate and throw off all other attempts at balance in one's life. Earlier in the novel, Brian says that "the complex of color" presents itself at some point or another as the ultimate "confusion" in every colored person's life; it appears to be an insurmountable obstacle that "gets in the way of his dreams, his education, his marriage, and the rearing of his children." He admits that "the ordinary job of living is bad enough," but adding to it "the thousand and one difficulties which follow simply in the train of being colored" can complicated matters to such an extent that it is liable to drive a person insane (179).

Fauset leaves us with a two-pronged dilemma: on the one hand, there is life with its attendant confusions, the need for correctives, and the struggle to balance the private and the public, ambition and self-sacrifice, personal freedom and close ties with others. On the other hand, there is the "inextricable puzzle" of race which becomes tangled with the other complexities of life. Whereas the problematic of balancing a deep concern for race with the attendant confusions of life is embedded in *There Is Confusion,* it is handled with greater depth in Fauset's next novel, *Plum Bun.*

Therein, Fauset more explicitly addresses the nearly impossible task of balancing the universal confusions of life and the particular extremes of the color line in America.

"LOOK HERE, THIS IS WHAT A MIXTURE OF BLACK AND WHITE REALLY MEANS!": MERGING PRINCIPLE WITH INDIVIDUAL DESIRE

Fauset's second novel, *Plum Bun* (1929) highlights the "interminable puzzles" of locating one's life between the oft-conflicted poles of racial identity and personal fulfillment and longing. With a five-part structure that follows the arch of the "Plum Bun" nursery rhyme, Fauset walks her main character, Angela Murray, through various stages of ignorance, disillusionment, and misconception to understanding, responsibility, and fulfillment. At first, individual and group identity are contrasted through Angela and her sister Virginia, who is constructed as her foil. Angela, an artist figure, is aligned with whiteness, selfishness, and eventually, loneliness; Virginia, the domestic angel, is aligned with family, blackness, and racial pride. Early on, however, Fauset shows this dichotomy to be seriously flawed, stressing, as she does in *There Is Confusion,* a necessary balance between these poles. She also problematizes the assumption that racial pride and individual fulfillment are necessarily opposed without oversimplifying the conflict that often results between them in people's lives. Going beyond the tentative conclusion of her first novel, Fauset illustrates in *Plum Bun* that neither color nor sacrifice need be experienced as a limitations. Instead, Angela comes to understand that principle can merge with individual desire if she moves beyond her longing for fairytale endings and puts in its place a more mature and responsible pride that nurtures yet transcends the self.

The movement of leaving home and returning (with a difference)—mirrored in the movement of the five sections of the novel, "Home," "Market," "Plum Bun," "Home Again," "Market Is Done"—is introduced early in the novel's first section when on Saturdays Angela and her mother, Mattie, exit home and black racial identity to "pass" in the tea rooms, department stores, theatres and hotel lobbies of upscale Philadelphia establishments. Angela, who increasingly values these passing experiences, is unaware that her mother, with "a keener sense of humour than her daughter," views them as "unnecessary and silly" and participates in them out of "a mischievous determination to flout a silly and unjust law" (15, 17). Angela's misreading of her mother's motivations and intentions, however, leads her to draw "certain clearly formed conclusions" about the value of passing and the superiority and desirability of whiteness, "which her subconscious mind thus codified" (17). Like Joanna's problematic reading, in *There Is Confusion,* of the moment of color blindness which she experiences with the racist white woman at the concert, Angela's attitudes about passing are fallaciously unaware. The repercussions of such ignorance are made evident when Mattie determines to never again allow passing to take precedence over her family after she had allowed her own husband and daughter to pass by her without acknowledging them: "But of this determination Angela, dreaming excitedly of Saturdays spent in turning her small olive face firmly away from peering black countenances was, unhappily, unaware" (19). Here the narrator links being "unaware" with being "unhappy," and as Fauset's previous novel has shown us, happiness is a key component in the struggle for racial pride and individual fulfillment.

Angela's unawareness becomes a more explicit unhappiness after her friend, Mary Hastings, shrinks in bewilderment upon discovering that Angela is colored. This first in a series of recognition scenes thrusts Angela into an early moral dilemma regarding racial identity and individual desire: "she began to wonder which was the more important, a patent insistence on the fact of colour or an acceptance of the good things of life which could come to you in America if either you were not coloured or the fact of racial connections was not made known" (46). The dichotomous structure of Angela's thought in this sentence reveals the root of her faulty reasoning; namely, Angela equates black "racial affiliations" with "restrictions" and a "narrow[ing] of her confines" (57, 67). Even when she imagines wealthy black people, she disdains their racial identification: "their thoughts, their actions were still cramped and confined; they were sitting in their new, even luxurious quarters, still mental parvenus, still discussing the eternal race question" (67). Longing for "a larger, freer world" (57), for the company of "people with a broad, cultural background behind them, or, lacking that, with the originality of thought and speech which comes from failing, deliberately failing, to conform to the pattern" (67), Angela, like Peter Bye in *There Is Confusion,* presumes this level of culture to exist only among white people, not, in her opinion, among the provincial and small-minded, middle-class black people with whom she was raised.

Because Angela thinks that "all the things which she most wanted were wrapped up with white people" and because "she possesse[s] the badge" of that power which is whiteness, she makes the conscious decision to use it in moving to New York, away from family, home and community, to pursue "clever people, people who do things, Art," which, the narrator tell us, "her voice spelt . . . with a capital" (73, 78). Yet shortly after she arrives in New York, at the beginning of the novel's second section, "Market," Angela realizes that although "she was getting acquainted with life in her own way without restrictions or restraint," although "she was young . . . temporarily independent . . . intelligent . . . [and] white," the freedom from limitations that she so desires also requires that "she must have money and influence . . . protection" (87–88). And this leads her to consider if "perhaps it would be better to marry . . . a white man" (ellipses in original, 88). When she begins dating the wealthy, white Roger Fielding, it seems to Angela that all her dreams are about to come true: "she was sure now that he loved and would want to marry her, for it never occurred to her that men bestowed attentions such as these on a passing fancy. She saw her life rounding out like a fairy tale" (130–31). The problem with fairy tales, however, is that in order for the distressed maiden to be rescued by a charming prince, the maiden must be wholly passive and dependent while the heroic prince acts courageously, providing everlasting protection and security. Angela's early life has been infused with and influenced by the fairy tale myth of her parents' relationship: "Mattie her husband considered a perfect woman, sweet, industrious, affectionate and illogical. But to her he was god. When Angela and Virginia were little children and their mother used to read them fairy tales she would add to the ending, 'And so they lived happily ever after, just like your father and me'" (32–33). Unfortunately, Angela has a long way to travel before she recognizes the contradiction between her desire for freedom from limitations and the road she chooses to get there, a narrow one constrained by dependence, deceit, and even worse, "a sick distaste for her [own] action[s]" (162).

In a scene that mirrors the early passing scene when Angela and her mother stand aside and let her father and sister walk by without acknowledging them, Angela disavows her sister whom she is to meet at the train station because of a chance run-in with Roger. Having discovered Roger's racism from an unpleasant experience at a café with a black couple, Angela is torn between allegiance and love to her sister and pandering to the ridiculous whims of the man upon whom she depends to give her the life she craves. In the "Plum Bun" section, rather than have her fairytale dreams fulfilled, Angela is rudely awakened to Roger's intentions to keep her as a mistress instead of making her his wife. This turn of events is a pivotal moment in Angela's development because it rids her of much of her naïveté and sheds new light on her notions of individualism and nonconformity. At first, Angela decides to sleep with Roger but promises herself that she will accept no money from him. Throwing caution to the wind, trying on the rôle of the new modern woman, Angela decides to "live her life as an individualist, to suit herself without regard for the conventions and established ways of life" (207–08). However, the heady intensity of this experience, which she mistakes for happiness, proves itself the stalest of plum buns (204). Although painful, this experience makes Angela reconsider her stake in being "an individualist," in disregarding all "conventions and established ways of life": "And she began to see the conventions, the rules that govern life, in a new light; she realized suddenly that for all their granite-like coldness and precision they also represented fundamental facts; a sort of concentrated compendium of the art of living and therefore as much to be observed and respected as warm, vital impulses" (228). With this new appreciation for the old, Angela returns "Home Again" in section four, accompanied with the thought that "her sum total of the knowledge of life had been increased" and with "a great nostalgia for something real and permanent" (245, 250).

Angela's return home, however, by no means marks a point of full maturity although in many ways it resembles the point at which Joanna arrives by the end of *There Is Confusion,* willing to sacrifice ambition and independence for a deeper emotional connection with others. For all her growth, however, there is still much room for development regarding her attitude toward race and awareness of the need to balance the desire for individual fulfillment with the security and companionship of family, love and group identity. An indication of Angela's inability to think deeply about the decisions she has made regarding racial identification and to balance individual growth with being a member of a group is revealed in the following passage:

> her thoughts skirted the subject [of color] warily for she knew how immensely difficult living could be made by this matter of race. But that should take secondary place; at present life, a method of living was the main thing. . . . Companionship was her chief demand. No more loneliness, not even if that were the road that led to the fulfillment of vast ambition, to the realization of the loftiest hopes. And for this she was willing to make sacrifices, let go if need be of her cherished independence, lead a double life, move among two sets of acquaintances. (252)

With her thoughts firmly fixed on the safety and shelter she hopes a reunion with her sister will bring, Angela's mind, "suddenly as on a former occasion," travels to marriage "as a source of relief from poverty, as a final barrier between herself and the wolves of prejudice . . . as a means of avoiding loneliness" (262). Angela's motivations for wanting to marry reveal much about her initial return home: she is fleeing responsibility and relinquishing rather than bolstering moral courage. In a nod to the earlier fairytale-like description of her mother, Angela tells herself that "she was sick of being courageous, she wanted to be a beloved woman, dependent, fragile, sought for, feminine; after this last ordeal she would be 'womanly' to the point of ineptitude . . ." (ellipses in original, 296–97). With a nostalgic desire to return to a simpler childlike state, Angela still regards marriage as a fairy tale in which her role is the dependent, selfless woman: "It would be a relief to have some one on whom to lean; some one who would be glad to shield and advise her—and love her!" (264). But Angela will not be ready for a mature, fulfilling love until she comes to terms with her self as both an independent being and one who is part of a larger whole, until she carefully considers the consequences of her actions instead of finding ways around taking responsibility with such unthinking and passive evasions as "when it seemed best to be coloured she would be coloured; when it was best to be white she would be that" (253).

At the end of this section, while paying a visit to her sister in Harlem, Angela, who has decided to make "no further effort to set up barriers between herself and coloured people," still unconsciously distances herself from identifying with "these people whose blood she shared but whose disabilities by a lucky fluke she had been able to avoid" (325–26). The free indirect discourse that permeates the entire novel allows us to examine the language of certain passages in order to uncover what Angela hides from herself: "she had never closed her eyes to its disadvantages, to its limitedness! What a wealth of courage it took for these people to live!" (326). The repeated use of "these people" and her focus on only the negative aspects of identifying as black show that Angela has indeed begun to "think about colour" but not with any degree of complexity.

However, when the final section, "Market Is Done" commences, we again find Angela thinking about "her anomalous position," and while she begins with the same evasive mindset, she eventually takes her thoughts a step further to ask some pertinent questions (332). She thinks of all the times her blood has boiled as she held her tongue against "the peculiarly brutal terms which white America affects in the discussion of [coloured people]" and imagines making a "grand gesture" in just such a moment by revealing her racial heritage:

> But life she knew had a way of allowing grand gestures to go unremarked and unrewarded. Would it be worth while to throw away the benefits of casual whiteness in American when no great issue was at stake? Would it indeed be worth while to forfeit them when a great issue was involved? Remembering the material age in which she lived and the material nation of which she was a member, she was doubtful. Her mother's old dictum recurred: "Life is more important than colour." (333)

This "old dictum" sounds very much like Philip's advice to Joanna in *There Is Confusion,* yet without undoing the importance of this "old dictum," Fauset goes a step further in *Plum Bun* by exploring in greater depth the ways in which principle and desire, racial pride and individual fulfillment, need not be opposed. Like a true cosmopolitan thinker, Fauset keeps her novel and her readers in a paradoxical place of tension between what is often contradictory and at the same time not necessarily so. The most important lessons in Angela's development, for instance, are that while color is often experienced as a limitation it is also experienced as a gift; personal sacrifice, too, can be a restriction, but it can also lead to individual fulfillment.

Through Angela's sister Virginia, the Du Boisian figure Van Meier, and a few other minor characters, Fauset has offered these lessons as suggestions throughout the novel, but because Angela's consciousness controls the novel's point of view their importance is not highlighted until she reaches maturity. For example, in the first section of the novel during a conversation with her peers, Angela disagrees with Frank Porter: "'No, I don't think being coloured in America is a beautiful thing. I think it's nothing short of a curse.'" Porter's thoughtful reply complicates the either/or mentality that could keep this conversation running in circles: "'I think its being or not being a curse rests with you. You've got to decide whether or not you're going to let it interfere with personal development and to that extent it may be harmful or it may be an incentive'" (53). Angela does not digest this at the moment, answering instead with the naïve query, "'Doesn't anyone think that we have a right to be happy simply, naturally?'" (54). She has not yet learned what Philip in *There Is Confusion* advises, "happiness has to be deliberately sought for, gained" (288); it is never a given, no matter the color of one's skin. Rather, like Du Bois's "double consciousness," there must be an attempt to straddle different modes of being at the same time. Being colored in America can be a curse, but it can also be a gift—and to be more precise, it is never just one or the other but both. Therefore, when Angela is faced with the "interminable puzzles" of trying to choose between her own desires and the "racial pride" about which she hears Van Meier lecture, she must learn to think along the lines of her friend Arthur Sawyer's advice: "'If you're coloured you've just got to straddle a bit; you've got to consider both racial and individual integrity'" (69). For "racial pride" counteracts the debilitating aspects of double consciousness, the "constant yielding to an invisible censorship" to which Sawyer objects. As the Du Boisian Van Meier explains in a lecture which Angela attends, racial pride "enables us to find our own beautiful and praiseworthy"; it enables "find[ing] completeness within its own group" (219).

The most important lesson Angela finally comes to learn, then, is that personal sacrifice, for the sake of principles that are greater than the self, is not in opposition to but rather complements desire and enhances individual growth. As Virginia argues with Angela in the novel's first section, hiding her racial heritage should "'[seem] sort of an insult to yourself. And then, too, it makes you lose a good chance to do something for—for all of us who can't look like you but who really have the same combination of blood that you have'" (79). By linking this personal affront with something greater than the self, Virginia implies that being a strong individual and being a member of a group can work in productive tension with each other, benefiting and enabling the growth of each. She continues, "'since in this country public opinion is against any infusion of black blood it would seem an awfully decent thing to put yourself, even in the face of appearances, on the side of black blood and say: "Look here, this is what a mixture of black and white really means!"'" (80). Thus, when Angela finally reveals her racial heritage to a group of newspaper reporters in order to help a fellow artist, she sees her action not merely as a sacrifice of her own funding but rather an assertion of racial pride. As she had noted previously about Anthony Cross, the man she loves, she experiences this action less as a sacrifice than "a general house-cleaning" of her "mental chamber" of "the chaff of deception and confusion" (340). Similarly, when Angela decides to let go of her dreams of marriage for the sake of others in her life and to instead focus on becoming a fully realized person on her own by traveling to Paris to pursue her artistry, the moral dilemmas of her life sort themselves out because she is finally able to strike a balance between individual development and a concern for that which is larger than the self. Ultimately, Angela Murray does learn that "a mixture of black and white" can come to mean a merging of principle with individual desire.

"UNPERTURBED BY THE WORLD'S STANDARD OF WEIGHTS AND MEASURES": AN INCIDENTAL MORAL

In *The Chinaberry Tree: A Novel of American Life* (1931), Fauset turns the basic premise of her two previous novels on its head in order to explore similar problematics from a different angle. Both Joanna Marshall and Angela Murray begin by trying to throw off convention, putting independence and non-conformity above all else, yet inevitably learn to temper desire with a new-found respect for convention, family life and sacrifice. However, the main characters of Fauset's third novel, Laurentine Strange and Melissa Paul, begin with a desire for the most conventional lives they can imagine, ready to conform to public opinion without question.

Fauset attests, in her 1931 Foreword to the novel, "Nothing . . . has ever been farther from my thought than writing to establish a thesis."[15] Yet by the end of the Foreword, she admits that "in spite of other intentions I seem to have pointed a moral" (xxxii). What occurs in between those to two statements relates to the novel directly, but it also suggests a larger argument regarding the nature of art itself, namely, that intention aside, the very acts of description and narration carry moral meaning. Fauset suggests that because art and politics cannot be easily separated, art is always already political.[16] If the very fact of being "a Negro in America posits a dramatic situation," as Fauset writes in the Foreword, then it also means that it posits a situation rife with artistic possibilities as well as political meanings (xxxi). While racial identity is seemingly less of an issue for the characters of *The Chinaberry Tree* than for those in *Plum Bun* (for example, one character is said to have "absolutely no feeling about color"), the novel is no less weighty in its socio-political implications.

Fauset shifts focus from the overt problematics of the color line to the less openly discussed but no less controversial topics of miscegenation and intraracial prejudice in order to explore another dimension of the problem of the color line. Thus, Fauset's is a two-part project: one, to show the "breathing-spells," the "in-between spaces where colored men and women work and love and go their ways with no thought of the 'problem,'" so that readers might see that "[the colored American] is not so vastly different from any other American, just distinctive." The second part of Fauset's project is to show that even when skin color is not the apparent focus, the color line is so pervasive a problem in America that "the elements of the play fall together involuntarily; they are just waiting for Fate the Producer to quicken them into movement. . . . The mere juxtaposition of the races brings into existence this fateful quality" (xxxi).

The Chinaberry Tree begins with a past action that reverberates long and low into the present day of the novel: white Colonel Halloway and black Sarah (Aunt Sal) Strange had a life-long love affair and a child, Laurentine Strange. The two lovers might disregard the color line, Colonel Halloway finding "nothing incongruous" with buying "a white lady birch" chinaberry tree for "this Negro maid who waited on his mother" to remind her of Alabama (1). But the rest of the town of Red Brook, while "not tak[ing] too open a stand against the Halloways," also "never forgot [the great scandal]." Colonel Halloway dies, but Aunt Sal, still sits under the chinaberry tree, keeping his memory alive and "car[ing] nothing about" the town's hushed yet disapproving tones (2). Not so for Laurentine, who having worked so hard to be "no longer a pariah, rather some one choice, unique, different," prays with all her might, "'Give me peace and security, a home life like other women, a name, protection,'" adding later, "'Oh God, you know all I want is a chance to show them how decent I am'" (20–21, 36). Unlike Fauset's first two novels, it is the older generation who disregard conventions while the younger generation, fearing the stigma of nonconformity, hold fast to appearances and the whim of public opinion.

Part of what Fauset puts under scrutiny in this novel is a social obsession, which some individuals internalize, with having "a blameless family life" instead of judging others based on personal merit. Thus, Laurentine, who "personally had been as pure as snow, as chaste as a nun," frets over her first boyfriend "Phil with his fear, which she had always sensed rather than known of being caught in the toils of her—she had to face the words—disreputable family" (59, 63). While Aunt Sal finds true love and happiness in a relationship that does not grant "the assurance of her place in the world" because it is not socially sanctioned, Laurentine places this assurance and stability over all else (85). Recalling the insulting elitism of Joanna Marshall when she calls Maggie Ellersley a "nobody," Laurentine exclaims to Stephen Denleigh, her future husband, "'I'm just—nobody, not only illegitimate, Stephen, but the child of a connection that all America frowns on. I'm literally fatherless'" (121). What is even more disturbing in this instance, however, is the fact that Laurentine has so internalized social taboos that the name-calling is self-directed. Fortunately, Stephen, who is a moral center in the novel, tries to set her straight by explaining that "the facts of life, birth and death are more important than the rules of living, marriage, law, the sanction of the church or of man" (121). This speech contrasts quite strongly with the passage from *Plum Bun* when Angela reconsiders her decision to "live her life as an individualist" and wonders whether conventions might be as or even "more important than the fundamental impulses of life . . . a sort of concentrated compendium of the art of living and therefore as much to be observed and respected as warm, vital impulses" (228). The contrast between these two passages shows us something essential to Fauset's cosmopolitan practice, namely, her unfailing effort to maintain tension between seemingly contradictory states of being, to illustrate for her audience the kind of movement that is necessary in order to try to understand life in all its complexity. By modeling this back and forth movement, Fauset shifts attention from the idea that one must choose either to follow conventions and communal norms or stake out a life of one's own based on desire and individual experience to a more complex understanding of the spectrum along which they meet.

Having explored these choices from the perspective of protagonists who begin as uncompromising individualists, Fauset unsettles their learned respect for conventions and a concern for community over self by exploring the perspective of protagonists who need to learn that values must be deliberately sought and gained from individual experience rather than blindly accepted from society at large. Thus, Stephen defends Aunt Sal and Colonel Halloway's relationship to Laurentine:

> "You must remember the times in which he lived and the social slant. It probably never entered his head to buck the concentrated opinion of his entire group by offering marriage. But he did everything else—[Colonel Halloway] let the world know that your mother was his woman. He provided for her and for you. And in any event Laurentine it was their affair. It's over and done with. We've got nothing to do with it." (122–23)

Stephen calls on Laurentine not only to be more respectful of the strength it takes to stand firm in a relationship that breaks social taboos but to focus on her own life experiences and to develop the values that will guide them.

Like Laurentine, Melissa Paul, Laurentine's younger cousin, values above all else "conventionality, security, a certain narrow beauty, definite position," and she finds these embodied in Malory Forten, who "care[s] a lot about class, about family" but "differently from the manner in which she did because he had always had it" (136, 175). Similar to Laurentine's first boyfriend, Malory "want[s] his roses dewy, his woman's reputation, not to say her virtue, unblemished and undiscussed" (252). Moreover, "in birth, gentility, decency, Malory believed, complacently, no one could surpass him" (256). Malory's complacent attitude toward his position in the world, one that has been inherited without effort rather than earned, and his blind adherence to conventional ideas about women make him out of touch with a reality which will eventually overtake him when the appearance of things fades away to reveal his family's own sordid past and the fact that he and Melissa are half-brother and sister.

In particular, Malory's ideas regarding gender roles are absurdly unrealistic. Even Melissa, who has a lot of growing to do, recognizes the problematic nature of a statement such as "'actually, Melissa, every fellow does want his wife to be on a pedestal; he'd like to think of her as a little inviolate shrine that isn't ever touched by the things in the world that are ugly and sordid.'" To this Melissa replies, "'I haven't had such a lot of experience, but it seems to me, Malory, that while all this about shrines and pedestals and things like that are awfully pretty, really beautiful, that life doesn't permit you to keep things like that in your head'" (265). Even though Melissa wants a conventional life, she still recognizes that life is too complex for the narrow roles of convention to encompass the residuum of experience. In addition, the narrator's subtly ironic tone when detailing domestic ideals suggests an even more critical assessment of them as patriarchal fantasies which even the most conventional of female characters do not internalize as the fixed limits and bounds of their existence.

The notion of "normal" life these fantasies instill is shown to be nothing more than the flat surface of a stage setting when the narrator describes Malory "plodding his way through the soft-falling clinging snow" of Christmas Eve and coming upon a vision of a cozy house nestled in a picturesque setting and containing a perfectly happy family unit:

> Somehow the accuracy, the truthfulness of the scene to type both magnified and appeased the pain in his own young aching heart. Like many boys and men, Malory had a very definite sense of what a home should be . . . perhaps if in his home there had been the warmth, the jollity and the light which one expects on Christmas Eve, he might have with sheer masculine perversity, turned both his thoughts and footsteps elsewhere and sought a far different and less suitable means of spending the occasion. As it was, thwarted, baffled, embittered by the presence of the increased gloom which the holiday season seemed to bring to his cheerless household, he would have sacrificed every hope almost that he had for the future to have been able to see enacted within his walls the scenes which he was sure were being enacted in every normal household in Red Brook that night. (ellipses in original, 187–88)

Malory's penchant for holding up life to types in order to judge its truthfulness instead of the other way around makes him an object of the narrator's scorn. This scorn is taken even a step further when the narrator extends Malory's foolishness to "many boys and men," in effect linking domestic ideals to patriarchal fantasies. Because Malory is "thwarted" in his own home from having these expectations met, he places even more weight in the belief that they are "enacted in every normal household." Yet the narrator's charge of "sheer masculine perversity" implies that to have these expectations and fantasies fulfilled would result in nothing more than a manifest indifference towards a presumed norm.

Lest we think that Fauset blindly accuses all men of this fallaciousness, however, we have the characters of Stephen Denleigh and Asshur Lane, the future husbands of Laurentine and Melissa, respectively. Both men serve as moral centers for the people in their lives and guides for the readers of this novel in scrutinizing the conventions informing gender roles and the blind adherence to social norms. Asshur's exemplary ways are highlighted, in particular, by contrast with Malory. While Melissa's "determined preferences" require "a man of different profession from what Asshur's would be and also of different color" (Asshur's skin is darker than Malory's), the narrator reminds us that there is much to be admired and valued in these traits (69). Asshur's choice to become a farmer links him with the soil and fundamental human industry: "farming seemed to him an essential industry; kingdoms, governments, business corporations might come and go but the earth and its productivity would always remain." Moreover, Asshur, unlike Malory, has a "catholicity of standard. Life, according to young Lane, was a gift to be relished. You might start out with a particular end in view, but there was no reason why you should not enter and enjoy an occasional by-path" (131–32). Asshur accepts and even welcomes the residuum of life as it comes to him rather than holding it up to a preconceived type. Thus, even when Melissa tries to forget Asshur in order to pursue Malory and all that he represents to her, she has nagging misgivings, "thought[s that come] to her insistently," about how much "Asshur cared for her, and for her only. No amount of scandal, no degree of misbehavior connected with her relatives, no libel circulated about herself would change Asshur. He would see her with his clear, strong, young eyes and somehow nothing else would enter his field of vision. Vaguely the thought of him comforted her, strengthened her" (212). Asshur's individual strength, his firm sense of personal values, and his appreciation of the unexpected qualities of life and experience, rather than occlude others' personalities, actually strengthens and supports them in discovering these qualities for themselves. Similarly, Laurentine tells Stephen, "'You restored me; you made me respect myself. You made me alive to my own inner resources,'" whereas Malory thinks that Melissa "would never be a finished product; he would always have to mould her and shape her" (204, 228).

After the devastating climax of the plot when it is revealed that Melissa and Malory are half-brother and sister, the narrator recounts that "it was Asshur who restored them. He it was, who with his nice, keen sense of values unperturbed by the world's standard of weights and measures, brought them healing" (336). The novel comes to a close with the image of Aunt Sal, Asshur, Stephen, Laurentine and Melissa happily united and sitting under the chinaberry tree, each thinking his or her own separate thoughts. Having opened the novel with Aunt Sal, the narrator turns to her final thoughts to mark the distance these characters have traveled in their development to a more fulfilling sense of self and community. Earlier Aunt Sal, "who had once flung every convention, every phase of normal living to the winds," finds herself, "for the sake of her child," having to revel "in every action that seemed to mark her and hers as being no different from the rest of mankind" (198). It is with a sigh of relief that she puts aside a concern for conventions and normalcy in the final scene of the novel. Sitting under the chinaberry tree, she is "free to think of her dead lover,—with ease and gratefulness and the complete acceptance which always made their lack of conformity of absolutely no moment. She had always been willing to pay the Piper. Now . . . she was at liberty to recall the Piper's tune" (339–40). As with previous endings, Fauset brings this one to a close on a note of freedom for the central women of her novel. This freedom is not one of a complete disregard for conventions and society but rather one that allows her female characters to develop their individuality and values in conjunction with, rather than against, a dedication to family and community.

"SHE WAS A GIRL WITHOUT A COUNTRY . . . DEPRIVED OF HER RACIAL BIRTHRIGHT": THE RAVAGES OF THE COLOR LINE

Fauset's last published novel, *Comedy: American Style* (1933), like the dark humor of Langston Hughes's *The Ways of White Folk* published the following year, is her most pointedly acerbic and uncompromisingly dark treatment of the "dramatic situation" the color line "in America posits" (*Chinaberry* xxxi). More than in her previous fiction, Fauset satirizes both comedic form and "American style" by showing the implausibility of the conventional marriage plot when the tragically absurd contradictions of color obsession are involved.[17] Unlike the characters of her previous novels who ultimately discover the possibility of home as a place where individual growth can be nurtured, a space where one can be connected with others and still have the freedom to be one's "true self," in *Comedy* home is a place of constraint, cruelty and alienation from self and others. My focus will be on two central female characters, Teresa Cary and her mother Olivia: one, a figure for the rootlessness and alienation of modern life, and the other, a figure for a color obsessed and white supremacist America. In presenting such a bleak and rootless portrait of America and a more general modern condition, Fauset implores her readers to seek remedy in a critical nationalism and a rooted cosmopolitanism. As exemplified in this study by the work of Langston Hughes and Albert Murray, Fauset's call is one to which subsequent writers will respond as they extend her cosmopolitan longings for and explore her critical questioning of these United States.

The novel opens with a psychological and developmental portrait of one of its key players in a section titled, "The Plot." When a young Olivia first realizes that, due to the comments of a thoughtless teacher, her skin color does not correlate with assumptions regarding her racial identity, she approaches her mother with the seed of an idea that is not yet fully formed but which will eventually become her way of life. "Struggling with an idea destined to become the cornerstone of many a latter-day cult," Olivia surmises, "'if you really are one way and people see you another way, then it's just as easy for you to be their way as your way.'"[18] Strangely resonant with Jean Toomer's fateful journal entry which reads, "In a very truthful way it is a fact that we are not only what we think of ourselves but equally what others think of us," Olivia cultivates this seed, "daily cherishing within herself the idea of emerging into a world which knew nothing of color," until fully mature, it takes the form of "one consuming ambition and that is to be white" (11–12, 23). This section ends with the catalyst for the rest of the plot, Olivia's obsession with color or, more precisely, its absence, grimly manifested in her desire for its literal embodiment: "They would have white children. . . . So at last she would obtain her desire. And for that reason and no other she married Christopher Cary" (29).

Seeing blackness as nothing but a curse, Olivia becomes, in a sense, a figure for white supremacist attitudes in America. It is this particular "American style" that Fauset's satire targets, and Olivia is both the offspring and the perpetrator of the destructive havoc it wrecks. This prejudiced "American style" is illustrated near the beginning of "Teresa's Act" at, of all places, a liberal northern boarding school that Teresa attends with other "white" girls. Upon learning that the first openly black student is to be admitted to this haven of educated liberals, the girls sit around discussing how terribly difficult and awful to be black it must be until one exasperated girl exclaims,

> "Why should it take any courage to acknowledge you are what you are? That girl probably doesn't mind being colored, because, oh, because—how can I make you see? Being colored is being her natural self and she can't imagine being any other way. Any more than I can imagine being a boy, or a giant, or a Scandinavian or what have you!" (78)

To show how overvalued whiteness is in American culture, even amongst the educated and supposedly liberal population, Fauset's narrator describes the girls' reactions with satirical wit: "They were all silent a little, trying to adjust their minds to this entirely revolutionary idea" (78).

The effects of white supremacist attitudes are not always so obvious and are, therefore, often more insidious, particularly when internalized by black people themselves. Thus, Fauset acknowledges intraracial color prejudice amongst educated middle-class black people, some of whom, like the older generation of Blakes and Carys, consider themselves "strong 'race people'" (190, 194). Grandfather Cary, for example, teaches Teresa's younger brother, Oliver, "that greatness kn[ows] no race, no color," yet "neither of [the Cary grandparents] would have married, nor would they have wanted their sons to marry with Negroes of unmixed blood" (193, 190). Color prejudice also seeps into the "more democratic" and "more catholic" Blake household where "there was little talk of race. . . . One heard in the same breath of Roland Hayes and John McCormack. Oliver learned of Crispus Attucks, as he learned of Paul Revere, of Sojourner Truth and Susan B. Anthony, of Burghardt DuBois and Morefield Storey." Although color does not matter in their discussions of great people and events, the narrator tells us that "in matters of moment" the Blakes "were really . . . strong 'race-people.'" However, evidence of this is given in a satiric inversion of the Carys' prejudice: "Janet, junior, particularly was in the habit of declaring bluntly that when it came to marriage, no white colored men need apply" (194). Absurd contradictions abound in all attempts to maintain a color line, and Fauset uses these contradictions as grist for her satiric mill. The Jacob White's School, for example, where the children of Philadelphia's best colored families are in attendance, "was the forerunner of the 'separate school' in Philadelphia which, while not based on the truest spirit of either brotherhood or the much-vaunted Quaker fairness, had yet its points" (191).

The satirical humor recedes, however, when the more blatantly devastating effects of color prejudice are explored through Olivia's stranglehold on Teresa's life.[19] Early in "Teresa's Act" she considers, "How wonderful it would be to live, act, breathe, *be* one's very own self . . ." (italics and ellipses in original, 87). But because of Olivia's influence, Teresa is instead alienated from herself and "estranged" from others, black and white alike. She repeatedly considers that there is no place where nor people with whom she is "at home" (88). Nonetheless, Teresa's college life is enriching; it "was fuller, maturer, more sophisticated. Lectures used universal terms. Their attitude was more cosmopolitan. . . . The student body, too, was much fuller, and more varied. . . . Teresa found herself rubbing shoulders with Canadian, Mexican, Russian, Italian, several Chinese and Japanese, and an occasional French or English girl" (first ellipses in original, 114). At the same time, the text is deeply ambivalent about the kind of cosmopolitanism this liberal white world offers. While Teresa is "indignant" in "discussions of overt acts against Negroes," "as a humanitarian might be indignant," she is coldly removed from an imaginative sympathy with their plight (89). In this sense, Teresa must repeat her mother's unfeeling detachment from the philanthropic causes with which she is involved.

Another target of Fauset's satire, Olivia's failure to be truly kind, warm or giving to those closest to her while she devotes countless hours to "her precious welfare committees" is also closely linked to her passing for white. In her obsession with color, Olivia "never paused to think of the thousands of unsuccessful white families pressing in on her from every side. With all her will, and wit and native intelligence she never once saw that the fate of these indigent people . . . might so easily be hers" (206). Whereas Olivia is "always referring" to "the eternal advantages" of whiteness, Teresa becomes increasingly frustrated with what she thinks of as "this nebulous world of near whiteness," which has "shut out the expression of her true self" (146). She longs to "mak[e] a home for herself and Henry [her fiancé] and Oliver [her brother who is neglected by Olivia because of his skin color], a home in which she could be real and from which she could by example, even more than precept, make clear what her attitude was to be on a certain moot question" (145). Of course, this "certain moot question" regards her desire to leave behind the "morass of secrecy, of deceit" and to be part of a community, "which for all of its limitations imposed from without was yet a free one within" (146). More than anything, Teresa decides she wants to identify as black even if that means "she ha[s] to wear a placard." Yet along with her growing awareness and broadening world view, she "revolt[s] at the general idiocy of a scheme which could make such an idea possible." She is able, for the first time, to see "brightly and clearly" "this senseless prejudice, this silly scorn, this unwelcome patronage, this tardiness on the part of her country to acknowledge the rights of its citizens . . ." (ellipses in original, 124).[20]

The textual ambivalence that surrounds acquiring a wide range of experience, developing an individuated self and cultivating a more cosmopolitan world view becomes clearer when we realize the absolute rootlessness of Teresa's life, the fact that she is at home nowhere in the world. For a strongly developed sense of individuality and a broad perspective of the world is not enough to build a rich and happy life. The cosmopolitan must also be rooted through the cultivation of connections within larger circles than the self. Teresa's situation, then, is deeply regrettable:

> Emotionally, as far as race was concerned, she was a girl without a country. . . . Later on in life it occurred to her that she had been deprived of her racial birthright and that was as great a cause for tears as any indignity that might befall man.
>
> With no conscious volition on her part a metamorphosis had been achieved. She had become, and she would always remain, individual and aloof, never a part of a component whole. (ellipses in original, 89)

Olivia, herself the victim of a color-obsessed America, destroys Teresa's chance for meaningful connection when she robs her of "her racial birthright." Not only is Teresa forced to inhabit a "nebulous world of near whiteness" which requires continual deceit and secrecy, but Olivia also ruins Teresa's chance for connection with Henry, the man she loves, because he is not white. Henry had represented to Teresa the possibility of a nurturing home, a space where she could develop as an individual and be an integral "part of a component whole," both on the level of family and racial community. Instead, she remains quite literally "without a country" when Olivia arranges her marriage to a "cold-blooded" and "insular" French man named Aristide Pailleron who Teresa discovers has his own share of color prejudice (181–82). "Teresa's Act" comes to a close on a note of tragic absurdity, cut off from the people she loves in America and not "know[ing] what to make of her life" in France with her "vapid, unimaginative" husband, "her scolding mother-in-law," and her only bit of solace, the kindness of the maid, "an ignorant peasant woman." All of Olivia's "ambitions" and her obsession with whiteness have amounted to this "colorless, bleak and futile" existence for her daughter. As the curtain falls, Teresa's only thought regarding this outcome is "Absurd but true" (183).

Teresa's case speaks specifically to the plight of mixed race individuals in a country determined to maintain a color line. It is also clear that such an investment in a color line is fundamentally tied to an investment in a racial hierarchy that holds whiteness supreme. White supremacist attitudes, moreover, have as their consequence the inner if not the literal death of those with darker skins. Oliver, Teresa's younger brother, becomes a figure for this inner decimation that in turn manifests itself in outward form when he commits suicide as a result of his mother's hatred of blackness.

Additionally, the obsession with whiteness which Olivia embodies in *Comedy: American Style* resonates beyond race to speak figuratively to a condition in America that with the rise of modernity was becoming increasingly dire. This modern condition is the "dusty desert of dollars and smartness" which Du Bois describes in *The Souls of Black Folk* as the state of America.[21] It is the colorless and soulless condition of assimilation to a rootless standard of "Americanization" that shuns particularity and individuality rather than the "ultimate assimilation *through* self-assertion, and on no other terms" with which Du Bois credits Frederick Douglass.[22] Likewise, New York intellectuals, such as Waldo Frank and Randolph Bourne, who identified themselves as Young Americans, railed against the spiritually bereft state of America, its "doctrine of success with its subsidiary Puritan morale," insisting instead on the need to accept the particularism and distinctiveness of American life and "to assert a higher ideal than the 'melting pot'" in order to investigate "what Americanism may rightly mean."[23]

Fauset, too, is concerned with this critique of America. While deeply patriotic, her nationalism, like other New York intellectuals,' is a critical nationalism that coexists with a cosmopolitan worldview.[24] Moreover, like many New Negro writers and artists, she offers black cultural heritage and a dedication to national ideals as antidotes to the spiritual wasteland of an acquisitive and colorless America. Embedded in the narrative of *Comedy: American Style* are the thoughts of a minor character, Alex, who thinks that "America might by now try to live up to some of the tall saying and implications of her founders." Even with "his national quota of materialism," which makes him prefer living in America, "a practically free Negro . . . in relative security and comfort," over living in France or England, "a technically free, but starving, Negro," he still longs to find a way to show America "the spiritual waste which annually she inflict[s]" on black Americans (91). As Jane Kuenz suggests in "The Face of America: Performing Race and Nation in Jessie Fauset's *There Is Confusion,*" the cultural politics of African-American modernism provide a counternarrative to a white world "in collapse" through a sense of a "living [cultural] tradition." Furthermore, Kuenz claims that the "vitality" of black cultural traditions gives the lie to a modernist sense of dissolution by exposing the threat of "the loss of 'civilization'" as "in fact losing the right or ability to ignore or squelch difference" (102).

A key player in early African-American modernist cultural politics, Fauset's project is two-fold: one the one hand, she works through the distinctiveness of African-American culture and politics, while on the other hand, she focuses, not on the folk or the black masses, which literary critics have tended to align with modern conceptions of black identity, but on an emerging black middle class who share the bourgeois values of a rapidly modernizing nation. In negotiating the space between these two, Fauset illustrates the centrality and inextricability of African-American citizens to the defining ideals and cultural traditions of America. A cosmopolitan intellectual in the spirit of Du Bois, Fauset explores the intersections of racial particularity, Americanism, and universal humanism, while negotiating the protocols of race with personal desire and subjective experience, individual development with communal connections, the public sphere with the domestic sphere, and finally, bourgeois values with a racialist agenda. Using the forms of domestic and sentimental fiction, Fauset considers the "interminable puzzles" of the twentieth-century, and in doing so, she illustrates the ways in which class, gender and race inform a sense of national identity. Fauset's work, while "anomalous," to borrow Tate's description, within the black modernist canon, is an initial foray into the exploration of the tensions and continuities between universal ideals and the particular concerns of race, class, gender and national identity. As we shall see, subsequent black cosmopolitan writers and thinkers, like Langston Hughes and Albert Murray, will extend Fauset's project toward understanding these broad categories of experience as often in conflict with one another but not necessarily opposed.

Chapter Three

The Aesthetics of Particularity and the Politics of Integration

The Ways of White Folks and Langston Hughes's Work with *Common Ground* in the 1940s

In tracing the nearly fifty-year span of Langston Hughes's eclectic career as poet, novelist, short story writer, social activist, reporter, dramatist, essayist, translator, editor, librettist, folklorist, and newspaper columnist, critics (and even Hughes himself in his autobiographies) tend to emphasize disjunctions or to identify distinct and often contradictory phases of his oeuvre. My focus for this chapter, however, will be on the essential continuities throughout the various stages of Hughes's career. Other critics have noted important patterns and connections: Raymond Smith locates a continuous attempt "to resolve the dilemma of divided consciousness" throughout Hughes's poetic works; R. Baxter Miller identifies a tragicomic mode as "the hidden unity" in Hughes's writing; and Monika Kaup recognizes, in Hughes's poetry, "the fluid dynamic of the Black Atlantic" in "an ongoing rhythm" between "an abstract state of exile and . . . homecoming and national inclusion."[1] I argue that what some critics might identify as a mutual exclusivity in Hughes's career between the primarily aesthetic and formal concerns of a black vernacular or blues poetry and the less aesthetically focused but more politically engaged and socially radical writing[2]—consider, for example, the difference between Hughes's 1927 collection of poetry *Fine Clothes to the Jew* and his 1938 pamphlet of radical verse *A New Song*—can also be framed as elements of an ongoing cosmopolitan project that he continued to refine throughout his life as a writer.

As we will see, the modernist aesthetics of Hughes's early career in which the celebration of a black cultural distinctiveness is foremost, proved to be, like *Cane* for Toomer, some of his most highly praised work but also some of the most personally problematic in its after-effects; this was due to the various impulses and forces motivating and funding this celebration, namely in the form of Hughes's patron, Mrs. Mason, otherwise known as "Godmother." Her thinly veiled condescension along with her unreflective desire for the primitive seemed to drive Hughes in the different direction his writing took in the 1930s with its focus on politics and social causes and an ostensible move away from modernist aesthetic concerns and black cultural distinctiveness. Without a doubt, throughout his career Hughes inflected these elements differently, placing varying degrees of emphasis on them and reordering their priority, as he wrote for specific audiences, from specific historical moments, and with specific literary interventions in mind. Yet it is my aim in this chapter to show how, as Hughes came to terms with the psychic and artistic stresses of his early career (which, I might add, he was able to do more successfully than Toomer was) he achieved that delicate balance, the sign of a true cosmopolitan, between the aesthetic particularities of a black cultural distinctiveness and the more universal concerns of a politics grounded in a critical cultural nationalism.[3]

As I examine the nature of Hughes's literary project across the various genres he employed, I will focus on his short story collection, *The Ways of White Folks* (1934), as an important transitional moment in his career for its explicit illustration of his coming to terms with, in order to move beyond, some of the lingering bitterness and pain that resulted from the trials of his early career. I eventually locate the culmination of Hughes's literary cosmopolitanism in the seamless blending of his aesthetics (often identified with his writing of the 1920s) and his socialist politics (given emphasis in the 1930s) in the black vernacular and critical cultural nationalism of his writing from the 1940s, a representative sampling of which appeared in *Common Ground* (1940–49), a little magazine that published more of his writing than any other magazine of the decade.

AESTHETIC IDEALISM AND SOCIAL RELEVANCE

Possibly the best known statement of Hughes's artistic career is one that also marks its inception, the 1926 essay which appeared in the *Nation* as "The Negro Artist and the Racial Mountain." Written six months after the publication of his first volume of poetry, *The Weary Blues* (1926), this essay was, in part, responding to George Schuyler's "The Negro-Art Hokum," which had sparked debate and controversy when it appeared a week earlier in the same publication.[4] From one angle it appears that Hughes simply argues for the aesthetic value of expressing racial particularity over an unraced American standardization that is, by implication, banal, colorless, and lacking a distinct individuality which lends a certain vitality to art. This racial particularity, which can "furnish a wealth of colorful distinctive material for any artist," is to be found, according to Hughes, among "the low-down folk, the so-called common element"[5]—not, as he would later write in 1927, among "the best Negroes" with "their slavish devotion to Nordic standards" ("Bad New Negroes," *Essays* 38). In fact, it is in large part the black middle class's negative reactions to his poetry, in particular his second volume *Fine Clothes to the Jew* (1927), and their accusations that he is not representative enough of Negro progress that requires Hughes to continue to lay out his aesthetic agenda in social terms.[6] Hughes counters the negative criticism of his second volume of poetry by stating that he never intended to write propaganda for the Negro. Rather, he wished to artistically interpret and record the racial life of the Negro masses (*Essays* 39).

But close attention to some finer distinctions in his unpublished essay "These Bad New Negroes: A Critique on Critics" (1927) should make us consider the unrefined and youthful nature of Hughes's conception of his literary project at this point in time. He writes, "I do not pretend, or ask anyone to suppose, that I officially represent anybody or anything other than myself. My poems are my own personal comments on life and represent me alone. I claim nothing more for them" (*Essays* 40). This statement is not entirely accurate when we consider Hughes's first two collections of poetry closely. Take, for example, the lines that begin each stanza of the "Proem" to *The Weary Blues* (1926): "I am a Negro . . . I've been a slave . . . I've been a worker . . . I've been a singer . . . I've been a victim . . . I am a Negro."[7] The "I" of these lines is less a clearly outlined poet-persona than a racially representative speaker for an historically African-American experience. Similarly, the first eight "Blues" poems of *Fine Clothes to the Jew* (1927) encompass a variety of representative voices from blues culture, such as the "Bad Man," the man with "Hard Luck" and the "Homesick Blues" man, as well as the woman in "Misery" about to commit "Suicide" or kill the "man that done me wrong" (12) for having taken "ma last thin dime" and left her all alone ("Gypsy Man" 14). Hughes admits, furthermore, in a letter to the editor of the *Nation* in direct response to Schuyler's essay, "Until America has completely absorbed the Negro and until segregation and racial self-consciousness have entirely disappeared, the true work of art from the Negro artist is bound, if it have any color and distinctiveness at all, to reflect his racial background and his racial environment" ("American Art or Negro Art?" *Essays* 552). To some extent, then, Hughes recognizes, although not in a way that he articulates in terms of the aesthetic project he has embarked upon, that his work is racially representative and socially relevant.

We might note this shift from an aesthetic idealism to a deeper concern for the socially relevant in the difference between two short unpublished pieces on Claude McKay. In the first, "Negro Art and Claude McKay" (1931), still very much in the vein of the essays on Negro art from the mid-1920s, Hughes reiterates his chastisement of Negro readers and critics for considering, "even in art," white people first, while he praises McKay's writing for its truthful depictions of both the beauty and faults of poor Negroes (*Essays* 46). But just a few years later, "Claude McKay: The Best" (1933?), Hughes criticizes McKay's second novel *Banjo* for not being representative enough of the proletarian masses, for being too individualist and primitivist. "One puts [the novel] down in the end," writes Hughes, "with an impression of mingled back to Africa, pagan, O-how-joyous-Negroes-are-even-as-dock-rats-stuff, mixed with the conclusion that the strong almost always win out, therefore let the individual fight for his own life in no matter what the social order. It is Claude McKay turned pagan and individualist, vagabond and race-chauvinist" (*Essays* 55). Yet it is important not to obscure the fact that alongside this strong sense of social responsibility rests Hughes's concern for the aesthetic merit of the work as well. It is "heavier and more seriously patterned" but "move[s] with less verve and life" than McKay's first novel, *Home to Harlem*. Moreover, it is artless in its "pages of slow-moving conversations that are really the author's own philosophical dissertations on the ways of our age" (55).

What accounts for this distinct shift in just a few years, as has been well documented by countless critics, is revealed near the end of the paragraph containing the criticism quoted above. "There is nothing of the revolution in *Banjo*," writes Hughes; "nothing of the spirit of the Moscow from which McKay had but shortly returned to Europe; and nothing of the workers of the world uniting to break their chains" (55). In short, "[McKay] hasn't yet had the need of the Internationale knocked into him" (56). Clearly, Hughes has, and this accounts for his shift in emphasis from racially particular aesthetic concerns to international and interracial social responsibilities. In 1931, Hughes traveled to Haiti and visited the Scottsboro Boys in prison in Alabama. Then in 1932, he traveled to Russia to participate in a film project on race relations in the United States, and although the project failed, he stayed a year in the Soviet Union.[8] It was also during this year that he began publishing what is often referred to as his "radical verse," poetry that was markedly differently from his previous volumes in its blatant call for international worker solidarity and class revolution, as in "Good Morning Revolution":

Together,
We can take everything:
Factories, arsenals, houses, ships,
Railroads, forests, fields, orchards,
Bus lines, telegraphs, radios,
(Jesus! Raise hell with radios!)
Steel mills, coal mines, oil wells, gas,
All the tools of production,
(Great day in the morning!)
  Everything—
And turn 'em over to the people who work.
Rule and run 'em for us people who work. (35–46)

Such calls for redistributing the means of production, added to the angry tone of a poem like the controversial "Goodbye Christ," were seen as threatening enough to bring Hughes under investigation in 1944. (Eventually he was made to testify before McCarthy's subcommittee on subversive activities in 1953.) In fact, in 1941, Hughes still found it necessary to counter the misguided readings of "Goodbye Christ" as simply anti-Christian (and by extension, anti-American). Hughes explains that this poem, written in the form of a dramatic monologue, brings together

> what seemed to me the declared and forthright position of those who, on the religious side in America (in apparent actions toward my people) had said to Christ and the Christian principles, "Goodbye, beat it on away from here now, you're done for." I gave to such religionists what seemed to me to be their own words merged with the words of the orthodox Marxist who declared he had no further use nor need for religion. ("Concerning 'Goodbye, Christ,'" *Essays* 208)

Following what must be a disappointing and tedious task for any poet of underlining the irony many readers had failed to recognize, Hughes continues in a weary tone, explaining the difference between the "I" of poetic persona and the autobiographical "I" by referencing his blues poems of the 1920s, where the "I" is "the poor and uneducated Negro of the South—and not myself who grew up in Kansas." Similarly, the "I" of "Goodbye Christ," explains Hughes, "was the newly liberated peasant of the state collectives I had seen in Russia merged with those American Negro workers of the depression period who believed in the Soviet dream and the hope it held out for a solution of their racial and economic difficulties" and not Hughes himself who was attacked for expressing anti-Christian sentiments

(208). Failing to read poetically or to consider Hughes's more overtly political poems in light of his other poetry, readers missed the irony and satire of "Goodbye Christ," as well as its connection to his other work, which had included, according to him, "many verses most sympathetic to the true Christian spirit for which [he had] always had great respect" (208).

Directly addressing Christ, the poem's speaker begins by proclaiming the passing of a time when the Biblical story of Christ worked in powerful ways for people. Now, due to insincere overuse, its validity and meaning have been lost:

> But it's dead now,
> The popes and the preachers've
> Made too much money from it.
> They've sold you to too many
> . . . .
> You ain't no good no more.
> They've pawned you
> Till you've done wore out. (6–9, 14–16)

Following this ironically critical mode, one that indirectly attacks the rhetorical use of true Christian sentiment for despicably selfish causes, the speaker shifts tone in the third stanza from criticism to solution: "Make way for a new guy with no religion at all— / A real guy named / Marx Communist Lenin Peasant Stalin Worker ME—" (20–22).

While such communist solutions as the redistribution of the means of production or the replacement of old value systems and institutions with new ones might have been a major factor in Hughes's difficulty with finding a publisher for what he called his "proletarian poems," his close friend and literary supporter, Carl Van Vechten, thought it was the quality of the poems themselves. In a letter of March 1934 to Hughes, Van Vechten writes candidly that he finds the collection of poems *Good Morning, Revolution* (later renamed *A New Song*) "lacking in any of the elementary requisites of a work of art. This opinion," he adds, "has nothing to do with the opinions expressed therein." Rather, the poems, whether considered "as art, as propaganda, as anything you may care to mention" are "Very Very Weak," Van Vechten confides.[9] But clearly Hughes has not left behind aesthetic concerns for the social and political matters of the day. A brief glimpse at some of his expressions of praise for other proletarian art of this period reveals a steady concern for the aesthetic alongside the social. In "Moscow and Me," a 1933 essay published in *International Literature,* Hughes contrasts the aim of filmmakers in Moscow to make "art for the advancement of certain ideas of social betterment" with the aim of Hollywood filmmakers "to make money" (*Essays* 58–59). Yet social importance is not the only concern in Soviet art, as Hughes makes clear in his explanation of the abandonment of the film project about race relations in the United States, on which he had traveled to the Soviet Union to work. First and foremost, the project was postponed for aesthetic reasons: "the best minds of the Soviet film industry declared the scenario of *Black and White* artistically weak and unsound" (59). Because of its artistic shortcomings, they also "felt it could not do justice to the oppressed and segregated Negroes of the world, or serve to further enlighten Soviet movie audiences" (59). And in his 1934 article, "Tamara Khanum: Soviet Asia's Greatest Dancer," in *Theater Arts Monthly,* only after a lengthy discussion of the artistic roots of traditional Uzbek dance and a description of the aesthetics of her performance does Hughes state that Tamara Khanum "illustrates very clearly what Soviet critics continually speak of—art that is also a social force, that changes life, that makes it better." Her "brave and creative" art "break[s] down old taboos" and, through its example, "help[s] others to break them down," too (*Essays* 127). Moreover, Hughes attributes the revolutionary quality of Tamara Khanum's art to its being rooted in folk materials and to the fact that, as a woman, she is breaking traditional taboos by even appearing on stage. Hughes's attention, then, is still focused on the formal origins of the art and the subject position from which it is performed as much as on its social or political content.

If, as Hughes suggests, the revolutionary potential of art is in its folk roots and the agency it grants marginalized subject positions, such as women, blacks, and the poor, by offering a space in which to control their own representation, then it is possible to argue that his blues poetry of the 1920s is just as revolutionary (if not more so) as his proletarian poems of the 1930s. With this in mind, we might also reconsider the source of charges that Hughes's radical poetry lacks aesthetic merit since such judgments may stem from an unreflective desire for an authentic racialized representation of self rather than the interracial or international perspective of communism. Anthony Dawahare suggests that "in his radical poetry, [Hughes] consistently replaces the 'black, like me' self-identification of his Harlem Renaissance period with a class-conscious sentiment that might be paraphrased 'worker, like me.'"[10] In "failing to express the 'essential identity' of the black American" and in "embrac[ing] an internationalist perspective that is critical of the black nationalist or Pan-Africanist ideology attributed to his earlier Harlem Renaissance poems," Hughes elicited negative responses from his usually supportive critics, such as Carl Van Vechten and Blanche Knopf. In other words, Hughes's poetry of this period did not meet the criteria that had made his earlier poetry acceptable and marketable, because recognizable, as Negro poetry. Dawahare locates the crux of the matter in the wider poetic context of the exclusion of proletarian literature from academic canons, which he identifies as a New Critical achievement. "1930s radical poetry was disqualified as poetry," writes Dawahare, "since it was not—nor ever aimed to be—self-referential."[11] Charges that Hughes's radical poetry lacks artistic merit, then, stem more from a bias, one that not only values and rates the self-referential as the properly poetic but regards the socially relevant as inartistic, than from any real distinction between the aesthetic value of Hughes's blues poems and his proletarian ones of the 1930s.[12]

This assumed separation of aesthetics and politics is precisely what Hughes counters with more and more efficacy as he refines the techniques, conceptions and aims of his art throughout his career. Even in the 1920s, a period Dawahare describes as subordinating the political to cultural nationalism,[13] I argue that Hughes, although most apparently focused on the formation of a black aesthetic, still conceived of his poetry as bearing social importance and revolutionary potential because it is rooted in the folk and gives voice to the socially and economically marginal.[14] By the 1930s, Hughes's focus noticeably shifted to social concerns as he developed a new proletarian poetry, yet this shift does not mean he entirely leaves aesthetic matters behind. Elizabeth Davey argues that by 1931, after a visit with Mary McLeod Bethune, black educator and president of Bethune-Cookman College, Hughes had a new "educational mission" to bring poetry to a mass black audience and "to introduce black audiences to the possibilities of literature representing their own creativity, aspirations, and experiences."[15] In order to do so he not only had to bring his "poetry within the financial reach of economically marginalized black Americans" but he also had to make it accessible to their daily lives.[16] Rather than "'[aim] at the heads of the high-brows'" as he had with his writing in the 1920s, Hughes said that he would go for "'the hearts of the people.'"[17] Thus, Davey argues that in the 1930s Hughes "presented himself to his critics as a reformed poet," acknowledging their objections "to the experimentalism of projects such as his blues poetry" and shifting his emphasis to a more accessible form and content.[18]

Hughes's social concerns are exhibited in his statements on the role of Negro art in this period, such as the speech he prepared for the first American Writer's Congress in 1935, where he asserts an imperative to use art practically, i.e. in the Du Boisian sense of propaganda, and insists on the duty of Negro art to "expose" the lies and hypocrisy that stand in the way of obtaining true social, political and economic equality (*Essays* 132).

Hughes clearly finds a primary focus on aesthetics to be socially irresponsible: "Write about the moon if you want to. Go ahead. This is a free country. But there are certain very practical things American Negro writers can do. And must do. . . . Something has got to change in America—and change soon. We must help that change to come" (133). Yet he continues to refine and clarify his sense of the proper relationship between aesthetics and politics. For instance, in a speech he made at the Paris Meeting of the International Writers Association for the Defense of Culture in 1938, "Writers, Words and the World," he opens with an emphasis on social responsibility: "Words must now be used to make people *believe and do.* Writers who have the power to use words in terms of belief and action are responsible to that power *not* to make people believe in the wrong things" (*Essays* 198). He further modifies this when he states, "The best ways of word-weaving, of course, are those that combine music, meaning and clarity in a pattern of social force" (*Essays* 198). The final note of his speech, however, still places emphasis on the social and political power of words: "But we must use words to make them believe in life, to understand and attempt to make life better. To use words otherwise, as decent members of society, we have no right" (199).

RETICENCE AND INDIRECTION: THE MODERNIST AESTHETICS OF *THE WAYS OF WHITE FOLKS*

Keeping in mind these statements from Hughes on the aesthetic and political values of art, I now turn to Hughes's prose fiction of the 1930s, in particular the short story collection, *The Ways of White Folks,* published by Knopf in 1934. Unlike the negative responses many of Hughes's critics levied against his poetry of the period, this collection received some of the highest praise of all his writing. Carl Van Vechten, for example, wrote to Hughes on December 15, 1933, regarding the manuscript, "I read the book through at a sitting and was THRILLED. I think it is superb from beginning to end (including the magnificent title). In fact I think it is the best thing you have done and I am PROUD of you" (*Letters* 115). And a few days later, he follows up with a postcard: "I hope you got a letter from me telling you how crazy I am about The Ways of White Folks. . . . Blanche [Knopf] is crazy about it too. Who won't be?—Everybody is sure to love it!" (*Letters* 116). To Blanche Knopf, Van Vechten writes, "All of it is good and some of it, I should think, is great. . . . I am glad to feel this way after my reaction to that communist book of poetry" (*Letters* 115). Van Vechten's contrasting responses to the short story collection and the proletarian poetry is telling, especially when considered in light of the only criticism included in his letter to Hughes of

December 15, which pertains to the story "Little Dog." Van Vechten suggests this story would be stronger if the last sentence were deleted. He writes, "In fact always your tendency is to say too much rather than too little and you might think about this in going over your text. Reticence is more powerful in literature than shouting" (*Letters* 115). If we consider Hughes's proletarian poetry in light of this advice, it becomes clear that its supposed aesthetic weakness lies precisely in its shouting, its lack of reticence. Hughes, however, is both fully aware of the aesthetic difference and purposefully committed to his reasons for it. Thus he writes Blanche Knopf, asking her to release his "manuscript of verse, 'A NEW SONG,'" about which he feels "it is important . . . that the proletarian poems therein be published soon, and that they be published in a form available to a working class audience, that is, in a cheap edition" (*Letters* 123).[19] Rather than having made poor aesthetic choices, then, Hughes knowingly shaped his aesthetic designs, making different artistic choices when writing for different audiences with specific aims in mind for what he would accomplish.

Nonetheless, the guiding aesthetic principle of the critically acclaimed *The Ways of White Folks* is, indeed, reticence. A sense of holding back, of keeping a precarious and tautly stressed tension from snapping, of laughing to keep from crying—or from raging with fury—is at the heart of what Arnold Rampersad describes as "the presiding consciousness in this collection," a consciousness that, in contrast to Hughes's novel, *Not Without Laughter* (1930), is "adult and unromantic, disillusioned and frankly bitter."[20] Rampersad adds, moreover, that because of what he identifies as the book's militancy and defensiveness, *The Ways of White Folks* is also "more modern and accurate as a description of the Afro-American temper as it was emerging."[21] More specifically, the bitterness and disillusionment of the collection represent a coming to terms with in order to move beyond many of the frustrations that accompanied the opportunities and successes of Hughes's early career. In relation to white patronage, publishing opportunities and artistic success within a framework of continued social inequality, I identify four overarching themes around which Hughes's major grievances could be aired and purged: 1) humanitarian concern, in either an exemplary display or (often hypocritical) lack; 2) miscegenation, regarded from different perspectives and with varying degrees of acceptance and denial; 3) primitivism within different combinations of art, sexuality and spirituality; and 4) the double standards applied to the realms of art and culture and the social and/or economic sphere.

Cutting across these larger thematic groupings is one of the main targets of this collection's scorn: the unwittingly hypocritical liberal white. A specific manifestation of this type can be found in the Pembertons of

"Poor Little Black Fellow." This story, which combines the themes of Christian charity and miscegenation, treats the liberal white Pembertons and the New England community they represent with a tone of disdain and anger that is barely held in check. At the beginning of this story, Arnie, the son of two black servants to the Pembertons, is left behind after his parents die. The Pembertons, as part of "their Christian duty," decide to raise Arnie as "*their very own*" because being "one of New England's oldest families, one of the finest," they "were never known to shirk a duty."[22] It is quickly revealed, however, that the Pembertons' kindness towards Arnie and his parents, Amanda and Arnold, is the result of a thinly veiled racism and the sense of superiority the Pembertons garner through their sense of having helped those less fortunate (because inherently less gifted) than themselves. They like Arnie's parents so much "because they thought they saw in Amanda and Arnold the real qualities of an humble and gentle race" (130). Thus, their charity rewards black people who "keep their place" and at the same time ensures that place is a subservient one. Their superior attitude is revealed through their language, as the narrator disdainfully underscores when Grace Pemberton says, "'In memory of Arnold and Amanda, I think it is our Christian duty to keep it, and raise it up in the way it should go.' Somehow, for a long time she called Arnie 'it'" (131).

A tense and bitter irony boils beneath the surface of the narration as discrepancies between liberal rhetoric and harsh realities are revealed. For example, consider the following descriptions: "Arnie, in church, a little black spot in a forest of white heads above stiff pews. Arnie, out of church, a symbol of how Christian charity should really be administered in the true spirit of the human brotherhood" (132). While Arnie symbolically serves to reinforce the community's investment in believing itself a model of Christian charity, the bitter reality of Arnie's alienation (ironically, a result, in part, of his being treated as a symbol) is highlighted in his figuration as an insignificant and lonely black spot. Although it is reiterated time and again that the Pembertons "treat him as their very own," the narrator shows us, rather, their hypocritical treatment of Arnie, on whom they bestow token gestures of kindness while reinstating his status as a lesser being who will perform the work of a servant for them without pay.

The narrator accomplishes such displays of disjunction through the employment of free indirect discourse. The following passage illustrates the way in which the narrator moves in and out of the unwitting minds of the liberal white community, subtly underscoring their unacknowledged hypocrisy with slight shifts in perspective and tone.

> The church and the Pembertons were really a little proud of Arnie. Did they not all accept him as their own? And did they not go out of their way to be nice to him—a poor little black fellow whom they, through Christ, had taken in?
>
> Throughout the years the whole of Mapleton began to preen itself on its charity and kindness to Arnie. One would think that nobody in the town need ever again do a good deed: that this acceptance of a black boy was quite enough.
>
> Arnie realized how they felt, but he didn't know what to do about it. He kept himself quiet and inconspicuous, and studied hard. He was very grateful, and very lonely. (133)

At the start of this passage, phrases such as "did they not" and words like "really" and "little" indicate an almost seamless shift in perspective from an omniscient narrator to the inner workings of the minds of the Pembertons and other white members of the community. Their condescension is revealed through trite language, barely masked doubt and uncertainty, and their demeaning characterization of Arnie as "a poor little black fellow" from which the title of the story is taken. The narrator then pulls away from this narrow point of view to a view of the community from a distance, indicated by the sentence beginning, "Throughout the years the whole of Mapleton. . . ." From the distanced perspective of "one would think," an incriminating judgment of the community is implied in word choices like "preen" and "quite enough." The beginning of the next paragraph indicates another shift, this time to Arnie's point of view, with the phrase "Arnie realized." Arnie is fully aware of the community's feelings toward him, but he clearly does not share these feelings. Through the use of free indirect discourse, then, the narrator manages to make a significant yet subtle point: namely, the community's view is myopically narrow because limited to its own unreflective and biased perspective while Arnie, endowed with a double consciousness of sorts, has sympathetic knowledge of the communal consciousness ("he was very grateful"), in addition to his own thoughts and experience ("and very lonely"). The fact that everyone is "over-kind" to Arnie alienates him and makes him so self-consciousness that he keeps himself as "quiet and inconspicuous" as possible.

In the eyes of the community, however, "everything might have been all right forever had not Arnie begun to grow up" (133). As Arnie enters adolescence, the community is faced with, what is for them, an insurmountable difficulty: "There were parties to which Arnie was not invited—really couldn't be invited—with the girls and all." This sentence begins with the narrator's neutral reporting of a fact, but after the first dash it moves into the communal consciousness, signified by words like "really" and evasive expressions like "and all." Through this narrative technique, the community's attempts to occlude all responsibility and to avoid, at all costs, any degree of reflectiveness are underscored. Since the community refuses to acknowledge its responsibility for maintaining and policing a color line, it finds itself instead "beset" with a "problem": "And after generations of peace the village of Mapleton, and the Pembertons, found themselves beset with a Negro problem" (133). Thus, because the liberal rhetoric in which the Pembertons and others have invested themselves clashes with an irrational fear of miscegenation, to the extent that its potential is not even acknowledged, agency remains unassigned in this sentence. Neither Arnie nor the community is blamed, but rather, unrest and disruption are vague conditions carrying with them a sense of invasion from without.

But the vagueness takes on an unbearably definite outline for the Pembertons once miscegenation is not a mere potentiality but an all-too-palpable reality. In fact, the narrator states that it is with the conflict that ensues when the Pembertons take Arnie to Paris where he meets his first colored friends, as well as artists and intellectuals of all creeds and colors, that the "tale begins" (140). This mixture of creeds and colors among the fashionable artists and intellectuals with whom Arnie becomes involved through Claudina, a beautiful, light-skinned Negro dancer who occupies a room on the same floor of the hotel in which the Pembertons stay while visiting Paris, is just one aspect of what the Pembertons find upsetting about his new friends.

> A lot of young Negroes, men and women, shiny and well-dressed, with good sophisticated manners, came at all hours to see Claudina. . . . They were a little too well dressed to suit the Pembertons. They came with white people among them, too—very pretty French girls. And they were terribly lively and gay and didn't seem dependent on anybody. . . . They would be a bad influence. (140–41)

What becomes apparent is that the Pembertons object to well dressed, sophisticated, high class Negroes as much as they object to the mixture of colors among this lively group. Free indirect discourse, indicated through words and phrasings we have by now come to associate with the Pembertons' way of characterizing what is unpleasant or distasteful to them, such as "a little too . . ." and "terribly," brings us, again, inside their thoughts, leading us to their final assessment of Arnie's new friends as "a bad influence" on him. By this point, we are also able to infer their reasoning for this assessment; namely, that these new Negroes are not the "poor little black fellow[s]" who know and keep their place, which is of course one of subservience and dependence on whites for subsistence, education and culture. For the Pembertons, however, the final straw in this tale remains, not the distantly imagined and much feared possibility of miscegenation, but its all-too-real manifestation when Arnie refuses to "keep his place" and enters an intimate relationship with Vivi, a white Romanian woman. The final rift between Arnie and the Pembertons is caused by Arnie's blurring the categorical distinctions that allow liberal whites like the Pembertons to be the benevolent Christians meting out charity to "poor little black fellows," those lesser beings who could never make their way in the world without assistance and who most certainly could never occupy a position of social equality with those equipped to assist.

Ultimately, it is a fear of social equality that is signified by real or even imagined miscegenation. The fact of miscegenation forces people who would maintain categorical distinctions based on race to see reflections of their own selves in those who they suppose to be fundamentally different and inferior. In other words, refusing to recognize and sympathize with an other's full humanity, or denying others the consideration (and treatment) one would like for oneself, becomes exponentially more difficult when miscegenation enters the equation. Other stories in *The Ways of White Folks* make this point but through an entirely different cast of characters and setting. Take, for example, Clarence, a white sailor who is back in a small Florida port town and who is going to visit Betsy, in "Red-headed Baby." Betsy, a "young yellow girl," who was seventeen and inexperienced at their last encounter, now lives with her mother who prostitutes her out to white men (124). In the present time of the tale Betsy has a red-headed child, also named Clarence, who is clearly the product of their last encounter. The older Clarence, however, refuses to recognize this blatant reality because it would destroy categorical distinctions upon which his way of ordering the world rests. Stylistically, the narrative employs modernist techniques in shifting from first-person point of view to free indirect discourse, mainly from Clarence's perspective. The result is a stream of consciousness technique that reveals more than Clarence would consciously recognize or admit. For instance, in response to young Clarence's advances, the older Clarence says/thinks in a jumble of confusion, "Get him the hell out of here pulling at my legs looking like me at me like me at myself like me redheaded as me" (127). The physical resemblance between father and son causes a sense of panic in Clarence, who would deny, to the point of psychic breakdown, his own reflection in a non-white other.

"Father and Son" is another story of a man who does not abstain from sexual relations with non-white women yet would deny to his last dying breath his own reflection in the non-white children that result from these relations.[23] At the opening of the story, Colonel Thomas Norwood awaits his son Bert's return from college, but we are immediately informed that Bert is "not his real son, for [he] had no real son, no white and legal heir to carry on the Norwood name; this boy was a son by his Negro mistress, Coralee Lewis, who kept his house and had borne him all his children" (200). Moreover, "Colonel Norwood never would have admitted, even to himself, that he was standing in his doorway waiting for this half-Negro son to come home. But in truth that is what he was doing" (200). Like Clarence, Colonel Norwood is disturbed not so much by the fact that he has a son but because Bert is "nearly light enough to pass for white" and the "spittin' image of his father, too," as folks said (215). The physical resemblance is compounded by the fact that Bert is impetuous; he has "a temper and ways like white folks, too" (215). In fact, it is because Bert is "handsome and mischievous, favoring too much the Colonel in looks and ways," that he has been sent off to school and not allowed to return for six or seven years (201). The Colonel, however, a plantation owner and slaveholder, must maintain categorical distinctions of race at all costs, so that even though he might recognize striking resemblances—"'He's too damn much like me. . . . Quick as hell. . . . leading his class at the Institute"—this father cannot be proud of traits that have passed from himself to his son (203). Instead, the Colonel must frame obvious signs of intelligence and strength in terms of categorical difference: "'Well, anyway, he must be a smart darkie. Got my blood in him'" (204). But, if Bert will not "keep his place"—and he refuses to do so time and again, from calling the Colonel "papa" in front of white people (203), to trying to shake hands with Colonel Norwood upon returning from school (206), from refusing to "talk like a nigger should to a white man" (233), to ultimately refusing to die "like a nigger" when he shoots himself so the mob cannot lynch him—the community of southern whites will force some other Negro to symbolically "keep his place." Thus, this tale ends with the lynching of Bert's subservient brother Willie, one who always "kept his place," even in death.

In this revision of the trope of the "tragic mulatto," Hughes employs a tragicomic sensibility; his movement between the comic and the tragic is mirrored, moreover, in the movement of his critical eye, which roams from rich to poor, from Northerners to Southerners, and from black to white communities and individuals throughout this collection of short stories. This continuous shifting between comic and tragic modes and among various subject positions challenges readers to resist either blaming or lauding entire groups of people and, ultimately, to resist the impulse to fit all people into groups in the first place.[24] Keeping this in mind, I turn to another tale with miscegenation at its center in surveying the responses it elicits from various folks. So far we have considered the fictional perspectives of New England liberal whites, a white southern plantation owner, and a white sailor. In "Mother and Child," it is the response of a black community to miscegenation that falls under scrutiny. In this story, a married white woman, who has been having sexual relations with a black man named Douglass, has a baby whose skin is tellingly dark. The narrative is told through the dialogue of several black women, who are less than sympathetic towards Douglass, the white woman and the child because they fear that the black community will have to pay for the "sins" of this couple. By including this tale among the others concerned with miscegenation, Hughes shows that miscegenation is not simply anathema to whites; nor are prejudice and the capacity for self-absorbed cruelty the province of whites alone.

"Mother and Child" further serves to offset other stories in the collection that revolve around the theme of humanitarian concern or Christian charity and the lack thereof. Most of these tales exhibit white people as lacking basic Christian charity (even while they claim it) or showcase black people with a well-developed sense of the common human bond. An example of the former can be found in "One Christmas Eve" where Arcie, a Negro servant for a white family, wants to leave work on time so that she can buy Christmas presents for her son Joe before the stores close. The white folks not only come home late; they also do not have the full amount of money they owe Arcie, nor are they much concerned. When Arcie takes Joe downtown with her, he decides he wants to see Santa Claus, but the theatre where Santa is does not allow colored folks inside. Needless to say, this Christmas tale is decidedly short on Christmas spirit. "Berry," on the other hand, is quite a different tale. While Milberry Jones realizes the white folks who run a home for crippled children "only [speak] to him when they [have] some job for him to do" (178), have him "doing far too much work for the Home's eight dollars a week" and "[impose] on him in that taken-for-granted way white folks do with Negro help" (174–75), Milberry himself is a model of Christian charity and human kindness. He is the only worker at the home, in fact, who genuinely cares about the children, spending time over and above his assigned work to tell the children stories and sing them songs.

Interestingly, both the title of this collection and its epigraph, "The ways of white folk, I mean some white folks. . . ." are taken from this story. Milberry speaks these words upon discovering that he receives less pay than the previous worker who had his position and was white. Out of exasperation over his blatant exploitation, Milberry says to himself, "Besides . . . the ways of white folks, I mean some white folks, is too much for me. I reckon they must be a few good ones, but most of 'em ain't good—leastwise they don't treat me good. And Lawd knows, I ain't never done nothin' to 'em, nothin' a-tall" (175). The "ways of white folks" seems to signify here cruelty, lack of human kindness and Christian charity, and oppressive mistreatment. And at first glance there are plenty of examples throughout the collection of stories to support this interpretation without question. However, upon closer inspection, Milberry corrects himself at least twice in the quote above. Qualifying the easy and obvious conclusions he has reached from the way white folks have unjustly treated him, Milberry imagines, first, white folks who might not fit this description and, then, the possibility that the very white folks who have treated him badly might have the capacity for doing good. In giving white folks the benefit of the doubt without concrete proof for doing so, Milberry exercises his sympathetic imagination and, at the same time, distances himself from merely repeating the same unjust behavior he criticizes. Unlike "some white folks" in this collection who lump all Negroes together in one undistinguishable mass, seeing only a type of their own construction, Milberry, in at least imagining the possibility of distinctions, allows for differences and the complexity of individuality amongst white folks.

Now that we have considered its meaning in context, we should further consider the significance of Hughes's having chosen this particular quote as the epigraph to his collection of stories. We might first mention the significance of choosing an epigraph, not from an outside source, but from within the collection itself. In referencing the wisdom of his own created characters, Hughes implies two related points: 1) that there may not be a literary precursor to the kind of representation he sets out to compose, and 2) that the source of such insight is often located in unlikely people and places. We might even discover we have something to learn from the most common of men, such as Milberry Jones, who although uneducated has "plenty of mother wit and lots of intuition about people and places" (174). While "the grown-up white folks" who run the home for crippled children "kidd[ed] him about being dark, and talking flat and Southern, and mispronouncing words," Hughes challenges readers to be more like the children in this story, who "didn't care how [Milberry] talked" but merely appreciated him and "loved his songs and stories" (178). (And we might also ask whether there is an ironic significance in the fact that while these children are white they are also crippled, possibly removing the hindrance of privilege while affording a kind of second sight or insight.)

My analysis of the story "Milberry" and its significance as the source of this collection's epigraph suggests that, unlike Hughes's proletarian poetry of the 1930s, the intended audience for *The Ways of White Folk* was not necessarily the common folk; rather, it was more likely the educated, relatively privileged, black and white bourgeoisie who had also been the audience for Hughes's first two collections of poetry associated with the Harlem Renaissance writing of the 1920s. This should help us understand its modernist aesthetics of indirection and implication, the critical cultural nationalist politics to which its aesthetics is inseparably linked, as well as how different both are from the international, socialist and proletarian poetry of the same period. Ultimately, I argue that, in considering the overall development of Hughes's artistic career, it is strikingly significant that the 1930s are the time in which these most radically dissimilar products of Hughes's writing style appear. As Arnold Rampersad notes in his biography of Hughes, "[l]ike many writers responding to the Depression, Langston was altering his aesthetic to accommodate social reality."[25] After his involvement with the Scottsboro trial and his experiences in Cuba, Russia and Haiti, Hughes felt it necessary that he reach a mass audience. Besides still needing to rid himself of the bitter taste in his mouth after breaking with his wealthy patron Mrs. Mason, Hughes had also watched the passing of the heyday of the Harlem Renaissance and the vogue for all things Negro that brought not only white money and support to black art but negative repercussions, too, particularly with regards to artistic control, as well as more elusive psychic and emotional effects. It is not surprising, then, that the transition in Hughes's style was not a smooth one.

While his early disdain in "The Negro Artist and the Racial Mountain" for audience consideration, which critic Raymond Smith describes as a "philosophy of artistic distance," still lingers in *The Ways of White Folks,* it is essentially gone from the proletarian poems of the same period.[26] Rampersad frames this transitional period of Hughes's career as one in which "he faced a paradox: to reach the black masses, his writing had to be not radical but genteel, not aggressive but uplifting and sentimental. In effect, he was becoming at least three different writers—radical . . . commercial . . . and genteel." Furthermore, Hughes's decision to make a living from his writing without a patron put him "at the mercy of the marketplace, which, he would later," Rampersad claims, "sometimes seem to confuse with the people." Whereas Rampersad interprets all this as having "an enormous strain on [Hughes's] integrity as an artist" and "endanger[ing] his independence," I argue otherwise.[27] It is my contention that Hughes was actively struggling for his independence as a writer but had not yet settled into an aesthetic to satisfy his ever-evolving politics. As a result, the radically different styles of his writing from this period reflect his various impulses (ones he would eventually integrate by the 1940s) as they appear in separate works intended for separate audiences.

LAUGHING TO KEEP FROM CRYING: PRIMITIVISM AND PATRONAGE IN *THE WAYS OF WHITE FOLKS*

Before moving on, then, to Hughes's more fully integrated, aesthetically and politically mature writing of the 1940s, it is necessary to grapple with the interlinked aesthetics and politics of *The Ways of White Folks* and the ways in which this collection of short stories is, in part, Hughes's response to the vogue for Negro writing in the 1920s. In doing so, I turn to a discussion of two closely related themes: primitivism within different combinations of art, sexuality and spirituality, and its complex intersection with the double standards of lauding and promoting black Americans in the realm of culture while oppressing and exploiting them in the socio-economic sphere.

I begin with "The Blues I'm Playing" because it is most obviously and directly linked to Hughes's own experience with his patron, Mrs. Mason or "Godmother," as she wished to be called, and his working through some of the frustration and bitterness that resulted from their relationship.[28] In this story, Mrs. Dora Ellsworth is the white patron of Oceola Jones, a black pianist. "At first," the narrator relates, "it was hard to get Oceola to need anything. Mrs. Ellsworth had the feeling that the girl mistrusted her generosity, and Oceola did—for she had never met anybody interested in pure art before. Just to be given things for *art's sake* seemed suspicious to Oceola" (100). Even more insidious because unconsciously committed is the fact that Mrs. Ellsworth "was sometimes confused as to where beauty lay—in the youngsters or in what they made, in the creators or the creation" (96). Oceola knows that Mrs. Ellsworth's interest in her talent "for art's sake" is an insufficient explanation. She might even suspect that Mrs. Ellsworth is using her not only to get close to her idea of authenticity but to wield power over one less fortunate than herself, in much the same way the Pembertons did with Arnie in "Poor Little Black Boy." As it turns out, Oceola's suspicions are not unfounded, given the fact that Mrs. Ellsworth expects her to sacrifice, all for the sake of a narrowly defined idea of art, important parts of her life, such as her love for a medical student, her desire to have children, and her love for blues music. Oceola, on the other hand, does not see why "children and music couldn't go together" (106), but Mrs. Ellsworth goes so far as to demand that Oceola "learn to sublimate her soul" (109).

Similarly, there were periods when the fickle "Godmother" would chastise Hughes for not working around the clock, even going so far at times as to resent his close relationships with others. We might draw a further connection, then, with Oceola's decision to marry and her patron's response: "When [Mrs. Ellsworth] saw how love had triumphed over art, she decided she could no longer influence Oceola's life." This leaves Oceola to wonder, "Why did white folks think you could live on nothing but art? Strange! Too strange! Too strange!" (117). Hughes, too, experienced Godmother's disfavor when she realized she could not control his life. Whereas Mrs. Mason's other "godchildren," Zora Neale Hurston and Alain Locke, successfully duped her with insincerity and, therefore, continued to reap the benefits of her support and encouragement, Hughes's honesty cost him not only her favor but her financial support.[29]

When Mrs. Mason finally abandoned him in 1930, which Hughes took "to be a result of [her] displeasure over his unwillingness to return to work following his return from Cuba," she went so far as to "accus[e] him of ingratitude and disloyalty."[30] It was this unfair presumption, coupled with "the idea that she would tell him when and where to work [that] chilled him."[31] He had written Mrs. Mason earlier,

> So far in this world only my writing has been my own, to do when I wanted to do it, to finish only when I felt it was finished, to put it aside or discard it completely if I chose. . . . I have washed thousands of hotel dishes, cooked, scrubbed decks, worked 12 to 15 hours a day on a farm, swallowed my pride for the help of philanthropy and charity—but nobody ever said to me "you must write now. You must finish that poem tomorrow. You must begin to create on the first of the month."[32]

Hughes's chilliness turned to a raw and aching wound when Mrs. Mason went even further in her accusation. Louise Thompson, Hughes's close friend and secretary, recounts from Hughes's telling a final quarrel he had with Mrs. Mason over his taking a trip to Washington, D.C., rather than staying home and writing, "The way she talked to Langston is the way a woman talks when she's keeping a pimp. 'I bought those clothes you are wearing! I took care of you! I gave you this! I gave you that!'"[33] Eventually, however, the deep hurt Hughes experienced from Mrs. Mason's unwarranted accusations turned to a slowly simmering rage that would need release in order for him to move beyond Mrs. Mason's influence and to continue developing as a writer. For a time, Hughes was so full of repressed rage that he admitted, "Violent anger makes me physically ill. I didn't feel any of those things consciously—for I had loved very much that gentle woman who had been my patron. . . . But now I was violently and physically ill, with my stomach turning over and over each time I thought about that morning at all. And there was no rationalizing anything. I couldn't."[34] But Hughes would eventually work out that anger through the indirection of art and, specifically, through several stories in *The Ways of White Folks* that give voice, as Louise Thompson later put it, to the idea "that someone because they have money can do to you as they wish and talk to you as they want to. How *dare* they!"[35] In a letter to Claude McKay, Hughes put it another way: he "had gotten awfully bored," he wrote, "with LITERATURE and WHITE FOLKS and NIGGERS and almost everything else."[36]

Hughes's linking of "literature," "white folks" and "niggers" in this sentence is revealing, and in order to understand what holds these three larger-than-life abstractions together in Hughes's career as a writer, we might turn to another story from the collection, "Slave on the Block," which introduces the linchpin of primitivism. While the relationship between a wealthy white patron and a black musician in "The Blues I'm Playing" most obviously parallels aspects of Hughes's experience with Mrs. Mason and some of his feelings about the "art for art's sake" aesthetics of the Harlem Renaissance heyday, the connection with "Slave on the Block" is more subtle, lying beneath the surface of the details of the story. In it, the Carraways, Michael and Anne, are not patrons of the arts but are themselves artists who "went in for the Art of Negroes":

> They were people who went in for Negroes. . . . But not in the social-service, philanthropic sort of way, no. They saw no use in helping a race that was already too charming and naïve and lovely for words. Leave them unspoiled and just enjoy them, Michael and Anne felt. So they went in for the Art of Negroes—the dancing that had such jungle life about it, the songs that were so simple and fervent, the poetry that was so direct, so real. They never tried to influence that art, they only bought it and raved over it, and copied it. For they were artists, too. (19)

Besides their love for the primitive in art, the Carraways like to have Negroes around, so they employ two Negroes as servants, one, an older woman, and another, an attractive young man named Luther. Their appreciation of the art and vitality of the primitive becomes confounded, then, with their interpersonal relations with and "appreciation" of Luther. By turning Luther into an abstraction of the racialized body, the Carraways, and Anne in particular, essentialize and sexualize him as "the essence [of Negro] in the flesh" (21–22). Regardless of Anne's own belief in her liberalism, her sense of entitlement and her tendency to see individual Negroes as representative types to be appreciated or critiqued like works of art are fully revealed when she decides she must paint Luther as "representing to the full the soul and sorrow of his people. She wanted to paint him as a slave about to be sold. And since slaves in warm climates had no clothes, would he please take off his shirt" (24). In this passage the connection between art, "white folks" and "niggers" begins to become clear. All three are abstractions and, therefore, in some sense, tools for reinforcing racial categories and securing a racial hierarchy in which all things and people associated with the Negro are either infantilized or sexualized, just as Luther becomes the literal representation of "the nigger" in Anne's painting of "The Slave on the Block." "Art," or "literature" in Hughes's original triad, is also kept at a remove from the particular and local realities of actual people and the social and economic conditions in which they live. "White folks," in turn, are as much abstractions as "niggers," or in other words, one category engenders the other. Even if "the ways" under scrutiny in this collection are only those of *some* white folks, as the epigraph makes clear, in relation to their treatment of black folks, the point remains that the unfair and generalized treatment of the Negro as a monolithic abstraction becomes associated with another monolithic categorical abstraction, "white folks."

Hughes, of course, did not escape unscathed the 1920s New York art world vogue for All Things Negro. Primitivism, or the essentialist aestheticization of "the Negro" during the Harlem Renaissance, was part and parcel with the condescending liberalism of a philanthropic "appreciation" of "the primitive."[37] A brief glance at some of the correspondence between Mrs. Mason and Hughes discloses her sense of entitlement in coloring and shaping Hughes's artistic productions to fit her own racial ideology. Like the character Mrs. Dora Ellsworth of "The Blues I'm Playing," who wished to control and define the art and artist she financed, Mrs. Mason demanded that Hughes reproduce her particular ideas of "primitive" peoples. "What [Mrs. Mason] considered good fiction," writes H. Nigel Thomas, who conducted a comprehensive study of her correspondence with Hughes through the various drafting stages of his 1930 novel *Not without Laughter,* "was not necessarily writing that employs a diverse number of techniques but rather writing that dramatized her own ideology."[38] Thomas, therefore, disagrees with Rampersad's interpretation of Mrs. Mason's criticism as primarily of an aesthetic nature. She may very well have couched her criticism in terms of literary technique, as she did when she said of *Not without Laughter,* "The whole book needs literary welding together," or when she complained, "The quality of the writing at that point becomes self conscious, and has the air of the author's propaganda."[39] Thomas shows, however, that these aesthetic critiques only thinly veil her ideological mission. Her accusations of "propaganda utterances" that mar the "dark beauty" of the text, then, usually indicate some "controversial detail" that makes her uncomfortable,[40] such as "scenes that deal with white bigotry."[41]

In his autobiographical *The Big Sea,* Hughes explains Mrs. Mason's essentialist ideology: "Concerning Negroes, she felt that they were America's great link with the primitive, and that they had something very precious to give to the Western World. She felt that there was mystery and mysticism and spontaneous harmony in their souls. . . . She felt that we had a deep well of the spirit within us and that we should keep it pure and deep" (316). Although Hughes does not revisit in detail his break with Mrs. Mason, nor even mention much that their correspondence reveals, he does suggest that he was not primitive enough for Mrs. Mason: "She wanted me to be primitive and know and feel the intuitions of the primitive. But, unfortunately, I did not . . . so I could not live and write as though I did. I was only an American Negro—who had loved the surface . . . and the rhythms of Africa—but I was not Africa. . . . I was not what she wanted me to be" (*Big Sea* 325). Mrs. Mason, moreover, required many of her patrons to call her Godmother, which prompted Zora Neale Hurston, in her typical double-speak, to address her once as "'Guard-mother who sits in the twelfth heaven and shapes the destinies of her primitives.'"[42] Mrs. Mason certainly did infantilize "her primitives" in both addressing and treating those she patronized as children. Take, for example, her letter to Hughes of 5 June 1927, where she refers to him as "My winged poet child who as he flies through my mind is a noble silent Indian chief, shining messenger of hope for his people and then again a previous simple precious child with his pockets full of bright, colored marbles looking up at me with his dear blessing eyes."[43] Another letter of 19 June 1927 is even more overblown in its rhetoric of the nurturing mother and the helpless child, in addition to various forms of "primitive" worship:

> Godmother prays to the sun to keep her boy free from any germs and dry up the foul air. You see, Langston, you will forget about yourself while you are absorbing the colors of all kinds and types. And all I have to depend upon to have my boy preserved are those great Gods that sit in space, who, while they set his spirit free to absorb must protect his body from harm. And so, Langston, find in your make-up the Indian song that preserves you from all evil and disease, and sing it with your whole heart. Surely Godmother's great love and belief in you she hopes may be a little protection too.[44]

Because Hughes depended on Mrs. Mason's money and because a part of him did desire to please her, he often humored her wishes and altered his writing to reflect her views, removing or rewriting what she objected to as "propaganda."[45]

Hughes briefly touches upon one of the more poignant examples of his compliance with Mrs. Mason's primitivism in *The Big Sea* when he writes about the sociological study of Lincoln University he conducted during his senior year as a student there. "There was something I wanted to prove," he admits, regarding "Lincoln's own peculiar color line." Hughes was dismayed not only by "the fact that there was an all-white faculty for an all-Negro student body" but by the fact that many students agreed with this situation because they thought that "there was something inherently superior in white teachers" (306–07). Without the least bit of dissembling, Hughes states, "I wanted to prove that the students believing this were wrong, and that Lincoln was fostering—unwittingly, perhaps—an inferiority complex in the very men it wished to train as leaders of the Negro race. I wanted to show that the color line in not good on campus or off" (307). However, in the following very short section of *The Big Sea,* titled simply "Extra Page," he relates without explanation his addition of "a kind of poetic foreword" to this study, one that had "no place in a sociological survey" (311). He gives the foreword in full:

> In the primitive world, where people live closer to the earth and much nearer to the stars, every inner and outer act combines to form the single harmony, life. Not just the tribal lore then, but every movement of life becomes a part of their education. They do not, as many civilized people do, neglect the truth of the physical for the sake of the mind. Nor do they teach with speech alone, but rather with all the acts of life. There are no books, so the barrier between words and reality is not so great as with us. The earth is right under their feet. The stars are never far away. The strength of the surest dream is the strength of the primitive world. (311)

Hughes follows the reproduction of his foreword and concludes this section of his autobiography with only the briefest of remarks: "This meant, I suppose, that where life is simple, truth and reality are one" (310). This sentence sheds very little light upon the apparent inexplicability of the foreword, unless we read Mrs. Mason's influence between his closing line and the first word of the next section's title, "Patron and Friend."[46]

Such evidence of his complicity with Mrs. Mason's primitivism, however, does not mean that Hughes was uncritical of his patron's views or that he had no way of distancing himself from them. It is my contention that to understand more completely Hughes's apparent sycophancy, we must put his impulse to please in the context of *The Ways of White Folks,* his first book-length work published after the complete break with Mrs. Mason. Not only did he pull the foreword from the finished draft of the study of Lincoln University, but he also composed pointed critiques in *The Ways of White Folks* of the kind of primitivism wealthy "white folks" went in for. Two stories, in particular, perform precisely the kind of critique of Mrs. Mason's "ways" with which Hughes never directly confronted her.

In "A Good Job Gone," Mr. Lloyd, a wealthy white man with an invalid wife in White Plains, New York and an apartment in the city for his affairs with various women, falls for Pauline, a "sugar-brown" woman from Harlem. The story is told from the point of view of Mr. Lloyd's servant in whom Pauline confides and who reports, "But she knew what it was all about. Don't think she didn't. 'You've got to kid white folks along,' she said to me. 'When you're depending on 'em for a living, make 'em *think* you like it'" (59). And after Pauline drives Mr. Lloyd crazy by leaving him, she scoffs, "'Just because they pay you, they always think they own you. No white man's gonna own me. I laugh with 'em and they think I like 'em . . .'" (62). In life, Hughes might not have explicitly expressed such feelings of resentment about his own relationships, but he could mitigate them through the indirection of art. Fiction, in other words, could provide an outlet for Hughes's anger and resentment over having been a "kept man" in relation to Mrs. Mason and the money she could always choose to withhold if displeased or not sufficiently reassured of his love for her. Significantly, too, the spurning that takes place in "A Good Job Gone" is reversed in terms of color: rather than the white Mrs. Mason abandoning Hughes, Pauline drops the white Mr. Lloyd, which places her in a position of power. However, that position of power, whether in the form of an abandoning mother or a scornful lover, is still occupied, perhaps tellingly, by the female in the scenario.

Hughes reserves his most derisive treatment of Mrs. Mason's primitivism, however, for the story "Rejuvenation through Joy," a darkly comical tale.[47] By employing laughter to deflect yet provide release for the pain and anger he had been holding inside since that final devastating morning between himself and Mrs. Mason, Hughes finally alleviates some of the feelings that had made him "violently and physically ill, with [his] stomach turning over and over each time" he thought of it (*Big Sea* 327). That morning, Mrs. Mason's Park Avenue drawing room, which "had been so full of light and help and understanding for [him], suddenly became like a trap closing in" as he realized—more unconsciously than not—that he, as the title of this section of *The Big Sea* suggests, was "Not Primitive" enough for her (325). "Rejuvenation through Joy" critiques a faddish new-age cult of the primitive, reminiscent of Mrs. Mason's own beliefs, as well as the Gurdjieffian-style spirituality of which Harlem Renaissance writer, (Eugene) Jean Toomer, was a major proponent and after whom the central character Eugene Lesche, a former circus star and con man of sorts, is modeled. More particularly, however, Hughes's sarcasm is aimed at the very rhetoric of the primitive he had employed in some of his own writing, such as the foreword to the Lincoln University study and his letters to Mrs. Mason. For example, while a jazz band plays "Mood Indigo" at the exorbitantly expensive Colony of Joy, Lesche intones, "'*See how the Negroes live, dark as the earth, the primitive earth, swaying like trees, rooted in the deepest source of life*'" (84). Behind the scenes, writing these rhetorically overblown speeches is "a smart young man from Yale," possibly modeled on Toomer's friend and mentor Waldo Frank, "who prepared a program of action for a high brow cult of joy—featuring the primitive" (77–78). In order to create this pricey blend of self-help for the soul and the modernist primitivism of Negro jazz, "the Yale man" sits in a room "surrounded by books on primitive art, spiritual guidance, Negro jazz, German eurhythmics, psychoanalysis, Yogi philosophy, all of Krishnamurti, half of Havelock Ellis, and most of Freud, besides piles of spirituals, jazz records, Paul Robeson, and Ethel Waters, and in the midst of all this—a typewriter" (80). The disingenuousness of this carefully orchestrated production is apparent throughout the piece in its wry tone, as well as the juxtaposition of speeches like the one quoted above and the strategic planning that accompanies it. "'Then I'm gonna have 'em all rise and sway,'" adds Lesche while practicing his speech. "'That ought to keep 'em from being bored until lunch time'" (84).

The rich white folks who subscribe to the Cult of Joy claim its success is based on the primitive, soul-expanding element of "movement," which makes it far surpass the other cults to which they have belonged, "cults that had never satisfied" (86). They ask with amazement, "How did it happen that nobody before had ever offered them Rejuvenation through Joy? Why, that was what they had been looking for all these years! And who would have thought it might come through the amusing and delightful rhythms of Negroes?" (87). But the narrator's seethingly ironic tone reveals these rich white folks as ridiculous and easily duped by anyone with enough ingenuity to cash in on their emptiness and ennui. They are made to look especially foolish when feeling "all a-tremble in the depths of their souls after they had done their African exercises," "those slow, slightly grotesque, center-swaying exercises" that accompany Lesche's absurd inspirational speeches (88). "'We need to *live* up,'" says Lesche while directing his audience to sway,

> "point ourselves at the sun, sway in the wind of our rhythms, walk to an inner and outer music, put our balance-points in motion. . . . Primitive man never sits in chairs. Look at the Indians! Look at the Negroes! They know how to move from the feet up, from the head down. Their centers live. They walk, they stand, they dance to their drum beats, their

> earth rhythms. They squat, they kneel, they lie—but they never, in their natural states, *never* sit in chairs. They do not mood and brood. No! They live through motion, through movement, through music, through joy! (Remember my lecture, 'Negroes and Joy'!) Ladies, and gentlemen, I offer you today—rejuvenation through joy." (68–69)

I bring this section on *The Ways of White Folks* to a close, then, with a representative example of the sardonic humor that operates throughout the collection. This derisive laughter, through the indirection of art, allowed Hughes to attack the presumptuous naivety and ignorant essentialism of a primitivism that he had faced in the early stages of his career as a Negro writer in a white-dominated cultural sphere, one that was crazy for Negro art but only within the parameters which would keep a social hierarchy in place. As Hughes consciously entered a new phase of his career, which would prevail throughout his writing of the 1940s, he harnessed this dominant mode of *The Ways of White Folks*—a laughter that keeps one from crying or, be it as it may, seething with rage—in order to expand the particular trials of the Negro writer to the more general concerns of attaining democracy in an America that would recognize, without exception, all colors and creeds.[48]

HUGHES'S COSMOPOLITANISM AND *COMMON GROUND*

By the late 1930s, a new group of young Negro writers were making just such a turn from the particular concerns of African Americans to the more universal concerns of a nation (and world) in turbulent transition. Richard Wright's essay, "Blueprint for Negro Writing," which first appeared in *New Challenge* in 1937, opens with a criticism of the current relationship between black writers ("inferiority-complexed Negro 'geniuses'") and "burnt-out white Bohemians with money," as well as "the fact that Negro writing has been addressed in the main to a small white audience rather than to a Negro one."[49] Wright's next move was to urge Negro writers to distance themselves from the "specious and blatant nationalism" of the 1920s, manifest in Harlem Renaissance art and black nationalist movements, like Marcus Garvey's, based on essentialist notions of black identity, and to accept, instead, "the nationalist implications of Negro life."[50] Informed by the internationalist perspective of socialist and Marxist movements of the 1930s, the nationalism Wright promotes is a return of sorts but with a major difference. Coming out of a heritage of Negro folklore, the nationalistic literature Negro writers develop will replace a "reactionary nationalism" with "a nationalism whose reason for being lies in the simple fact of self-possession and in the consciousness of the interdependence of people in modern society."[51] Wright emphasizes integration and commonality that spans yet respects differences when he concludes his essay by stressing "the necessity for collective work . . . *among* Negro writers as well as *between* Negro and white writers" on "the American scene."[52] This collective work will draw upon the differences and particularities of various groups but ultimately aim towards attaining democratic freedom and human rights for all, regardless of race, color or creed. Ralph Ellison, too, in his first published piece of writing, a review of *These Low Grounds* by Waters Edward Turpin, reflects Wright's charge. "It is the Negro writer's responsibility," Ellison asserts, "as one identified with a repressed minority, to utilize yet transcend his immediate environment and grasp the historic process as a whole, and his, and his group's relation to it."[53]

Likewise, Hughes begins a speech for the Third American Writers' Congress in New York in 1939, entitled "Democracy and Me," by speaking "as a Negro and a writer, and secondarily as an American—because Negroes are secondary Americans" (*Essays* 203)—but he ends, in the interest of "a finer and more democratic America," by transcending the language of "mine" and "yours." It is imperative, contends Hughes, to address the problem of secondary Americans as "ours" because it makes "a weak and imperfect democracy" for all Americans (206). By the early 1940s, moreover, it is clear that Hughes has shifted his focus from Marxism and labor to a concern for the state of democracy in America. This shift, of course, is not so much a drastic change in philosophy or belief as it is a matter of emphasis, of prioritizing certain elements that while always present to his thinking take on different relevance when considered in a different historical moment. And, as Hughes notes in "Democracy, Negroes, and Writers," in 1941, "Negroes, like all other Americans, are being asked at the moment to prepare to defend democracy" (*Essays* 211). With another world war raging and America's full involvement just months away, Hughes's attention was drawn to "the democratic ideals for which we are urged to be ready to die" and the fact that "Negroes would very much like to have a little more democracy to defend" (211). Hughes would ceaselessly return to this point throughout the decade, arguing it from various angles and within different genres, but he would never leave it alone. In fact, one of his main contentions was that "democracy is achieved only through constant vigilance, struggle, and the educational processes of the written and spoken word" (211). He saw his role as a writer, therefore, very much at the center of this process, "expos[ing] to public view" "the harsh and ugly aspects of our life . . . in order that they might be changed and remedied" (211). Writers, Hughes believed, would be a key component in "call[ing] for and work[ing] toward the realization of full democracy in regard to people of all colors," for another of his main contentions was that "if we wish to preserve democracy, we must not only defend it but *extend* it" (210–11).

In this chapter's final section, then, I will explore what I consider a representative grouping of Hughes's writing in the 1940s—not a collection of short stories or poetry but generically various and eclectic pieces of writing published in *Common Ground,* a quarterly that ran from Autumn 1940 to Autumn 1949. Because *Common Ground* had its brief but, nonetheless, influential existence over the span of the 1940s, it captures a very specific response to and agenda for wartime and postwar America. Given Hughes's interest and involvement in the publication (he joined its advisory editorial board by the Spring 1942 issue and published more of his writing in it than in any other magazine of the decade), we might assume its objectives accurately represent Hughes's own ideas about how best to confront the historical moment as a writer and activist for social change.

Printed on the inside of every cover was the mission statement of the Common Council for American Unity, *Common Ground*'s publisher and source of funding.[54] Its first paragraph focuses on the commonality and unity of all Americans:

> To help create among the American people the unity and mutual understanding resulting from a common citizenship, common belief in democracy and the ideals of liberty, the placing of the common good before the interest of any group, and the acceptance, in fact as well as in law, of all citizens, whatever their national or racial origins, as equal partners in American society.

The paragraph following this one, however, shifts emphasis to the particularity and diversity of Americans: "To further an appreciation of what each group has contributed to America, to uphold the freedom to be different, and to encourage the growth of an American culture which will be truly representative of all the elements that make up the American people." This shift from commonality to particularity is crucial in understanding the magazine's role in the context of similar publications of the decade. As Abby Arthur Johnson and Ronald Maberry Johnson note, "Integration became the dominant emphasis during World War II and in the postwar years, as seen in contemporary events and as dramatized by Afro-American magazines of the period."[55] They quote "Cosmos," a poem by Roger Woodbury, published in 1945 in *Opportunity,* as exemplary of this integrationist spirit:

On common ground we'll learn to stand
And till the common soil
And reap the harvest hand-in-hand
And share the fruits of common toil.[56]

The themes represented here of "common ground," "common toil" and sharing the harvest that will result are pervasive throughout the decade, as are watchwords such as "integration," "unity" and "common humanity." What makes the periodical *Common Ground* unique, then, is its particularly cosmopolitan spirit, which emphasized that the only kind of unity worth attaining is one that respects and recognizes diversity. In other words, the kind of integration promoted in *Common Ground* is not synonymous with assimilation to a dominant group but required an active acceptance of diversity as the defining feature of American identity and strength.

Featured in the magazine's first issue is an essay "This Crisis is an Opportunity"[57] by Louis Adamic, the magazine's founder and chief editor for the first year and a half of publication.[58] Adamic maintains, "The central educational or cultural effort . . . should be not toward uniformity and conformity to the prevalent, as it was in the 'Americanization' drive of twenty years ago . . . but toward accepting and welcoming and *exploiting* diversity, variety, and differences." Concerning our involvement in the war abroad and our national life at home, Adamic stresses, "we must not imitate, however mildly, Hitler's own and his fellow dictators' frenzy for uniformity and regimentation, and for stamping out diversity; and we must not succumb to their idea of the superiority of one group of humanity over the others."[59] Referencing Emerson, who said, "It is the 'not-me' in my friend that charms me," Adamic reinforces his claim for "Americanism . . . as an *expanding concept*" that invites rather than shuns difference in others because difference "contribute[s] to the evolving culture and civilization."[60]

Distinguished from other civic unity and race relations groups that either promoted the assimilationist "melting pot" theory or focused on the needs and concerns of a particular group, the CCAU and *Common Ground* were influential but did not have mass appeal. The most subscribers *Common Ground* ever had numbered 8,800 in 1946, whereas the *Nation*'s subscribers that year numbered 42,297 and *Survey Graphic*'s 33,847. "Nevertheless," William Beyer remarks, "the CCAU staff were consulted regularly by the federal government and local social service agencies for advice regarding foreign language groups, immigration policy, and intercultural education."[61] When the results of a questionnaire were published in the Summer 1942 issue of the magazine, its impact on readers was revealed in comments like the following:

> "Being a Southerner, my viewpoint has been broadened, my sympathies deepened through reading *Common Ground*," writes a Southern newspaper editor.
>
> A New Jersey teacher says: "As an individual it has widened my appreciation of the peoples who make up America. As a teacher it has given me an interesting 'handbook of Americanism' to place in the hands of students who really want a country where brotherhood exists but don't know enough about groups who differ from them."
>
> A Judge of the Superior Court in California writes: "I have come to know better the foreign-born who come before me as witnesses, jurors, parties to litigation, and applicants for naturalization. I can better understand their viewpoint and process of reasoning."
>
> "I have learned what 'national unity' in this United States implies," writes a Swedish immigrant in California. "It informs me of matters where I am ignorant (and where one shouldn't be, as a citizen of this great nation). It has stimulated my inborn interest in people and peoples and also naturally widened my sympathy."[62]

From these testimonials, we see that Hughes's desire to speak to everyday people through his writing and in a way that would affect everyday life could be met, in part, through a publication like *Common Ground*.[63] In addition to its ideological content, Hughes was also attracted to the aesthetic standards of the magazine, which Margaret Anderson, who replaced Adamic as chief editor until the magazine ceased publication, described as "a literary quarterly with a theme, a thesis."[64]

The writing Hughes contributed to the magazine is representative of nearly every genre in which he worked. Early examples of poetry Hughes published in *Common Ground* are the blues poem, "Evenin' Air Blues," sung by a man whose hopes in moving north have been almost dashed to pieces yet who manages to "do a little dancing / Just to drive my blues away" (13–14), and the dramatic monologue, "Merry-Go-Round," spoken in the voice of a "colored child at carnival" who wonders, "Where's the Jim Crow section / On this merry-go-round?" (1–3).[65] Later, in the summer 1943 issue, Hughes published "Madam to You!: Four Poems Concerning the Life and Times of Alberta K." in which he celebrates black women and the heroism of everyday folk, who work hard, face setbacks bravely, and although fallible in many ways, are kind, generous, perceptive, and indomitable in spirit.[66]

"What Shall We Do About the South," one of two companion pieces addressing the current climate of race relations in the South under the heading, "Democracy Begins at Home," is acerbic and uncompromising in its criticism of the inconsistency between fighting a war abroad in the name of democracy and the reality of racial inequality in the U.S.[67] Hughes begins the essay with "a New Yorker of color" who discovers, in riding a train south from New York City, that "the South begins at Newark," where a Negro customer cannot sit on a stool to eat the hamburger he bought at a street-corner stand. The restrictions only multiply as the train travels further south. When Hughes offers solutions to the problems of "the South," then, readers should consider the title's question in a broader context: if the "the South" is not limited to a geographical region but to any place Jim Crow policies appear, then the problem is potentially everyone's in America. All the solutions Hughes offers, moreover, involve the federal government's responsibility to instate "pro-democratic education . . . from the first grade to the universities" (4). Hughes's tone is unapologetic and, at times, he verges towards condescension in suggesting that "Southerners" are in sore need of basic education. Take, for example, the following statements: "It must be due to some lack somewhere in their schooling"; "Governor Dixon of Alabama and others of like mentality need a little education"; "I go on the premise that Southerners are reasonable people, but that they just simply do not know nowadays what they are doing, nor how bad their racial attitudes look to the rest of the civilized world" (4–5). In order to carry the message of freedom and democracy to the world, "war's freedom train," writes Hughes, cannot include "a Jim Crow coach. No matter how streamlined the other cars may be, that coach endangers all humanity's hopes for a peaceful tomorrow" (6).

While not as openly caustic in tone, another essay Hughes wrote for the Winter 1944 issue of *Common Ground,* "White Folks Do the Funniest Things," managed to hit a more sensitive nerve in American racial politics.[68] Like the earlier essay, this one also underscores the disparity between an American rhetoric of freedom and democracy for the war abroad and its Jim Crow practices at home. As most of Hughes's writing throughout the 1940s attests and as Beyer astutely notes, Hughes felt "this duplicity must be faced as a basic part of American self-definition and not merely as a minority problem or a regional question" (34). What is more, the essay's title, "White Folks Do the Funniest Things," recalling the ironic mode Hughes employed in *The Ways of White Folks,* alerts us to the seamless blending between political objectives and aesthetic technique that I argue Hughes mastered in his cosmopolitan and democratic literary intervention of the 1940s. The opening sentence, too, calls attention to the particular humor of laughing to keep from crying as it reminds readers that while "Negroes laugh at many of the same things white Americans do, they also laugh for *different* reasons at different things" (42). In exploring the peculiar nuances of "Negro humor" that have developed as a result of the absurd and tragic quality of life under Jim Crow laws, Hughes's descriptive terminology ranges from "macabre" to "heart-stopping," "desperate" and "grotesque" (44–45). The central joke around which the essay revolves is taken from a cartoon that appeared in *The People's Voice of New York* after the Detroit riots of 1943. Hughes describes the cartoon as follows: "Two little white boys are standing looking at one of the boys' father's collection of hunting trophies hanging on the wall of Papa's den—an elk head, a tiger head, a walrus. There among them, nicely mounted, is a human head—a Negro's. Proudly, the small son of the house explains, 'Dad got *that* one in Detroit last week'" (44). Hughes introduces the joke with an explanation of its reception: most Negroes, he claims, find it funny—they laugh, clip the cartoon, and send it to friends—yet he has not found one white person who so much as smiled when shown the cartoon. This macabre sense of humor, Hughes implies, is complex; rather than laughing away troubles, it is instead a way of confronting important political and social realities. According to Hughes, whites who would preserve racial inequality cannot afford to laugh at their own absurdities; rather, like Hitler who "has no sense of humor, either," "those most determined to Jim Crow me," concludes Hughes, must stay grimly focused on their killing, which, by extension, includes the killing of America (46). Lest he commit the same crime, however, Hughes carefully revisits the lesson of the epigraph to *The Ways of White Folk* by qualifying his essay's title in the final paragraph: "*Some* white folks do the funniest things! Personally, I know that not *all* white Americans practice Jim Crow at home and preach democracy abroad" (46).

Through his writing, Hughes repeatedly undermines racial and geographical classifications in order to defy their solidification in everyday life and to counter the oversimplified finger pointing that replaces the difficult work toward attaining democracy in America. By using the language of categorization, i.e. white folks, the South, Negroes, but at the same time, continuously qualifying the very terms of categorization out of existence, Hughes shows that action not essence is and should be the basis of identity. Not only, then, does he draw attention to the way categorization obscures exception from sight, but by constantly inserting exception into categorization, Hughes makes exception the rule. Thus, in the story "I Thank You For This," two Negro soldiers forced to ride in a Jim Crow car as they travel from Miami to New York by train are surprised by a kind old white man who offers them a seat at his table in the dining car.[69] When the steward protests, the white man defends the others as American soldiers and his guests. Hughes, therefore, challenges categorization by establishing this exception to the "ways of white folks" who would uphold the shameful practice of Jim Crow segregation. Furthermore, in having one soldier hail from the deep South and the other from Harlem, while the white man's son serves his country in the South Pacific, Hughes challenges race and region as the primary factors in forming bonds between people, for what brings these men together is their common belief in democracy and participation in wartime efforts.

Like the urban folk Madam poems which celebrate the heroism of everyday people, "Graduation," a poem that would be included under the heading "South Side: Chicago" in Hughes's 1949 collection of poems *One-Way Ticket,* lauds Mary Lulu Jackson for the hope she represents in having received her diploma.[70] This document symbolizes to Mary Lulu and her mama, who works in a kitchen, "Where the people all are icebergs / Wrapped in checks and wealthy" (8–9), the American dream of upward mobility with hard work. Even more, "The DIPLOMA bursts its frame / To scatter star-dust in their eyes" (23–24), as it comes to represent not only Mary Lulu's potential break away from kitchen work but the greater possibility that "The colored race will rise!" (26). Significantly, however, the poem's hopeful sentiments for progressive change are expressed in terms of being just over the horizon and, as "star-dust" suggests, maybe never to arrive but to fade and dim as the framed diploma gathers dust and hopes are repeatedly thwarted. Thus, Hughes ends the poem with a pendulum swing between the up-tempo rhythm and hopeful possibility of "Mama says, / Praise Jesus!" and the slowed down, plodding lines of drudging reality, "Then, / Because she's tired, / She sighs" (27–31).

While tempered with a mature grasp of harsh realities and everyday struggles, the postwar poetry Hughes published in *Common Ground* makes clear that hope, whether for peace, integration, or social and economic equality, resides with the common folk. They are the heroes as well as the heralds of progressive change. "Peace Conference in an American Town," included in the Winter 1946 issue, focuses its attention not on governments and official committees but on the back fences of an American town where Mrs. Jones, Mrs. Greene, Mrs. Browne and their children come together to play, exchange information, and mull over the question, "When / is all this trouble / gonna end?" (22–24). Although "Colored, White," "Gentile, Jew," they call each other "Neighbor! Friend!" (26, 28, 20). The repetition in every other line of "At the back fence calling" indicates that this kind of mingling is no isolated event but an everyday occurrence across America. The final words of the poem—"At the back fence calling / You!" (31–32)—address readers directly as key players in the national struggle for peace and integration, in maintaining a sense of responsibility for and recognizing the importance of everyday interactions towards achieving a more fully integrated and democratic United States.

By the latter part of the decade, Hughes still employed an urban folk style, often with a particular complexion, yet he also conceived of his poetry in terms of a universality underlying the variety of particular surfaces that make America cause for celebration. A sampling of some of the poems Hughes published in *Common Ground* during its final two years illustrates the importance Hughes placed on maintaining a dialectical relationship between the universal and the particular. In "Songs for Our Nation of Nations," described in the magazine's blurb as "excerpts from . . . preliminary lyrics of an ensemble song for *Street Scene* . . . showing . . . the different nationalities in an American city, and presenting . . . their unity and friendship," "a regular Noah's ark" of children from the same classroom, who represent "Every race beneath the sun," have a "motto for graduation": "One for All and All for One!" (17–20).[71] Another poem in the series shows how the telephone book is "a record of America's worth": "There's no priority— / A millionaire like Rockefeller / Is likely to be behind me" (4, 6–8). Described as a "list of democracy," the telephone book signals that the dream "Of nations united as one" has begun (13, 10).

While Hughes writes in an unpublished essay of 1945, "I think the dreams in my poems are basically everybody's dreams," he adds, "But sometimes, on the surface, their complexion is colored by the shadows and the darkness of the race to which I belong" (*Essays* 255). Another poem Hughes published in *Common Ground,* "Ballad of the Seven Songs: A Poem for Emancipation Day," attests to this dark beauty and these troubled shadows by "Captur[ing] segments of [freedom's] history / In terms of black America" (7–8).[72] In singing the songs of "Seven men and women / From unrecorded slavery to recorded free"—Cudjoe, Sojourner Truth, Harriet Tubman, Frederick Douglass, Booker T. Washington, George Washington Carver and Jackie Robinson—the poem reminds readers that "Freedom is a mighty word, / But not an easy word. / . . . Maybe you have to win it all over again every generation" (18–19, 202–03, 206). And this message of holding fast and continuously struggling for freedom is implicit in another poem, "Second Generation: New York," that Hughes also wrote from a particular position, not as an African American this time but as the child of an Irish immigrant and a Polish immigrant. This child is aware of the difference between his mother's memories of "the four-leaf clover / And the bright blue Irish sky," his father's memories of the beauty of winter in Poland, as well as "pogroms / And the ghetto's ugly days," and his own memories of New York particularities, "the East River Parkway / And the tug boats passing by," "Third Avenue / And the el trains overhead," "Vocational High, / Park concerts, / Theatre Guild plays" (2–3, 22–23, 5–6, 8–9, 24–26). Yet while the child knows that "All I remember is here," he also knows enough to twice consider it "dear!" (15, 33).

Hughes's experimentation with a variety of voices, expressing particularities while still emphasizing universal themes, reflects an evolved aesthetic sensibility and coincides with the literary aesthetics of integration that dominated many magazines of the war and postwar years.[73] When asked by the editors of *Phylon* magazine in 1950 what he considered most heartening for the Negro writer in the field of contemporary letters, Hughes answered, "The most heartening thing for me . . . is to see Negroes writers working in the general American field, rather than dwelling on Negro themes solely" (*Essays* 310). Hughes's opinion corresponds with Alain Locke's announcement, in his 1950 retrospective review for *Phylon,* of "the rise of the universalized theme supplementing but not completely displacing the poetry of racial mood and substance."[74] "The necessary alchemy," Locke added six months later, "is, of course, universalized rendering, for in universalized particularity there has always resided the world's greatest and most enduring art."[75] Likewise, the "true artist," in Hughes's opinion, belongs "least of all (yet most of all)" to any one nationality. For instance, Kurt Weill, the composer with whom Hughes had collaborated on the Broadway opera *Street Scene,* was, for Hughes, the embodiment of the "universal folk artist" who communicates what he has to say "in the simplest and most direct terms, in the surface language of each country in which he lived, but in the universal language of that world beyond worlds to which all human souls are related" (*Essays* 349–50).

It is my argument that Hughes reached a point of literary maturity in the 1940s, signaled by a new balance between his interest in particular identities and universalized humanitarian concerns for democracy and racial cooperation. The writing Hughes published in *Common Ground* exemplifies his commitment to making democracy possible in an integrated America that loses none of its varied racial and ethnic particularity in the process. Hughes's writing of this period is infused with a sense of purposeful intervention prompted by the fight for democratic freedom in the Second World War and the ongoing struggle for civil rights in America. Thus, rather than diminish his involvement in the struggle for African American civil rights, Hughes's move toward what I identify as a cosmopolitan perspective places that particular struggle in a larger globalized context and actually strengthens his position as a representative leader of the black "folk." Just as Hughes relished the challenge of maintaining balance between the particular and the universal in his writing, he also celebrated and further challenged other writers to aspire towards a position of cosmopolitanism, transcending land, race, nationality and color without losing a sense of particular identities. In his paper for the First Conference of Negro Writers in March 1959, Hughes advised other Negro writers to "[s]tep *outside yourself,* then look back—and you will see how human, yet how beautiful and black you are. How very black—even when you're integrated" (*Essays* 382).[76] Moreover, Hughes continued to defend this position when others started talking about "the high price of integration" and moving toward an aesthetics of separatism and black cultural nationalism.[77] The fact that Hughes did not see integration in terms of sacrifice or loss soundly positions him within a cosmopolitan tradition of African American letters. As Hughes continued to both celebrate and transcend racial and ethnic particularities in his own writing for the remainder of his life, he also urged other writers to see that "the more regional or national an art is in its origins, the more universal it may become in the end" (*Essays* 382).

Chapter Four

The Fine Art Tradition of Albert Murray

Democratic Elitism and Rooted Cosmopolitanism

Scooter, the main character and narrator of Albert Murray's novel series—*Train Whistle Guitar* (1974), *The Spyglass Tree* (1991), *The Seven League Boots* (1995), and *The Magic Keys* (2005)—is reminded time and again by the elders of his community that he has been chosen for a special status which will extend beyond the accelerated classes of his primary schooling, into college and, finally, the world at large.[1] Scooter is "indelibly earmarked for Mister B. Franklin Fisher and his ancestral imperatives for the 'talented tenth,' to whom he said much had been given in raw potential, acknowledged or not, and from whom therefore much in commitment, development, refinement, and ultimate achievement would always be not only expected but required" (*ST* 5). In other words, the idea that "some are called and some are not" (*ST* 20) and that those "precious few" have "to make up for the many" (*ST* 127) is a central tenet of the southern black community in which Scooter's character is formed and his ideals and values shaped. Scooter relates "the hometown expectations" (*SLB* 325) that guide and shape him first as a schoolboy, then as a student in a Southern college modeled after Tuskegee Institute, as a musician in a jazz band not unlike Duke Ellington's, and finally as a graduate student at New York University who prepares to return South to teach at his alma mater: "*What was important to the folks in my hometown was not that you could have a good time among the so-called common people of Gasoline Point on the outskirts of Mobile, Alabama, but that such a place could produce people of extraordinary potential and achievement*" (*SLB* 326, italics in original). Being extraordinary means that Scooter does not simply fulfill expectations but rather extends and shapes his community's expectations by "raising the horizons of aspiration for the so-called common man" (*SLB* 325–26).

In raising the horizons of aspiration, though, Scooter must not disregard, forget or lose touch with his down-home up-bringing; rather, he must discover how to combine and incorporate the idiomatic particulars of his hometown of Gasoline Point, Alabama, with the fine art forms of Western tradition. Scooter is a composite of different types drawn from other literary figures such as Stephen Dedalus, Odysseus, and Brer Rabbit. Thus, Scooter's portrait is partly the artist as a young man, partly the witty adventurer of the picaresque story, and partly the legendary trickster of the folk tale. From this combination of diverse styles and traditions, Murray develops a unique style that is intricately connected to both black vernacular and Western literary traditions. For instance, Scooter speaks of his "own turret-tall spyglass tree above but never apart from the also and also of either the briar patch itself or any of the blue steel and rawhide routes hithering and thithering toward the possibility, however remote, of patent leather avenues in beanstalk castle town destinations yet to come" (*ST* 207). Here fairy tale imagery mingles with the language of a southern folk tale in the tradition of Uncle Remus to form Murray's own "blue steel, rawhide, patent leather" idiom, which, he explains, signifies "the prerequisite combination of patent-leather finesse, rawhide flexibility and blue steel endurance" to make it through the briarpatch with style and grace.[2]

By way of describing "the kind of fiction [he is] trying to write," Murray repeatedly references blues music as both a "poetics" or idiomatic style and a "frame of reference" or organizing metaphor for his content.[3] One of the most common formal features of blues music, repetition with a difference, points toward an even more profound relation in Murray's combination of the blues and the literary. As Henry Louis Gates, Jr. claims, one of the defining features of the black vernacular tradition is "Signifyin(g)" or "repetition and revision," yet this is also an identifying mark of the literary, or in Gates's words, "all texts Signify upon other texts" (xxiv).[4] Gates also makes a distinction between motivated and unmotivated signifying, or the difference between a kind of parody that "seems to be about the clearing of a space of narration" and a kind of pastiche that connotes "not the absence of a profound intention but the absence of negative critique." This distinction helps the critic address the resonances and references in Murray's work to other texts, the ways in which his constant riffs and stylized quotation of other writers "underscore[s] the relation of [his] text" to others. Gates writes, "The most salient analogue for this unmotivated mode of revision in the broader black cultural tradition might be that between black jazz musicians who perform each other's standards on a joint album, not to critique these but to engage in refiguration as an act of homage." Murray's literary riffs can be understood as examples of just this kind of unmotivated signifying that conveys "unity and resemblance rather than critique and difference."[5]

While Murray plays with the aesthetic resonances between blues music and the literary, he also explores the political implications of the way in which "the dynamics inherent in the blues idiom," which are "affirmative" yet unidealistically "alert to the political facts of life," are also particularly suited to the "ambivalent literary sense of human complexity" (*South* 251, 250, 253, 240). Murray's work ultimately shows that folk forms like the black vernacular blues tradition sit comfortably with "high art" literary forms; however, this does not mean that he disregards the tensions between the related fields of a "racial politics" derived from "social oppression and resulting protest" and the bourgeois privilege of higher education and access to "high art" forms, to follow Claudia Tate's formulation.[6] The "spyglass tree," a prominent figure in Murray's fiction, embodies this tension. Situated in the yard of Scooter's boyhood home from which he sees into the distance spatially, temporally and metaphysically, this chinaberry tree recalls Jessie Fauset's *The Chinaberry Tree* where it also signifies the "promise" of "the future" for the novel's main characters.[7] Scooter's chinaberry tree is the "turret-tall spyglass tree" of his youth, the "beanstalk" of his charmed travels and the "triangulation point" which he repeatedly references and to which he repeatedly returns. The elevated position he occupies in the "turret-tall spyglass tree" is at once "above but never apart from" the briarpatch, or life of the "so-called common people," recalling Du Bois's notion of a "Talented Tenth," which, like yeast, "rises and pulls all that are worth the saving up to their vantage ground."[8] This uplift impulse, which coincides with Murray's notion, borrowed from Kenneth Burke, of "raising the horizons of aspiration," is clearly elitist, based as it is, in the words of Du Bois, on a distinction between "the masses" and an "aristocracy of talent and character."[9] Nevertheless, another element counters the elitism of Scooter's elevated position, namely, the spyglass tree's roots, which are firmly planted in hometown soil, keeping Scooter connected to the everyday life of the so-called common people. That Scooter identifies this everyday life with the image of the briar patch is significant because it implies an acute awareness of the trials, snares, and often absurd nature of modern existence, crystallized in what Cornel West calls a "black tragicomic" sensibility.

In this chapter, I trace the seemingly distinct strains of Du Bois's elitism and West's black tragicomic sensibility throughout Murray's fictional and non-fictional work.[10] Mirroring Murray's ongoing conversation with other writers as he riffs on their sense and styles, I, too, draw extensively on the words of Murray's intellectual co-workers in order to elucidate the way in which Murray brings the exceptionalism of elitism and the everydayness of a tragicomic sensibility together in the same work while reveling in the tensions and contradictions that result. As I consider both how and to what ends Murray conjoins these two distinct impulses, I eventually conclude that, more important than reconciling elitism with a tragicomic sensibility, Murray would have us question an investment in perceiving them as necessarily at odds. True to the tradition of intellectual cosmopolitanism I have been tracing, Murray engages in the dialectical project of bringing seemingly irreconcilable impulses together, but rather than collapse their differences, he values and maintains the tensions that result from keeping them in difficult balance.

"ELEGANT IMPROVISATIONS": ELITISM AND A TRAGICOMIC SENSIBILITY

The first part of this chapter focuses on two strains of thought in Murray's work—one, a Du Boisian elitism, and another, a black tragicomic sensibility. I ask the question, to what extent might it be possible to believe in and even cultivate an elevated position without separating oneself from the everydayness of the briar patch and the tragicomic sense it facilitates? West, for instance, faults Du Bois's belief, stemming from an "enlightened optimism," in the notion of a self-appointed elite for promoting racial uplift and progress, as inevitably rendering him unable "to immerse himself in black everyday life." This inability, West claims, "precluded [Du Bois's] access to the distinctive black tragicomic sense and black encounter with the absurd."[11] Yet this assessment of Du Bois seems faulty for reasons other than the fact that West himself might be considered evidence of the possibility of merging elitism with a tragicomic sensibility.

Contrary to West's accusation that Du Bois fails to grapple with "the truth of modern tragic existence" and "modern absurd experience at the core of American culture," I argue that evidence of Du Bois's deep interest in precisely such elements of existence can be found in "The Revelation of Saint Orgne the Damned," his 1938 commencement address at Fisk University.[12] Questioning "life on his Commencement morning," Orgne asks whether "the dark damnation of color" will decide his destiny or if he should ignore "all seeming difference [and] rise to some upper realm where there is no color nor race, sex, wealth nor age, but all men stand equal in the Sun." The reply is dark but unevasive in its blues-oriented approach to life (a notion I will discuss at length later): "'In very truth, thou art damned, and may not escape by vain imagining nor fruitless repining. When a man faces evil, he does not call it good, nor evade it; he meets it breast-forward, with no whimper of regret nor fear of foe.'"[13] Orgne's confrontation of the darkly absurd truths that often accompany a life shadowed by the "damnation of color" is nothing if not an awareness of the tragicomic nature of "black everyday life."[14]

Yet that is not to underplay the strain of elitism in Du Bois's work nor its traces in Murray's own writing. In order to examine this I turn to the third novel of Murray's series, *The Seven League Boots,* in which a movie actress, Jewel Templeton, with whom Scooter has been living in Hollywood introduces him to the Marquis de Chaumienne. The presence of an old world aristocrat like the marquis serves, on the one hand, to underscore the elitist tendencies and aristocratic aspirations of other characters, not least of all, Scooter's. On the other hand, the marquis' presence marks a shift in the way elite status is attained, and by extension, in the very meaning it signifies. Instead of being born to family means and privilege, the marquis, evoking Du Bois's call for an "aristocracy of talent and character,"[15] "insists that to be truly representative of the possibilities inherent in the contemporary epoch one must not inherit but achieve one's aristocratic status" (*SLB* 206). Without naming it outright, then, one of Murray's aims in the novel is to set up an aristocratic class of cultural elites, who, regardless of their widely diverse backgrounds and upbringings, are joined through their acquired skills in reading and manipulating cultural symbols.

To identify as a member of this cultural elite is not contingent upon birth or class; rather, it is what one practices, the skills and knowledge one actively pursues. This marks a shift in the meaning of elitism itself, and it is through this redefined notion of elitism that Murray would have us understand his revaluation of aristocratic aspirations. In the commencement speech from which Murray's essay "Academic Lead Sheet" derives, he charges the class of 1978 graduating honors students at Howard University with "the indispensable responsibilities of being the elite of the generation now coming of age" (*BP* 16). This statement recalls Du Bois's commencement address of 1898 to the graduating class at Fisk University, when he reminds his audience of the responsibility that accompanies their elevated, college-educated status:

> Remember . . . that you are gentlemen and ladies, trained in the liberal arts and subjects in the vast kingdom of culture that has lighted the world from its infancy and guided it through bigotry and falsehood and sin. As such, let us see in you an unfaltering honesty wedded to that

> finer courtesy and breeding which is the heritage of the well trained and the well born.[16]

Du Bois links the "well born" aristocracy to the "well trained" elites who have achieved membership in "the vast kingdom of culture" through their liberal arts education. While Murray makes a similar connection between the marquis and Scooter as members of a cultural elite, he is also more sensitive to a contemporary distaste for elitism. In apparent anticipation of a negative response from his audience to the term, Murray repeats, "Elite. Yes, elite. And again elite. Don't allow yourselves to be faked out by epithets. If elitism bothers you, substitute the word specialist and get on with the mission" (*BP* 16). Murray's substitution of "specialist" for "elite" suggests that while most twentieth-century Americans might take issue with the word "elite," they not only condone but openly aspire to become specialists of one sort or another. Murray puts it another way:

> Can any group, based on whatever distinction, even survive, let alone develop and fulfill itself (to say nothing of transcending itself), without the benefit of its own elite corps of highly competent and dedicated intellectual, professional, and technical specialists? Obviously such an elite was what W. E. B. Du Bois had in mind when he advocated the development of what he called the Talented Tenth. Nor were Booker T. Washington's agricultural, technical, and normal school missionaries expected to add up to anything less than an even larger elite corps that was to include the big moneymakers. (*BP* 16)

Murray alludes to our contemporary faith in specialists of all kinds while gesturing toward an elite corps that, particularly in America, is often met with open distrust and even hostility—the cultural specialists or intellectual elite singled out by Du Bois as "the Talented Tenth." In the next sentence, however, Murray collapses the distinction between the historical antagonism (maybe more emblematic than actual) of the cultural elite associated with Du Bois and the technical and laboring specialists associated with Washington (to which Murray adds moneymaking specialists).

Nevertheless, he quickly withdraws from this it-takes-all-kinds reasoning to reassert his primary concern with cultural and intellectual specialists when, borrowing Kenneth Burke's phrase, Murray says, "The function of the elite is to provide the rest of society with *equipment for living* which is commensurate with the complexity and possibilities of the time in which they live" (my italics, *BP* 16).[17] Murray suggests that what artists and intellectuals can do for the rest of society is process experience into aesthetic statement; in other words, in "coming to terms with yourself, with your consciousness," and in making that realization accessible to others, artists and intellectuals "make other people aware of what they really live in terms of" (*BP* 182–83). The terms towards which Murray gestures here suggest fundamental human and moral truths we can derive from experience, provided we have access to the necessary tools for doing so. This again recalls Du Bois's commencement address and his claim that a liberal education affords "a glimpse of the higher life, the broader possibilities of humanity," to the student who, "amid the rush and roar of living, pauses four short years to learn what living means."[18] In his essay "A Brief for the Higher Education of the Negro," Du Bois's contemporary, Kelly Miller, also defends the importance of a liberal arts education to "strengthen the grasp on moral truth," claiming that higher education would "create a zeal for righteousness and truth."[19] Viewed in this context, Murray's theory that the primary concern of creators and students of art is "the quality of human consciousness" firmly places him in a line of tradition that sees a liberal arts education as providing essential equipment for living (*BP* 27).

Art, writes Murray, is about "the struggle of human consciousness against chaos, the void, entropy" (*BP* 40). It is "a means by which the raw materials of human experience are processed into aesthetic statement," and "to process is to stylize," he clarifies (*BP* 29). Murray's conceptualization of art as a processing of experience into *aesthetic statement* is, in other words, a creation of form (hence meaning) in the face of "chaos, the void, entropy," or the essential formlessness Murray identifies as that against which we spend our lives struggling. The implications of this are even weightier than Murray's original claim that artists and intellectuals provide equipment for living because here "he who creates forms and images creates the very basis of human values . . . and in doing so exercises immeasurable influence on the direction of human aspiration and effort."[20] Cornel West identifies similar motives and aspirations at the heart of the Talented Tenth's role as "self-appointed agents of Enlightenment" who see themselves, "the educated few," as servicing "the pathetic many" by "promot[ing] material and spiritual progress" in and through "shaping and molding the values and viewpoints of the masses."[21] Clearly, West is much more skeptical of this Enlightenment project and its assumptions "that highbrow culture is inherently humanizing, and that exposure to and immersion in great works produce good people" than writers such as Du Bois, Miller and Murray. "Du Bois holds," writes West, "that the educated elite can more easily transcend their individual and class interests and more readily act on behalf of the common good than the uneducated masses." Questioning these assumptions, West asks, "Is this so? Are they not just as prone to corruption and graft, envy and jealousy, self-destructive passion and ruthless ambition as everyone else? . . . Was not Du Bois himself both villain and victim in petty political games as well as in the all-too-familiar social exclusions of the educated elite?"[22]

West contrasts what he considers Du Bois's optimistic prose and detached elitism to a tragicomic sensibility in "profound black cultural efforts to express the truth of modern tragic existence and build on the ruins of modern absurd experiences."[23] In order to contextualize his theory of a black tragicomic sensibility, he draws a comparison between "the Russian sense of the tragic and the Central European Jewish sense of the absurd and the black intellectual response to the African-American predicament."[24] Moreover, his first examples of the black tragicomic sensibility are not from the field of literature but from "the black musical tradition." West explains,

> the intellectual response of highbrow black artists—most of whom are musicians and often of plebeian origins—probe the depths of a black sense of the tragic and absurd which yields a subversive joy and sublime melancholia unknown to most in the New World. The form and content of Louis Armstrong's "West End Blues," Duke Ellington's "Mood Indigo," John Coltrane's "Alabama," and Sarah Vaughan's "Send in the Clowns" are a few of the peaks of the black cultural iceberg—towering examples of soul-making and spiritual wrestling which crystallize the most powerful interpretation of the human condition in black life.[25]

With these illustrations of a black tragicomic sensibility in mind, I return to Murray and his conjunction with West's description of the tragicomic.

Murray's use of the briar patch as a metaphor for the tragic and absurd nature of contemporary life expresses both a tragicomic perspective on and a method for dealing with life. Scooter's cultivated finesse and flexibility, for instance, are enabled by the trials and snares of the briar patch, without which there would be no opportunity to exercise these skills.[26] In describing this relationship between the briar patch and the grace and style it enables, Murray borrows Ralph Ellison's phrase, "antagonistic cooperation," which emphasizes the way in which antagonism facilitates improvisation and provides the necessary risk that accompanies the possibility of success. Signifying within the tradition of Uncle Remus's folk tales, Murray recalls another name Scooter assigns himself as a boy: Jack the Rabbit, a legendary folk character who is born and raised in the briar patch. Murray asks, "*What makes the Alabama jackrabbit so nimble, so resilient, so elegantly resourceful? The briarpatch!*" (*BP* 6). In extending this metaphor for the elegance and grace enabled by antagonism beyond the legendary southern folk tale, Murray, like West, relies heavily on a black music tradition, as well as epic poetry, ritual, and even sports like baseball and bullfighting:

> Still, the captivating elegance that always seems so entirely innate to blues-idiom dance movement is something earned in a context of antagonism. Not unlike the parade-ground-oriented sporty limp walk of the epic hero and the championship athlete, it has been achieved through the manifestation of grace under pressure such as qualifies the matador, for example, for his suit of lights and his pigtail.[27]

The "context of antagonism" from which stylistic elegance may emerge, then, is any situation, be it tangible or metaphysical, presenting trials and snares, which, in turn, provide an opportunity for exercising improvisatory skill, hence Murray's reference to Hemingway's description of the matador's artistry as an exhibition of "grace under pressure." Moreover, that the risk-taking improvisation which accompanies the possibility of heroic action can be located across such diverse forms as blues music and bullfighting attests to something more fundamental in the various contexts of antagonism: a metaphysical condition, manifested in a basic formlessness, which threatens to breed chaos, absurdity, and ultimately, meaninglessness.

One of the characters in Murray's series, the Marquis de Chaumienne, elaborates on the idea of a fundamental connection underlying various modes of improvisation. The marquis, who is specifically concerned with the link between bullfighting and playing or "stomping" the blues (significantly distinguished from the blues themselves), claims that for the bullfighter the bull "*is nothing if not the blues made visible, the blues in the flesh, destruction on the hoof, chaos personified, the symbol of all dragons and monsters, in a word, anarchy!*" (*SLB* 314, italics in original). Thus, the dragons and monsters of fairy tales, like the bull, are personifications of an elemental chaos or formlessness that also lies at the root of the blues. The marquis describes the matador as "life's delicate child" (à la Thomas Mann), "*who must survive not by his strength and power, but by his flexibility, his wit, and his style.*" The matador, then, is "*very much the same as the musician who must contend with the blues*" because each develops "*elegant improvisations*" to combat a particular manifestation of elemental chaos. Whether we take our cues from the blues musician or the matador, the marquis underscores the importance of developing "*elegant improvisations*" which are "*so basically relevant to the disjunctures of contemporary life*" (*SLB* 314–15, italics in original).

Murray extends his characterization of contemporary life as disjuncture in an essay entitled "Academic Lead Sheet."[28] While he argues like Jean Toomer that disjuncture or a basic instability and rootlessness in contemporary life is a general human predicament exacerbated by "twentieth-century technological innovations," he emphasizes its heightened significance in an American context, positing that it has shaped "a basic American attitude toward experience or outlook at life" (*BP* 22–23). This attitude or disposition, Murray argues, stems from "the early American explorers, pioneers, frontiersmen, and homesteaders," who were conditioned "to regard disjuncture as a normal expectation" and therefore "develop[ed] the resilience that facilitates improvisation" (*BP* 22). And if we consider the central role improvisation plays in blues music, another figure emerges as a key component of this resilient American disposition toward disjuncture: the enslaved African.

Murray argues that the legacy of slavery in the United States is not one of misery but precisely that "attitude toward life that the blues idiom embodies": "a disposition of affirmation of continuity in the face of adversity." Blues music is not an expression of misery but a counterstatement that in the very act of defying misery and adversity is also a "confrontation or acknowledgement of the harsh facts of life" (*BP* 20). Thus, Murray comments on the tragicomic sensibility blues music exhibits above all else:

> This intermingling of tragic and comic elements in the blues is often as complex and as outrageously robust as the tragicomic texture of Elizabethan drama. . . . *In a fully orchestrated blues statement, it is not at all unusual for the two so-called elements to be so casually (and naturally) combined as to express tragic and comic dimensions of experience simultaneously!*" (*BDN* 203–04, italics in original)

"The blues," Murray continues, "require you to confront chaos as a fact of life and improvise on the exigencies of the situation, however dire, on the opportunities or the options that are also always there" (*BP* 21). Hence, blues musicians deliberately employ disjuncture in the form of "the break," regarded as both a disruption and an opportunity. It is "a moment of high jeopardy" but also "a moment of truth, the moment in which your response defines your personal quality and identity." Thus, the narrator in the Prologue of Ralph Ellison's *Invisible Man* discusses the ways in which a context of antagonism, or the trials and snares of his invisibility, have given him "a slightly different sense of time," providing him with the opportunity to "slip into the breaks" and improvise. "Instead of the swift and imperceptible flowing of time," he explains, "you are aware of its nodes, those points where time stands still or from which it leaps ahead. And you slip into the breaks and look around."[29] Elsewhere, Murray adds, "The break is the very thing that every American worthy of the name is supposed to make preparations to take advantage of" (*BP* 22). Blues music, then, represents a distinctly American idiom that expresses resilience, flexibility and "perpetual creativity" in the face of uncertainty and instability (*BP* 22), or according to the marquis in *The Seven League Boots,* "a basic disposition toward adventure and its requirement for improvisation" (*SLB* 205).[30]

"LITERARY COSMOPOLITANISM" AND "THE IDIOMATIC PARTICULARS OF A BROWN-SKIN BOY FROM ALABAMA"

Like Du Bois before him, Murray promotes an ongoing interplay between particular contexts and their universal implications, a kind of continuous mental exercise that does not end with the acceptance of a diploma. Thus, Murray charges the graduating honors students at Howard University:

> Your ambition should be to become as cosmopolitan as possible. Now, you reach the universal or the cosmopolitan through the particular. So obviously you do not have to abandon your idiomatic roots. Indeed the more you dig down into yourself and deal with your personal problems against the richest possible background (and thus in the broadest context), the more universal the implications of your most casual personal gesture is likely to become. (*BP* 19)

Having focused upon what are, in part, two distinct elements in Murray's work, a Du Boisian elitism and a tragicomic sensibility, this section's emphasis is on how these two impulses are *not* separate, how they tend to inform and even implicate each other. In addition to and as an extension of the way in which the folk sits comfortably with the cosmopolitan in Murray's writing, this section also examines the more specific admixture of idiomatic blues and southern folk expression with "high art" forms of literary modernism in Murray's fiction. For instance, in *The Seven League Boots,* the third novel of Murray's series, an initial point of intersection may be found in the marquis' poignant example of self-named aristocrats: "those literally fabulous jazz kings, dukes, counts, earls, and barons [who] have given themselves titles and obligations that they then are expected to live up to" (*SLB* 206). If, as the marquis suggests, one achieves aristocratic status by proving oneself an elegant improviser when faced with the "disjunctures of contemporary life," then those who best represent a cultural elite in Murray's eyes must necessarily be in touch with and apply a tragicomic sensibility. Murray's elite, who are best exemplified by such jazz musicians and self-named aristocrats as Duke Ellington and Count Basie, are precisely those equipped with both a tragicomic sensibility that enables them to hone the improvisatory skills and style most relevant to the contemporary situation and a knowledge of elite or high art traditions upon which they may simultaneously draw.[31]

For the most part, Murray champions specialists in the humanities and arts, but he distrusts the field of social science or what he calls "social science fiction." His criticism derives from what he sees as the "pretentious terminology and easy oversimplifications" of social science categories that are incapable of taking into account the actual complexities of human life and experience.[32] Murray's idea of identity resembles his characterization of contemporary life as full of disjuncture and discontinuity, meaning he does not believe people fit into neat categories or classifications. Rather, Murray's thinking is grounded in philosophical pragmatism's belief that any notion of the self must take into account the "incommensurable," or, in the words of John Dewey, "every existence . . . has something unique and irreplaceable about it . . . it does not exist to illustrate a principle, to realize a universal or to embody a kind or class."[33]

In his desire to resist limitations or the fixing of identity, Murray demands a certain comprehensiveness, which, he argues, the humanities and the arts, more than other modes of discourse, make possible. Comprehensiveness is achieved in part by providing a "sense of context," which in turn enables one to address "what experience is really like" and "how rich and exciting [human life's] possibilities are" (*OA* 44). Following the "comprehensiveness" of a humanities and arts-based liberal education, the artist or intellectual, who is to "approach life in universal terms," must reach for the universal through the contextualization of the particular, or as Murray would put it, you reach "the universal implications" by "deal[ing] as accurately as possible with the idiomatic particulars."[34] "Aesthetic statement," by which Murray means the processing or *stylization* of experience into form, may be precisely that which is "the universally appealing in art," but stylization is still "the extension, elaboration, and refinement of the *local details* and *idiomatic particulars* that impinge most intimately on one's everyday existence" (*BP* 3, my italics).

If art is a matter of stylizing or refining the idiomatic particulars of our everyday lives into some sort of universally recognizable and meaningful form, then it would seem that the universal is closely tied to form itself. When Scooter thinks about "the storyteller's traditional opening lines," he recognizes the universality of narrative conventions: "*Once upon a time in a place perhaps very far away, what came to pass among some people perhaps quite different from us in many ways, nevertheless applies to us in a very fundamental sense indeed*" (*SLB* 204, italics in original). The "fundamental sense," or universal significance, of what may on the surface appear "quite different," is not any specific idea or abstraction about human life; rather, it resides in the patterns, forms and structures of the aesthetic statement itself. Addressing the nature of the novel specifically, Murray's long-term friend, Ralph Ellison, agrees, "it achieves its universality, if at all, through accumulating images of reality and arranging them in *patterns of universal significance.*"[35] Both Murray and Ellison understand that to be as widely significant as possible, one must keep the chaos of particularity in constant interplay with the organizing forms of the universal. Ellison reiterates this point in his 1969 speech at West Point: "the role of the writer . . . is to *structure* fiction which will allow a universal identification, while at the same time not violating the specificity of the particular experience and the particular character."[36] The process of refinement which Murray calls stylization parallels Ellison's notion that a "specific part of life" may speak "metaphorically for the whole" "through the eloquence of its statement."[37] As writers and artists, they see their tasks as the arrangement of particular details or "images of reality" into universally significant forms and structures.

In emphasizing the refinement of experience into aesthetic statement, both Murray and Ellison exhibit a Paterian mode of thought that says we get the most from life through the appreciation of the aesthetic. "We have an interval," writes Walter Pater in his Conclusion to *The Renaissance,* "and then our place knows us no more. Some spend this interval in listlessness, some in high passions, the wisest . . . in art and song. For our one chance lies in expanding that interval, in getting as many pulsations as possible into the given time."[38] Du Bois also expresses this mode of thought in "The Revelation of Saint Orgne," where he claims that "the development and broadening of the feelings and emotions, through sound and color, line and form" allow one to discover "the fullest, most complete enjoyment of the possibilities of human existence." He adds, "It is technical mastery of the media that these paths and emotions need for expression of their full meaning."[39] Therefore, it is in the process of refining experience (or the appreciation of experience that has been stylized) that the realms of thought and feeling are expanded "in increasing circles of apprehended and interpreted Truth," or in other words, the universally significant emerges from the mingling of particular details and aesthetic form.[40]

Murray, however, would have us delineate varying degrees of universal significance in aesthetic forms; thus, he distinguishes fine art from folk and pop art. Using jazz musicians as an example, Murray claims they "develop[ed] the technique and sophistication necessary to transform folk and pop music into aesthetic statement that qualified as fine art and that has had the universal appeal, impact, profundity, and endurance of fine art" (*BP* 9). Fine art, in Murray's conception of it, exhibits formal characteristics that achieve universal appeal through stylization or the process of "extending, elaborating, and refining folk and pop material up to the level of fine art" (*BP* 9). In other words, fine art forms use the raw materials but transcend the local and regional particularity of folk art and "the platitudes of pop fare" (*BP* 13).

Highlighting the *interaction* between the vernacular and the sophisticated or learned traditions, the jazz musician is Murray's most frequent example of an artist who has mastered an aesthetic form that is "particularly and peculiarly American and universally contemporary at the same time" (*OA* 168). Murray also draws on examples from literature, namely Faulkner, Hemingway and Ellison, to illustrate his conception of a fine art that is both universally significant and particularly American. He likens Faulkner's "linguistic southernness" to Joyce's "unmistakably Irish idiom" and claims that the literature they generate is no less international or "immediate in the universality of its implications" because of its idiomatic particularities. Rather, Faulkner's "cosmopolitan literary awareness" and his avant-garde stylization "could make small-town down-home stuff, even Mississippi small-town down-home stuff, as universal as anything from anywhere else" (*BP* 72, 70).[41] Murray describes Hemingway's prose as "all-American in a Walt Whitmanesque sense" (*BP* 70) while his ultimate project is "firmly dedicated to the accurate definition of the eternal condition of man" (*BDN* 219). Perhaps Ellison is the most poignant example for Murray's purposes. Finding Ellison's novel *Invisible Man* as steeped in the vernacular as the blues and as stylized in fine art form and universally significant as jazz, Murray says,

> It was a first rate novel, a blues odyssey, a tall tale about the fantastic misadventures of one American Negro, and at the same time a prototypical story about being not only a twentieth century American but also a twentieth century man, the Negro's obvious predicament symbolizing everybody's essential predicament. And like the blues, and echoing the irrepressibility of America itself, it ended on a note of promise, ironic and ambiguous perhaps, but a note of promise still. (*OA* 167)

Ellison's novel manages to operate on many levels at once with the inevitable outcome of illustrating how interconnected those levels really are: to be American is to be representative of a twentieth century human condition and, what might appear a slightly more radical claim to some, to be African American is to be quintessentially American.[42] Ellison notes the novel's potential for conveying the inseparability of the particular and the universal in his essay "Going to the Territory," when he contrasts how "race and color have been basic determinants in structuring what is one of the most aggravating barriers to free communication in this society" with the way in which "readers of widely differing backgrounds were able to see elements of their own experience brought to a unifying focus" in his novel.[43]

The vehicle for this "unifying focus" of Ellison's novel is, in part, the particularity of the vernacular. Ellison conceives of the vernacular as precisely that which keeps tradition alive, vibrant, and relevant to contemporary life; therefore, the vernacular is "a dynamic *process* in which the most refined styles from the past are continually merged with the play-it-by-eye-and-by-ear improvisations which we invent in our efforts to control our environment and entertain ourselves." Ellison adds, "In it the styles and techniques of the past are adjusted to the needs of the present, and in its integrative action the high styles of the past are democratized."[44] In other words, the vernacular, as defined by Ellison, does not merely preserve "the high styles of the past" but improvises upon them, adjusting them to present needs and synthesizing them with new innovations, thereby making them relevant and accessible (i.e. democratizing them) in the process. Murray, too, argues that the vernacular is precisely that which allows tradition to endure when he claims that experimentation in the arts is "not an effort to escape or reject the past but a confrontation of the present" (*HB* 80). Experimentation is how "tradition adapts itself to change, or renews itself through change"; it is "the means by which the true and tested in the traditional regenerates itself in the vernacular" (*HB* 72). For Murray and Ellison, then, the vernacular is both the dynamic and integrative force behind the possibility of change and continuity in tradition and precisely that which keeps tradition relevant and contemporary.

Murray and Ellison take their cues from T. S. Eliot in "Tradition and the Individual Talent" when he states that "the past should be altered by the present as much as the present is directed by the past."[45] Both Murray and Ellison attended Tuskegee Institute in the 1930s, and it was there they began to cultivate the kind of "cosmopolitan literary awareness," which Murray would later characterize Faulkner as having (*BP* 72). Murray read voraciously and broadly in order to fashion himself into a "twentieth century literary cosmopolitan," as he calls James Joyce, who "always wrote out of a sensibility that became more and more sophisticated about the world at large only to become more and more Irish at the same time, even as [he] embraced the idea of timelessness in order to remain up to date" (*HB*

69). Similarly, one hears and senses the presence of the past in the literary echoes of Eliot, Proust, Joyce, Faulkner, Hemingway, Mann, and Malraux, to name just a few of Murray's most obvious influences. But just as, say, Joyce's Irishness and Faulkner's Southernness, when integrated with a cosmopolitan literary awareness, in turn, become part of the "sophisticated" literary tradition upon which subsequent writers draw, a "sophisticated" literary tradition is not the only or even the foremost presence informing Murray's writing. Murray integrates his own idiomatic roots and particularities, most prominent in echoes and metaphors of porch or fireside chats, church services, and blues and jazz music, with literary traditions. In keeping with Eliot's dialectic of the present and the past, then, Murray's incorporation of idiomatic particularities is as much directed by past traditions as those idiomatic particularities, in turn, alter the way the past is heard, making literary allusions resonate with more recent literary developments.

In Murray's first novel, *Train Whistle Guitar,* Scooter narrates his down-home upbringing and, in doing so, relates the various sources of influence that contribute to the metaphors and style that mark his narration:

> But if like me and Little Buddy you had been as profoundly conditioned by the twelve-string guitar insinuations of Luzana Cholly and the honky-tonk piano of Stagolee Dupas (*fils*) as by anything you had ever heard or overheard in church at school by the fireside or from any other listening post, you knew very well that anything, whether strange or ordinary, happening in Gasoline Point was, in the very nature of things, also a part and parcel of the same old briarpatch, which was the same old blue steel network of endlessly engaging and frequently enraging mysteries and riddling ambiguities which encompass all the possibilities and determine all the probabilities in the world. (*TWG* 106–07)

On one level, blues music, in this passage, is an organizing metaphor and frame of reference for an improvisational approach to contemporary human experience. Scooter has been "profoundly conditioned" by the blues musicians of his community to both acknowledge and combat the harsh realities and frustrating ambiguities of life, much as blues lyrics often "recount a tale of woe" while blues instrumentation simultaneously "mock[s], shout[s] defiance, or voice[s] resolution and determination" (*SB* 69). Scooter relates other sources of his outlook on and approach to life, such as church, school, the fireside and barbershop, which, aside from differences in form and context, are connected through the universal implications of the improvisational and flexible blues aesthetic. Metaphors of the briar patch and the railroads are also part of Scooter's idiomatic roots, just as the title of the novel itself invokes a network of meaning in its combination of train and guitar metaphors. "The image of the train," explains Murray in a 1997 interview with Charles Rowell, "was deeply embedded in the consciousness of [black] Americans" so that it could function as a metaphysical metaphor in church when "they talked and sang about 'getting on board'" or as a political metaphor for freedom when "they talked about the 'Underground Railroad.'" He continues, "So when you hear music from a blues guitar player, what do you hear? It's a train whistle guitar" (*BP* 185).

In addition to this intricate network of idiomatic metaphors, the literary influence of high modernists like Faulkner and Joyce resound in the stringing together of phrases and detail without punctuation and in the lyrical and rhythmic qualities of the prose. This modernist literary influence, moreover, is closely wedded to Murray's blues poetics. Repetition, the rhythmic patterns in phrases, such as "had ever heard" / "or overheard," "endlessly engaging" / "frequently enraging," "encompass all the possibilities" / "determine all the probabilities," and the mimicking of other techniques employed by blues musicians, such as call and response within the structure of the sentence by the placement of interspersed clauses like "whether strange or ordinary" and "in the very nature of things," are all part of Murray's blues idiom or poetics. The close link between sound patterns of the blues translated into literary devices and the sound of modernist literary technique affects how each is heard in relation to the other. Murray's ability to integrate the influence of "great works" of literary tradition with his idiomatic roots requires an intimacy with both "sophisticated" tradition and the vernacular, resulting in the mutual enhancement of each. The idiomatic particulars of Murray's style, then, are not only compatible with but become an integral part of his "literary cosmopolitanism" (to borrow his own formulation) in such a way that underscores the dynamic dialectical relationship between the present and the past, as well folk and fine art forms, in an ever-evolving literary tradition.

Even as Murray's prose stylistically exhibits "the idiomatic particulars of a brown-skin boy from Alabama," the implications of Scooter's words and actions pertain to fundamental experiences in contemporary human life (*BP* 6). Murray also develops the related dialectic of the particular and the universal in art when he explains that "you deal with . . . big abstract questions in terms of idiomatic particulars (that is, concrete details) that you actually experience." The development of Scooter's character throughout the series can be traced in his attempt to "find poetic images for the expansion of consciousness and the deepening and enrichment of insight" (*BP* 169). In this sense, Scooter is both a "literary device" for Murray's coming to terms with his own consciousness, as well as an exploration of American identity (*BP* 168).

COUNTERSTATING SOCIAL SCIENCE FICTION: RECENTERING BLACKNESS IN AMERICAN NATIONAL IDENTITY

Murray's fiction, like Ellison's *Invisible Man,* illustrates how interconnected the particular and the universal actually are and, more specifically, how the particularity of African-American culture informs American national identity by providing, in the words of Carolyn Jones, "a performative space that moves between the authorized discourse and the space of the people."[46] Moreover, in their attempt to fit African-American cultural forms into a global and modern perspective, Murray and Ellison display a distinctly cosmopolitan concern for representing a general human condition by way of "negotiat[ing] the racial particular and the unraced universal."[47] In Murray's *The Seven League Boots,* for example, the Marquis de Chaumienne, who is said to have a "cosmopolitan point of view," discusses the importance of "idiomatic authenticity" in playing the blues, but he stresses that "it is through the impact that it makes in the larger, richer, and more complex context of the outside world . . . that the vernacular achieves universality" (*SLB* 205, 310). Thus, it is the artful negotiation (not resolution) of the idiomatic and the universal and all the tensions and contradictions that arise therein that makes a relevant fine art tradition possible.

In many ways, then, Murray's ultimate project is to redefine both what is representative of America and what qualifies as fine art. Idiomatic authenticity in art comes to indicate an approach to the fundamental questions of human existence through lived experience rather than the established categories of official discourse. Once refined and stylized, the vernacular is precisely that which most constitutes fine art. This realization in turn affects the terms of what comprises a tradition of American art. Thus, Murray places jazz and blues musicians and bandleaders on a par with canonical American writers, like Twain and Whitman. He even compares the aesthetic stylization of great baseball players and boxing champions to the refined artistry of Henry James:

> *Jack Johnson . . . was himself an American Work of Art to compare with anything in the major phase of Henry James . . . Jelly Roll Morton and Fats Waller would have done better than hold their own with Mark Twain, jive artist become fine artist. Nor is it at all outrageous to assume that Walt Whitman would have been bewitched by the infinite*

> *flexibility of the Kansas City 4/4 beat of Count Basie . . . Or that Herman Melville having made what he made of the crew of the* Pequod *may have gained new dimensions and resonances from a world tour with the Duke Ellington Orchestra.* (*BDN* 226, italics in original)

Murray remaps cultural influence and ancestry along what he calls "*functional*" or pragmatic lines as opposed to "*the conventional flesh and blood and thus official or legal*" lines of ancestry (*SLB* 138, italics in original). Again, this evokes Du Bois's call in "The Revelation of Saint Orgne" "to create a new family group" with culture as its base rather than ties of "biology and blood" which are "entirely subordinate and unimportant" when compared to those of culture.[48]

One of the most important results of redrawing lines of influence and ancestry is that the color line, which is drawn so often in social and political spheres, is rendered utterly insufficient and irrelevant in the realm of culture. In a famous passage from *The Souls of Black Folk,* Du Bois implies that the kingdom of culture has no color: "I sit with Shakespeare and he winces not. Across the color line I move arm in arm with Balzac and Dumas. . . . I summon Aristotle and Aurelius and what soul I will, and they come all graciously with no scorn nor condescension. So, wed with Truth, I dwell above the Veil."[49] Lines of influence and ancestry are drawn in accordance with practice and self-identification. Murray argues from a similar point of view when he states that "white jazz musicians eagerly embrace certain Negroes not only as kindred spirits but also as ancestral figures indispensable to their sense of purpose and to their sense of romance, sophistication, and elegance as well" (*OA* 102). In this sense, then, Murray discredits the question of authenticity based upon racial identification. When asked if a white man can "really play Negro music," he replies, "Of course he can. . . . If he develops the same familiarity with its idiomatic nuances, the same love of it, and humility before it as the good Negro musician does" (*OA* 131–32). Cultural authenticity is based solely upon personal involvement, through study and practice, with the vernacular or idiomatic particularities of any cultural form, no matter its origins. Or put another way, authenticity requires a familiarity with the traditions and conventions of cultural practices, which comes from individual engagement and is in turn filtered through the idiosyncrasies of those who take up the difficult work of mastering those forms.

Following this logic, cultural identity becomes more a matter of choice than something that is racially or economically predetermined. Thus, when Murray's Scooter mentions "ancestral imperatives," he knows he is not talking about blood but choice. Scooter asserts that just as "the names that really matter when it comes to the determination of actual identity are the nicknames we choose for ourselves—or the ones we accept as appropriately definitive when suggested . . . by others, so it is with ancestors and their imperatives" (*SLB* 149). Names, identity, ancestors, and imperatives are some of the major preoccupations of Scooter's life and the most prominent themes of the text he narrates. Throughout the trilogy, there is much discussion as to how people receive their names and the appropriateness of them. Red Ella, for example, received her nickname not from the blood with which she was streaked after murdering her husband but from "not knowing that bad luck and disappointment meant not the end of the world but only that being human you had to suffer like everybody else from time to time"; in other words, murdering her husband earns her the name "Red" because it was the furthest thing from a blues-orientated response she could have had (*TWG* 122).

Scooter, significantly, has no original or family name (or if he does he appears unaware of it). On a visit back home from college, he explains the reasons for his nickname: "*Mama's little scootabout man, he back home from all the way over yonder amongst them,* [Uncle Jerome, the preacher] *said, Now there's a name, notion, and designation to conjure with*" (*ST* 6, italics in original). And Scooter also reminisces about telling Little Buddy Marshall about his name on their first meeting at the pump shed, "I still can't remember ever calling myself anything else and I also said to him, That's what I'm supposed to be able to do" (*ST* 6). Under this logic, a name is a literal designation of what one does. But the fact that he qualifies his memory with "it was *as if* I had been calling myself Scooter all of my life" underscores his mysterious origins and patrimony (*ST* 6, emphasis added). At the close of *Train Whistle Guitar,* the first part of the trilogy, Scooter overhears the woman he had always thought to be his mother reveal to a neighbor that he is someone else's child. While it turns out that Scooter knows the woman who is his flesh and blood mother, his father remains a mystery. Scooter's unknown patrimony is significant for several reasons, not least of which is the suggestion that his father could be one of the legendary blues musicians, such as Luzana Cholly and Stagolee Dupas, or the local baseball legend, Gator Gus—men whom Scooter had already looked to as father figures and models for emulation. Scooter's ambiguous origins also suggest "*the ultimate rootlessness that is the perpetual condition humaine,*" a certain unsettledness that makes him all the more appropriate as a representative American and twentieth-century epic hero of sorts (*SLB* 25).

Fashioning himself a modern day Odysseus and fairytale hero, Scooter, upon graduating from college, joins a jazz band and accepts the adventurous challenge of a rootless life on the road. The title of Murray's third novel in the series, *The Seven League Boots,* refers to the "seven-seaward" attitude of a fairy tale hero with magic boots which enable him to take superhuman strides. Thus, once the band members, who at first playfully call him Schoolboy, test Scooter's ability to exhibit grace under pressure in a jam session, they rename him, "Hey Boots, Yeah Boots what about Seven League Boots," based upon his heroic actions (*SLB* 27, 29). The metaphor of sailing the seven seas operates throughout the novel as an indication of Scooter's adventurous approach to life. Yet importantly, the fairytale hero/epic adventurer is always able to return home not with any magic key that suggests a triumphant solution or final conclusion but with the added insight and wisdom his experiences have yielded so that he may continue the ongoing struggle that is life:

> *Home again, home again, in again, out again. And do you come back bearing the Golden Fleece? The golden apples? The magic jewels? The magic wand? You do not. As Odysseus, the most masterful of voyagers, did not. What he brought was that which he had acquired in experience in due course of his meandering: perhaps more pragmatic insight into his own identity and a deeper appreciation of chance, probability, and just plain lucking out. As for magic keys, are they not always a matter of the cryptographic information you acquire about combinations?* (*SLB* 369, italics in original)

Keeping with the overall aesthetic of the work, Murray resists finality and conclusion even in a passage like the one above, which appears at the end of the novel. As Murray comments in a 1996 interview, "My narrative structure is not geared to a tightly knit plot. It is a picaresque story, more a matter of one thing following another than one thing leading to another. To me, the 'and then and then and also and also and next after that' of a picaresque reflects a sensitivity consistent with contemporary knowledge of the universe" (*Conversations* 13). In this ever-evolving and continuous structure, Murray picks up a note, such as "magic keys" at the end *Seven League Boots,* and plays a new variation on it in the following novel, *The Magic Keys.*

Indeed, the predominant narrative forms of Murray's fiction, the picaresque and the fairytale, inform and shape their content, enacting the cosmopolitan tenets and aesthetic statements of his non-fiction. Instead of foregrounding a particular line of action and development for Scooter's character, he discovers "*that regardless of your career objectives your own story was something that you make up as you go along*" (*SLB* 137, italics in original). The episodic nature of the picaresque storyline, in which one experience leads to another like repetition with a difference in blues music and variations on a theme in jazz, is complimented by the narrative form of the fairytale, where the notion of a world of "make-believe" is less about fantasy than it is a "self-made" world in the true Emersonian sense of such representative American figures as the frontiersman and the pioneer. As Scooter narrates in the language of "the self-made world of storybook princes" and "fairy tale aunts," the chinaberry tree transforms into a beanstalk leading to castletown adventures, and he learns that his "*obligations to hometown expectations*" are "*more and more a matter of existential implication and less and less obviously a matter of personal social and political progress as such, without becoming any less pragmatic than direct involvement in concrete action as such, precisely because they were concerned with that upon which such action at its best must be predicated*" (*SLB* 257, 137, italics in original). Or as Scooter puts it regarding the necessary balance that must be struck between individual development and the strong presence of ancestral imperatives, "for all your carefully laid plans and expert training and guidance, a picaresque story line was the perpetual frame of reference for all personal chronicles" (*ST* 170).

Like the picaresque storyline, which functions as a reminder of the ongoing improvisation that life requires, the blues idiom represents a resilient and creative response to the fragmented nature of contemporary life. Thus, Murray argues that the "*blues statement*" is characterized by its "*affirmative disposition toward the harsh actualities of human existence.*" The blues statement provides a model for a general aesthetic "*upon which (and/or a frame of reference within which) a contemporary storybook heroism may be defined*" (*BDN* 7, italics in original). Murray identifies the attitude toward experience that the blues tradition embodies as an acknowledgment of and confrontation with "the infernal absurdities and ever-impending frustrations inherent in the nature of all existence *by playing with the possibilities that are also there*" (*OA* 58, italics in original). The blues-oriented hero is, above all, a pragmatist, if we understand pragmatism as "creative revisionary practice," to borrow Posnock's phrase. Parallels between Murray's description of the blues-oriented hero and William James's pragmatism, which he variously described as "the instilling of a temperament, a mode of conduct," and "an 'attitude of orientation' that 'stands for no particular results,'" are striking.[50]

As he historicizes the blues tradition, Murray connects it to a basic resilience that develops in response to "the ever-shifting circumstances of all Americans" and, more specifically, as "a central element in the dynamics of U.S. Negro life style" (*OA* 59, 58). By making the blues idiom central to American tradition, Murray also resituates the African American within that tradition. This is all part of Murray's larger project, introduced in his first book-length work of 1970, *The Omni-Americans,* to "counter-state" what he calls "social science fiction," which overemphasizes "the negative aspects of black experience" while all but ignoring "the affirmative implications of their history and culture" (*OA* 6).[51] He introduces the title essay of *The Omni-Americans* as "a discussion of the so-called questions of black identity in terms of the cultural dynamics involved in the formation of the national character of the United States as a whole" and "an indictment of those theorists and social welfare technicians whose statistics-oriented interpretations of black experience add up to what functions as a folklore of white supremacy and a fakelore of black pathology." Instead, Murray will review "the actualities and potentialities of black American experience as such elements are reflected in the blues idiom, one of the art styles most characteristic of U.S. Negro self-expression" (*OA* 7). If the blues idiom is emblematic of a basic American attitude toward experience, and if that same idiom originates from a specifically African-American experience, then it follows, Murray suggests in drawing on Constance Rourke's 1931 study of American humor and national character, that an African-American vernacular style is as representative of an American national character as the resilient pioneer and backwoodsman of American folk tradition.[52]

This is the argument Murray forwards in his discussion of the fugitive slave as a representative American, for, he writes, "the Underground Railroad was not only an innovation, it was also an *extension* of the American quest for democracy brought to its highest level of epic heroism" (*OA* 18, italics in original). In placing Frederick Douglass alongside canonical American figures like Benjamin Franklin, Thomas Jefferson, and Abraham Lincoln, Murray designates him a "heroic embodiment of the American as a self-made man" (*OA* 20). He tweaks and questions the dominant American narrative to counterstate the notion that African Americans are victims and "that slavery and oppression have made Negroes *inferior* to other Americans and hence less American" (*OA* 36, italics in original). Murray would have his readers understand African Americans as *ideal* American citizens whose political behavior in such instances as the abolition and civil rights movements proves them "the true descendent[s] of the Founding Fathers—who cr[y], 'Give me liberty or give me death,' and who [regard] taxation without representation as tyranny" (*OA* 37).[53]

Murray also questions dominant American narratives when he points toward the fact that emphasis is rarely, if ever, placed "on the failure of white Americans to measure up to the standards of the Constitution" (*OA* 36). Instead, documents such as the Moynihan Report typify the failure of the African-American family and construct a picture of black pathology and oppression that, in Murray's words, "violate one's common everyday breeze-tasting sense of life" (*OA* 5). His primary motivation is to confront the "outrage . . . being committed against [his] conception of actuality" in what are considered official, definitive or authentic representations of African Americans (*OA* 9). Such representations, as Franz Fanon discusses in relation to colonialism, merely propagate stereotypes, sealing African Americans in a "crushing objecthood," and revealing authenticity as a weapon wielded for a kind of colonial control.[54] Hence, Murray's criticism of "social science fiction" and his construction of the aesthetic, to borrow Posnock's words, as the "deferral" of identity, "a wedge against 'group imprisonment'" and directly "oppose[d] to the disciplinary yoke of [racial] authenticity."[55]

Murray uses his formulation of the blues aesthetic as a tool for counter-stating and shifting sclerotic discursive norms about black deviation. First correcting misconceptions of blues music as simple expressions of misery and oppression, or the blues themselves, Murray illustrates how the blues tradition provides a model for an "open disposition toward change, diversity, unsettled situations, new structures and experience, that are prerequisite to the highest level of citizenship" in America (*OA* 37). Furthermore, the blues aesthetic is not only representatively American. It is also, according to Murray, universally significant in its compatibility with "the *human* imperatives of modern times," or put another way, it "is compatible with those facts that in instances when Negroes are not involved are generally assumed to represent the universal element in all human nature" (*OA* 60, 4). Characterizing contemporary life as unstable and disjointed, Murray writes, "As rootless as the pioneer or even the captive Africans were, contemporary mankind in the world at large may well be in a predicament that is basically worse," due in part to the "widespread result of twentieth-century technological innovations" (23). The predicament of modernity requires "a resilience that is geared to spontaneous exploration, experimentation, inventiveness, and perpetual readjustment," or put in terms of the blues aesthetic, "a blues-conditioned disposition to remain perpetually resilient and alert to the ongoing need for improvisation" (*BP* 21, 23). Like Du Bois's confrontation of the dark truths of existence in "The Revelation of Saint Orgne the Damned," Murray presents a blues-oriented approach to life as one that "require[s] you to confront chaos *as a fact of life* and improvise on the exigencies of the situation, however dire, on the opportunities or the options that are also always there" (*BP* 21, my italics).

Important as it is to counter-state the social science fiction of black pathology, Murray does not allow readers to rest assured in a simple reversal of discursive norms: placing black Americans in the position of true

Americans while wondering whether white Americans are somehow less American for taking constitutional ideals like "freedom, justice, equality, fair representation, and democratic processes" for granted (*OA* 37). Rather, his complex approach to American identity necessarily moves beyond "the sterile category of race" and instead looks toward the realm of culture. And American culture is nothing if not "irrevocably composite" and "incontestably mulatto" (*OA* 22). The title of Murray's first book, *The Omni-Americans,* makes precisely this point: "the United States is in actuality not a nation of black people and white people. It is a nation of multicolored people. There are white Americans so to speak and black Americans. But any fool can see that the white people are not really white, and that black people are not black. They are all interrelated one way or another."[56] Furthermore, Murray celebrates ethnic difference in the United States as the "very essence of cultural diversity and national creativity" (*OA* 3).

Ultimately, Murray refuses to contribute to a misleading discourse of racial authenticity, especially when it comes to discussions of American culture. With this in mind, we might better understand his repositioning the Negro at the center of American culture. "After all, Negritude," writes Murray, "as the mulatto exponents of Afro-Americanismus are wont to say, is only a state of mind," which is to say that "blackness" is, to some extent, "a cultural identity" (*OA* 135, 173). Culture is open to those who choose to engage it through practice and study, and Murray criticizes "any Negro writer who assumes that 'black consciousness' is only a matter of *saying* you're black while writing about black experience" (*OA* 141). Thus, he censures Claude Brown for relying on false notions of authenticity, identity, and experience (his "complexion, his street address, and police record") rather than committing himself to the hard work of writing with sensitivity, imagination, depth, keenness of insight, linguistic precision and eloquence (*OA* 100). "Being black is not enough to make anybody an authority on U.S. Negroes," writes Murray, "any more than being white has ever qualified anybody as an expert on the ways of U.S. white people" (*OA* 97). Thus, Murray takes his place in a long line of black intellectuals such as Du Bois, Charles Chesnutt, Kelly Miller, and Alain Locke, who, as Posnock notes, "emancipated themselves from the imprisoning rhetoric of authenticity with its inevitable racializing of culture" and instead work to "deracializ[e] culture by making one's relation to it a matter of present action not prior identity."[57] Murray reminds readers that there is no scientific relationship between physiological characteristics and behavior when he states simply, "Consciousness and race just don't correlate" (*BP* 160). He openly distrusts the very idea of "negritude" at other points in his writing because he believes it "not only tends to mistake tradition (or cultural inheritance) for racial inheritance (or racial mysticism), it also encourages the kind of esthetic nonsense" of the Black Arts movements "that can only make it even more difficult . . . to realize the infinite potential of the black dimensions of the *American* tradition" (*OA* 153). Simplistic notions of authenticity promotes a racialized culture and are precisely what Murray, in the footsteps of Du Bois, strives to avoid by deliberately cultivating the distance and autonomy of the intellectual while keeping such elitism in productive tension with a rooted particularity or vernacular tradition, refusing "to be limited to any single role."[58]

Murray's claims about American cultural identity are actually quite radical if considered closely. His basic assumption is that a cultural tradition provides a context for identity (*BP* 86–87), and his theorization of the blues aesthetic asserts a "Negro idiom" at the heart of American cultural tradition. Following this logic to its conclusion results in the discovery that American identity is deeply indebted to blackness. Ralph Ellison reaches a similar conclusion when he describes "an American Negro idiom" as "a style and a way of life" that is "inseparable from the conditions of American society . . . from its general modes or culture." But, Ellison continues, "If general American values influence us; we in turn influence them—speech, concept of liberty, justice, economic distribution, international outlook, our current attitude toward colonialism, our national image of ourselves as a nation."[59] In his essay "What America Would Be Like Without Blacks"—the title of which recalls Du Bois's question in *The Souls of Black Folk,* "Would America have been America without her Negro people?"[60]—Ellison emphasizes the centrality of a "Negro idiom" in American culture and claims that "whatever else the true American is, he is also somehow black."[61]

In an article on Murray, Henry Louis Gates, Jr. discusses the implications of Murray and Ellison's common assertion that "the truest Americans were black Americans" as he attempts to correct what he considers a misperception of the two men as conservative for their bourgeois values and aesthetic sensibilities, as well as in their pandering to a white sense of guilt, in contrast to a younger generation of more radical and unapologetic black nationalists. Gates writes:

> This [that the truest Americans were black Americans] is the lesson that the protagonist of Ellison's novel learns while working at a paint factory: the whitest white is made by adding a drop of black. For generations, the word "American" had tacitly connoted "white." Murray inverted the cultural assumptions and the verbal conventions: in his discourse, "American," roughly speaking, means "black." So, even as

> the clench-fist crowd was scrambling for cultural crumbs, Murray was declaring the entire harvest board of American civilization to be his birthright. In a sense, Murray was the ultimate black nationalist. And the fact that people so easily mistook his vision for its opposite proved how radical it was.[62]

Both Murray and Ellison, in shifting the focus on the American scene ever so slightly, radically revalue the cultural, social, and political contributions of African Americans to the maintenance and meaning of American ideals and ultimately to the construction of American identity itself. Thus, Ellison writes that "today it is the black American who puts pressure upon the nation to live up to its ideals. . . . It is he who insists that we purify the American language by demanding that there be closer correlation between the meaning of words and reality, between ideal and conduct, our assertions and our actions."[63] In pointing out the dishonesty of a mere rhetorical commitment to American ideals, like equality, justice and freedom, and their subsequent corruption in both language and reality, Ellison turns commonplace assumptions on their head. More often than not, discussions that address the idea of purification in language have posited the vernacular and idiomatic as the corrupting elements of a standard or traditional language. Ellison, instead, situates the vernacular as a purifying agent for maintaining the connection between language and people's sense of actual lived life and experience.

Like Murray, then, Ellison asks unexpected questions and draws unconventional conclusions. In a lecture, titled "What These Children Are Like," given at a seminar on "Education for Culturally Different Youth" in 1963, Ellison asks, "How can we keep the discord flowing into the mainstream of the language without destroying it?" Obviously, his main concern is not, as seminar-goers might have expected, how to squelch discord but how to incorporate it into the mainstream. "One of the characteristics of a healthy society," he continues, "is the steady filtering of diverse types and diverse cultural influences."[64] Rather than disparage tension and discord, Ellison assumes their necessity for the health and growth of the nation. Similarly, he recontextualizes the criteria for determining cultural wealth or cultural deprivation. "When a child has no sense of how he should fit into the society around him," explains Ellison, "he is culturally deprived—no matter how high his parents' income."[65] The subtle and eloquent shift at the end of this sentence is another characteristic Ellisonian move of subverting conventional notions, here of economic class and cultural wealth. One might anticipate from the first part of the sentence that Ellison refers to a culturally deprived black child with little access to the elite educational institutions of his country or community; however, Ellison overturns the assumption that economic status guarantees one's connection to culture and a strong sense of identity. Instead, he asserts a pragmatist notion of identity: that one *is* something only through active involvement with it and not because one's economic status grants one access nor because one's blood relations claim it for their own.

The issue of identity returns us to Murray's complaint concerning the inadequacy of sociological categories. Statistical data, like income, place of residency, or even family history, cannot provide an accurate measure for one's cultural status or sense of identity. As Scooter reminds readers near the end of *The Seven League Boots,* unlike the marquis who was born to his aristocratic status, Americans ideally have the opportunity to achieve an elite status through hard work and practice:

> I began thinking again about how the marquis was to the manor and manner of the château born, and about how Jewel Templeton and I and most other Americans were born wherever and however we were born to be reborn on campuses. *Certainly the most basic of all things about universal free public education in the United States is that for all its widespread and longstanding entanglement with racial segregation it is predicated on the completely democratic assumption that individual development, self-realization and self-fulfillment is a matter of inspiring learning contexts not of one's family background and certainly not a matter of one's ancient racial forebears. So assumed Miss Lexine Metcalf and Mr. B. Franklin Fisher, neither of whom ever confused race with culture.* (*SLB* 321–22, italics in original)

Nor do Scooter's academic influences, his schoolteachers and college roommate, confuse culture with economic or any other predetermined status. Instead, they see the opportunity to achieve elite cultural status as "a matter of choice . . . a matter of incentive and depth of personal motivation—a matter of horizons of aspiration" (*SLB* 352). Personal responsibility to raise one's own horizons of aspiration, as well as those of "the so-called common man," however, does not negate the importance of remaining in touch with one's roots and "learning contexts." In fact, Scooter represents the possibility of a balance between specialized elite cultural institutions and the idiomatic roots of a down-home vernacular. An exemplary figure, Scooter links the blues with the literary, experience with education, ancestral imperatives with individual development, and by extension, racial politics of protest with bourgeois values. Through this combination of diverse influences and elements, Scooter achieves the elite status of the cosmopolitan: able to travel the road and record with a popular jazz band; consort with the wealthy aristocrats, Jewel Templeton and the Marquis de Chaumienne; attend graduate school in order "to earn what would be equivalent to the seven league stride of the heroes in rocking chair story times"; and still be able to return home to the porch, fireside and barbershop chat sessions of his youth (*SLB* 104).

The last section of *The Seven League Boots,* "The Craftsman," follows "The Apprentice" and "The Journeyman" stages in Scooter's development to a cosmopolitan perspective and the cultivated status of a specialist. Aware of the fact that his craftsman status as a musician is not an end point or resting place, Scooter sees the skills and knowledge he has gained as tools to be applied to other pursuits in the picaresque "and then and then and also and also and next after that" which is contemporary life reflected in the ongoing improvisation of the jam session (*Conversations* 135). By the end of the novel, Scooter is gearing up for graduate school, and it is precisely this kind of unexpected pairing of the hip jazz musician with the prospective graduate student that marks Murray's rooted cosmopolitanism in his insistent incorporation of the vernacular and the traditional. Likewise, "The Dancing of an Attitude: The Footnotes of the One and Only ROYAL HIGHNESS," a book project upon which Scooter embarks at the end of *The Magic Keys,* plays on the academic and idiomatic resonances of various traditions.[66] With the characteristic praise which has come to typify the heroic rendering of Scooter's epic adventures, Royal Highness reminds Scooter that he and the other band members "could see for themselves that you as hip to what the band is about as you are deep in all that college and university jive," further proclaiming, "The dancing of an attitude! Now, that's saying something. Talking about not just what you say, but what you do and how you do it. . . . Footnotes on the insights and outlook. That's exactly what riffing the blues on the afterbeat is all about" (*MK* 233–34).

Murray uses Scooter as a literary device to resituate the representative American, redefine the meaning of "elite" and, by extension, revalue the very notion of "elitism" itself, turning it away from exclusivity and exception towards possibility. In keeping with Du Bois's claim in *Dusk of Dawn* that the "vaster possibility" and "real promise" of democracy lies in "tapping the great possibilities of mankind from unused and unsuspected reservoirs of human greatness," Murray asks us to consider the possibility and promise of "hitherto untapped sources of cultur[e]."[67] While promoting the idea of a cultural elite, Murray also combats an elitism that is blind to particularity and irreducible conflict—one that would claim a universalism that abstracts all individuality, leaving no residuum, only identity.[68]

Murray builds his aesthetic sensibility from a modernist foundation that is both interracial and interdisciplinary with artistic ancestors as diverse as Joyce and Faulkner, Duke Ellington, Fats Waller and Jack Johnson, yet he also resists "modernist conventions of blackness," which Claudia Tate identifies as "center[ing] around the familiar racial paradigm of social oppression and resulting protest."[69] A consideration of Murray's work within "the traditional black canon" is important precisely because it does not "conform to the protest agenda of black modernism." Works such as Murray's, Tate argues, "make visible the ways in which we readers have circumscribed black subjectivity and black textuality by a reductive understanding of racial difference."[70] When Tate asks, "What are the critical imperatives of a black postmodern canon?" we might turn to Murray's conceptualization of the development of Scooter's personal identity in terms that do not "simply reject race as a primary focus" but that "place racial proscriptions in a broad context among other social issues and personal concerns" for one possible answer.[71]

Murray's rooted cosmopolitanism insists on the importance of the idiomatic particularity and the tragicomic sensibility that the vernacular provides, just as it is in agreement with Du Bois's characterization of the complex and unreconciled relationship between the particular and universal. In "The Conservation of the Races," Du Bois writes, "as a race we must strive by race organization, by race solidarity, by race unity to the realization of that broader humanity which freely recognizes differences in men, but sternly deprecates inequality in their opportunities of development."[72] Ultimately, Murray's achievement lies in his extension of this dialectical relationship between the particular and the universal, as expressed through his rooted cosmopolitanism and his democratic elitism, into a "universally appealing . . . aesthetic statement . . . achieved through the local details and idiomatic particulars" of a blues-oriented way of life.

Notes

NOTES TO THE INTRODUCTION

1. My focus on the United States is not only because of my particular interest in the racial discourse that has formed from the historical experience of race relations in a specifically American context. It is also informed by a notion similar to David Hollinger, *Cosmopolitanism and Solidarity: Studies in Ethnoracial, Religious, and Professional Affiliation in the United States* (Madison, W.I.: University of Wisconsin Press, 2006) who argues that "the United States has been a major site for many of the processes that now produce the problem of solidarity elsewhere"; thus, it is "not so much a model for the world as an archive of experience on which the world can draw critically" (xxii). "Far from serving as a sterling exemplar of cosmopolitanism," he adds, "it is a site, like many other nations, for struggles over the problem of solidarity in which cosmopolitanism is an active but not a dominant player" (xxiv). A critic such as Eric Lott, *The Disappearing Liberal Intellectual* (New York: Basic Books, 2006) would argue (wrongly, in my opinion) that this "neoliberal" position "promotes nationalism, ignores globalization, and dismisses multiculturalism outright" (46).
2. Kwame Anthony Appiah, "The Case for Contamination," *The New York Times Magazine,* January 1, 2006, http://www.nytimes.com/2006/01/01/magazine/01cosmopolitan.html.
3. W. E. B. Du Bois, *The Souls of Black Folk* (1903; New York: Penguin, 1989), 1.
4. Mary Louise Pratt, "Modernity and Periphery: Towards a Global and Relational Analysis," in *Beyond Dichotomies: Histories, Identities, Cultures, and the Challenge of Globalization,* ed. Elisabeth Mudimbe-boyi (Albany: State University of New York Press, 2002), 21.
5. Phillip Brian Harper, *Framing the Margins: The Social Logic of Postmodern Culture* (New York: Oxford University Press, 1994), 21.
6. Ibid., 3.
7. Gertrude Stein, *Three Lives* (1909; New York: Penguin, 1990), 13, 60, 172.

8. Ann Charters, introduction to *Three Lives,* by Gertrude Stein (New York: Penguin, 1990), vii.
9. Donald B. Gibson, introduction to *The Souls of Black Folk,* by W. E. B. Du Bois (New York: Penguin, 1989), xxxv.
10. Du Bois, *The Souls of Black Folk,* 5.
11. Quoted in Ross Posnock, *Color and Culture: Black Writers and the Making of the Modern Intellectual* (Cambridge, M.A.: Harvard University Press, 1998), 23.
12. For a review of *Color and Culture,* see Arnold Rampersad, "The Legacy of Black Intellectuals," *Raritan* 18.4 (Spring 1999): 116–22.
13. For additional reading, see Ross Posnock, "The Dream of Deracination: The Uses of Cosmopolitanism," *American Literary History* 12.4 (Winter 2000): 802–18.
14. Appiah, "The Case for Contamination."
15. Other critics have discussed at length the intersection of modernism and cosmopolitanism but through writers centrally located in the modernist canon. See Jessica Berman, *Modernist Fiction, Cosmopolitanism, and the Politics of Community* (Cambridge, England: Cambridge University Press, 2001) for a discussion of James, Proust, Woolf, and Stein, who in response to the threat of totalitarian models of national community, "not only inscribe early twentieth-century anxieties about race, ethnicity, and gender, but confront them with demands for modern, cosmopolitan versions of community" (3); and Rebecca L. Walkowitz, *Cosmopolitan Style: Modernism Beyond the Nation* (New York: Columbia University Press, 2006) who reads Conrad, Joyce, Woolf, Rushdie, Ishiguro and Sebold for their skepticism "about political commitments defined by national culture and about efforts to specify and fix national characteristics."
16. Du Bois, *The Souls of Black Folk,* 5.
17. Posnock, *Color and Culture,* 6.
18. Ibid., 92.
19. Ibid., 6.
20. Amanda Anderson, "Cosmopolitanism, Universalism, and the Divided Legacies of Modernity," in *Cosmopolitics: Thinking and Feeling beyond the Nation,* eds. Pheng Cheah and Bruce Robbins (Minneapolis: University of Minnesota Press, 1998), 267. This essay is reprinted in Amanda Anderson, *The Way We Argue Now: A Study in the Cultures of Theory* (Princeton, N.J.: Princeton University Press, 2006), chapter 3, pp. 69–92. For further discussion of the progressive potential of detachment, see Amanda Anderson, *The Powers of Distance: Cosmopolitanism and the Cultivation of Detachment* (Princeton, N.J.: Princeton University Press, 2001). For a counterargument, see Stephen Eric Bronner, *Reclaiming the Enlightenment: Toward a Politics of Radical Engagement* (New York: Columbia University Press, 2004), chapter 8, pp. 133–50, who writes, "Cosmopolitanism requires engagement and conviction. 'Detachment' or 'estrangement' actually strips away the radical and critical character of the idea" (148).
21. Anderson, "Cosmopolitanism," 267.

22. Ibid., 272. For a collection of essays that asks whether in our rush to globalization we can sustain the geo-cultural ideal of cosmopolitanism, see Vinay Dharwadker, ed., *Cosmopolitan Geographies: New Locations in Literature and Culture* (New York: Routledge, 2001). For a collection of essays on the viability of a world politics based on shared democratic values, see Daniele Archibugi, ed., *Debating Cosmopolitics* (New York: Verso, 2003). For a collection of essays by political theorists "contributing to the task of defending a positive political philosophy of cosmopolitanism," see Gillian Brock and Harry Brighouse, eds., *The Political Philosophy of Cosmopolitanism* (Cambridge, England: Cambridge University Press, 2005), ix. For a special issue on cosmopolitanism and cities, see Mike Featherstone, ed., "Cosmopolis," *Theory, Culture & Society* 19.1–2 (Feb.-Apr. 2002): 1–253 (Special issue.). In his introduction, Featherstone argues that "we should endeavor to understand cosmopolitanism in the plural" so that we consider a wide spectrum of experiences from global elites to working-class migrants (2). The anxiety that cosmopolitanism is a stance only capable of accounting for an elite perspective is widely recognized and variously handled in the critical discourse surrounding the term. For one of the most prominent voices critiquing cosmopolitanism for "functioning as a relay for the center's values," see Timothy Brennan, "Cosmo-Theory," *South Atlantic Quarterly* 100.3 (Summer 2001): 659–91; reprinted in Timothy Brennan, *Wars of Position: The Cultural Politics of Left and Right* (New York: Columbia University Press, 2006), chapter 7, pp. 205–32. Brennan claims that cosmopolitanism is "the process by which one . . . expands his or her sensitivities toward the world while exporting a self-confident locality for consumption *as* the world" (206–07). For a broader, more systemic critique along these lines, see Paul Gilroy, *Postcolonial Melancholia* (New York: Columbia University Press, 2005), chapter 2, "Cosmopolitanism Contested," pp. 58–86. Gilroy discusses the ways in which the term "cosmopolitanism" and human rights discourse in general have been "hijacked and diminished" by "the unipolar global order created by the economic and military dominance of the United States" through "recast[ing] the ideal of imperial power as an 'ethical' force which can promote good and stability amidst the flux and chaos of the postcolonial world" (59). For a counter to this kind of critique, see Carol A. Breckenridge, Sheldon Pollack, Homi K. Bhabha, and Dipesh Chakrabarty, eds. and intro., "Cosmopolitanisms," *Public Culture* 12.3 (Fall 2000): 578–786 (Special issue), who explore the possibilities of the term. In the introduction, the editors stress a "minoritarian modernity," which would consider the perspectives and experiences of refugees, peoples of the diaspora, migrants and exiles over a global elite, providing "a source for contemporary cosmopolitical thinking" (582), in addition to the model feminism provides in "the situated rather than the universal subject" (583). Similarly exploring the possibilities and problems of cosmopolitanism, Camilla Fojas, in *Cosmopolitanism in the Americas* (West Lafayette, I.N.: Purdue University Press, 2005), discusses "cosmopolitanism from the margins . . . to establish equitable dialogues between centers and peripheries" (4–5).

23. Others have noted a similar connection between cosmopolitanism and racial discourse in the United States. See, for instance, Ian Finseth, "Evolution, Cosmopolitanism, and Emerson's Antislavery Politics," *American Literature* 77.4 (Dec. 2005): 728–60; C. C. O'Brien, "Cosmopolitanism in Georgia Douglas Johnson's Anti-Lynching Literature," *African American Review* 38.4 (Winter 2004): 571–87; and Malin Pereira, *Rita Dove's Cosmopolitanism* (Urbana: University of Illinois Press, 2003). "One contemporary articulation of cosmopolitanism," claims Pereira, is a "new black aesthetic," which is critical of the black arts movement not in "moving beyond blackness" but in realizing that perspective is shaped by "shared group experience," as well as "individual personal experiences" (74, 77). For a discussion of the dangers or illusions of a cosmopolitan perspective regarding racial discourse, see Simon Gikandi, "Race and Cosmopolitanism," *American Literary History* 14.3 (Fall 2002): 593–615; and Don Robotham, "Cosmopolitanism and Planetary Humanism: The Strategic Universalism of Paul Gilroy," *South Atlantic Quarterly* 104.3 (Summer 2005): 561–82. In their critiques of Paul Gilroy, *Against Race: Imagining Political Culture beyond the Color Line* (Cambridge, M.A.: Belknap Press of Harvard University Press, 2000), Gikandi argues that in Gilroy's "war against the absolutism of social and conceptual categories, most notably racialism and nationalism," he is "caught between the dream—or illusion—of cosmopolitanism and the reality of political interpellation," or the "tension between what is construed as individual agency and the apparatus of cultural formation" (593–94). Robotham faults Gilroy's liberal cosmopolitanism "since it will exist solely at the formal-legal and moral levels, masking the substantive power, wealth, and privileges enjoyed in practice by dominant classes, identities, and Great Power nations" (565).
24. Jeremy Waldron, "Minority Cultures and the Cosmopolitan Alternative," in *The Rights of Minority Cultures,* ed. Will Kymlicka (New York: Oxford University Press, 1995), 110.
25. Ibid., 112.
26. Ulrich Beck, in "The Cosmopolitan Society and Its Enemies," *Theory, Culture & Society* 19.1–2 (Feb.-Apr. 2002): 17–44., defines cosmopolitanism as "globalization *from within* the national societies." Rather than understand globalization as something that only happens out in the world, Beck conceives it as happening inside our nation and our selves, "transforming everyday consciousness and identities significantly. Issues of global concern are becoming part of the everyday experiences and the 'moral life worlds' of the people" (17). In turn, this creates a need for a "reinvention of politics" in a "transnational framework," or "cosmopolitan parties" which "represent transnational interests transnationally, but also work within the arena of national politics" (41–42). See also, Roy Boyne, "Cosmopolis and Risk: A Conversation with Ulrich Beck," *Theory, Culture & Society* 18.4 (Aug. 2001): 47–63. For a discussion of "the cultural logic of transnationality" and "human rights obligations," see Bryan S. Turner, "Cosmopolitan Virtue, Globalization and Patriotism," *Theory, Culture & Society* 19:1–2 (Feb.-Apr. 2002): 45–63. In the critical discourse surrounding cosmopolitanism,

tension often arises between cosmopolitan norms of universal justice, for instance, as governed by the 1948 U.N. Declaration of Human Rights, and democratic ideals of sovereign self-determination. For a discussion of the need to mitigate this tension and renegotiate these dual commitments, see Seyla Benhabib, *Another Cosmopolitanism,* with commentaries by Jeremy Waldron, Bonnie Honig, and Will Kymlicka, ed. Robert Post (New York: Oxford University Press, 2006). For an argument that, instead, reveals flaws in both human rights universalism and claims about the imminent decline of the nation-state, see Pheng Cheah, *Inhuman Conditions: On Cosmopolitanism and Human Rights* (Cambridge, M.A.: Harvard University Press, 2006); and Pheng Cheah, *Spectral Nationality: Passages of Freedom from Kant to Postcolonial Literatures of Liberation* (New York: Columbia University Press, 2003).

27. David A. Hollinger, *Postethnic America: Beyond Multiculturalism* (New York: BasicBooks, 1995), 4.
28. Posnock, *Color and Culture,* 16, 23.
29. Ibid., 24.
30. Walter Benn Michaels, *Our America: Nativism, Modernism, and Pluralism* (Durham: Duke University Press, 1995), 15.
31. Ibid., 66.
32. Posnock, *Color and Culture,* 24.
33. Michel Feher, "The Schisms of '67: On Certain Restructurings of the American Left, from the Civil Rights Movement to the Multiculturalist Constellation," in *Blacks and Jews: Alliances and Arguments,* ed. Paul Berman (New York: Delacorte, 1994), 275.
34. Ibid., 275–76.
35. Tzvetan Todorov, *On Human Diversity: Nationalism, Racism, and Exoticism in French Thought,* trans. Catherine Porter (Cambridge, M.A.: Harvard University Press, 1993), 387.
36. Seyla Benhabib, *Situating the Self: Gender, Community and Postmodernism in Contemporary Ethics* (New York: Routledge, 1992), 3. See also, Couze Venn, "Altered States: Post-Enlightenment Cosmopolitanism and Transmodern Socialities," *Theory, Culture & Society* 19:1–2 (Feb-Apr. 2002): 65–80.
37. Todorov, *On Human Diversity,* 4.
38. Posnock, *Color and Culture,* 113, 104.
39. Ibid., 118.
40. Quoted in Posnock, 113.
41. Posnock, 118.
42. Hannah Arendt, "Truth and Politics," in *Between Past and Future: Eight Exercises in Political Thought* (New York: Penguin, 1993), 242.
43. Hannah Arendt, *Lectures on Kant's Political Philosophy* (Chicago: University of Chicago Press, 1982), 42. Dialogue and imagination are central to discussions of cosmopolitanism. See, for instance, Kwame Anthony Appiah, *Cosmopolitanism: Ethics in a World of Strangers* (New York: W. W. Norton & Co., 2006) who writes, "Conversations across boundaries of identity . . . begin with the sort of imaginative engagement you get when

you read a novel or watch a movie or attend to a work of art that speaks from some place other than your own. So I'm using the word 'conversation' not only for literal talk but also as a metaphor for engagement with the experience and the ideas of others" (85).

44. See Ian Baucom, *Specters of the Atlantic: Finance Capital, Slavery, and the Philosophy of History* (Durham, N.C.: Duke University Press, 2005), chapters 8 and 10, pp. 213–41, 265–96. Baucom employs the term "cosmopolitan interestedness," explaining that a work of imagination asks us "to discern in the image of the miseries we never saw the melancholy 'facts' of history, a worldly knowledge of things 'as they are' and an obligation to act on that knowledge." "Liberal cosmopolitanism," then, is when we are asked "to watch, sympathize, and then move on, to compose ourselves . . . as an effect of the *idea* of our witness to the sufferings of another" (295–96).
45. Arendt, *Lectures on Kant's Political Philosophy*, 43. For further discussion of the artist as a typically cosmopolitanism figure, "who makes an imaginative, empathic leap into the minds and hearts of his fellows," see Christopher Sten, "Melville's Cosmopolitanism: A Map for Living in a (Post-) Colonialist World," *Melville 'Among the Nations,'* ed. Sanford E. Marovitz and A. C. Christodoulou (Kent, O.H.: Kent State University Press, 2001), 38–48. Sten argues that cosmopolitanism is "a defining activity of the imagination for Melville, in politics and in art" (47).
46. For further analysis of these figures and their interrelations see George Hutchinson, *The Harlem Renaissance in Black and White* (Cambridge, M.A.: Belknap Press of Harvard University Press, 1995); Werner Sollors, *Beyond Ethnicity: Consent and Descent in American Culture* (New York: Oxford University Press, 1986); David Hollinger, *Postethnic America* and *In the American Province: Studies in the History and Historiography of Ideas* (Bloomington: Indiana University Press, 1985); Thomas Bender, *New York Intellect: A History of Intellectual Life in New York City, from 1750 to the Beginnings of Our Own Time* (New York: A.A. Knopf, 1987); Edward Abrahams, *The Lyrical Left: Randolph Bourne, Alfred Stieglitz and the Origins of Cultural Radicalism in America* (Charlottesville: University Press of Virginia, 1986); Casey Blake Nelson, *Beloved Community: The Cultural Criticism of Randolph Bourne, Van Wyck Brooks, Waldo Frank, & Lewis Mumford* (Chapel Hill, N.C.: University of North Carolina Press, 1990); and Posnock, *Color and Culture.*
47. For further discussion of Royce's "provincial cosmopolitanism," see Leigh Anne Duck, *The Nation's Region: Southern Modernism, Segregation, and U.S. Nationalism* (Athens: University of Georgia Press, 2006), chapter 6, pp. 177–211. See also Tom Lutz, *Cosmopolitan Vistas: American Regionalism and Literary Value* (Ithaca, NY: Cornell University Press, 2004); and Tom Lutz, "The Cosmopolitan Midland," *American Periodicals* 15.1 (2005): 74–85, where he claims, "the central ethos of American literary culture" is "to balance the particular and the general, the provincial and the cosmopolitan, the local and the global" (81).
48. Quoted in George Hutchinson, *The Harlem Renaissance in Black and White*, 81.

49. Hutchinson, *The Harlem Renaissance in Black and White,* 87.
50. Waldo Frank, *Our America* (New York: Boni & Liveright, 1919), 200.
51. Randolph Bourne, *War and the Intellectuals: Essays by Randolph S. Bourne 1915–1919,* ed. Carl Resek (New York: Harper Torchbooks, 1964), 108.
52. Ibid., 114.
53. Ibid., 118.
54. Horace M. Kallen, *Culture and Democracy in the United States: Studies in the Group Psychology of the American People* (New York: Boni and Liveright, 1924), 118.
55. Ibid., 124.
56. J. E. Spingarn, "Criticism in the United States," in *Criticism in America: Its Function and Status* (New York: Harcourt, Brace: 1924), 305. Like Spingarn, Thomas Bender, in "The Boundaries and Constituencies of History," *American Literary History* 18.2 (Summer 2006): 267–82, acknowledges the creative potential of scholarship when he asks, "Can our work as writers and teachers affect and partially effect that spatial restructuring and the new patterns of affiliation in positive ways, making for a richer and more cosmopolitan culture and more open forms of citizenship?" (269). He urges scholars to "move beyond the nationalist ideology and historiography that was forged in the second half of the nineteenth century" in order to create "a history of a nation that [i]s attentive to, perhaps even shaped by, an awareness that a national history [i]s part of a larger history, that it [i]s, so to speak, a province in a larger global human community and history" (275, 277). Using Du Bois's scholarship as an intellectual example, he posits not a postnational history but a rooted cosmopolitanism that would "acknowledg[e] transnational causes and consequences" of major themes and events in a national history (279). For a critique of Bender, see Peter Fritzsche, "Global History and Bounded Subjects: A Response to Thomas Bender," *American Literary History* 18:2 (Summer 2006): 283–87. A common critique of cosmopolitanism is that attention to a hybrid and global culture is somehow also a claim for the death of nationalism. See, for instance, Timothy Brennan, *At Home in the World: Cosmopolitanism Now* (Cambridge, M.A.: Harvard University Press, 1997). I maintain, with Bender, that a critical cultural nationalism need not be at odds with a cosmopolitan perspective, that we can be "rooted in local polities and thus a form of national citizenship, yet also openly engaged with and self-consciously dependent upon more extensive affiliations" (271).
57. Ralph Waldo Emerson, *Selections from Ralph Waldo Emerson: An Organic Anthology,* ed. Stephen E. Whicher (Boston: Houghton Mifflin, 1957), 65.
58. Bourne, *War and the Intellectuals,* 14.
59. Van Wyck Brooks, "The Critics and Young America," in *Criticism in America: Its Function and Status* (New York: Harcourt, Brace, 1924), 121–22.
60. Bourne, *War and the Intellectuals,* 108; Brooks, "The Critics and Young America," 126. For a discussion of critical cultural nationalism and its convergence with a cosmopolitan perspective in the work of Henry James, see John Carlos Rowe, "Henry James in a New Century," in *A Companion to*

American Fiction, 1865–1914, eds. Robert Paul Lamb and G. R. Thompson (Malden, M.A.: Blackwell, 2005), 518–35.

61. The recognition of a living legacy of a black cosmopolitan intellectual tradition is all the more important in light of Cornel West's statement, in *Keeping Faith: Philosophy and Race in America* (New York: Routledge, 1993), regarding "the dangling status of black intellectuals [which has] prevented the creation of a rich heritage of intellectual exchange, intercourse and dialogue. There indeed have been grand black intellectual achievements, but such achievements do not substitute for tradition" (72).
62. Quoted in Thomas Bender, *New York Intellect: A History of Intellectual Life in New York City, from 1750 to the Beginnings of Our Own Time* (New York: Knopf, 1987), 233.
63. Bourne quoted in Bender, *New York Intellect,* 236.
64. Theodor Adorno, "The Essay as Form" in *The Adorno Reader* (Malden, M.A.: Blackwell, 2002), 16–17.
65. Ibid., 16.
66. Ibid.
67. Ibid., 11.
68. Ibid., 13.
69. Ibid., 16.
70. Ibid., 17.
71. Barbara Christian, "The Race for Theory" in *Within the Circle: An Anthology of African American Literary Criticism from the Harlem Renaissance to the Present,* ed. Angelyn Mitchell (Durham, N.C.: Duke University Press, 1994), 351, 349, 355.
72. Ibid., 352.
73. Judith Butler, *Bodies That Matter: On the Discursive Limits of "Sex"* (New York: Routledge, 1993), 182.
74. Benhabib, *Situating the Self,* 5–6.
75. Shamoon Zamir, *Dark Voices: W. E. B. Du Bois and American Thought, 1888–1903* (Chicago: University of Chicago Press, 1995), 3.
76. For a relevant discussion of Oscar Wilde's cosmopolitan criticism, see Julia Prewitt Brown, *Cosmopolitan Criticism: Oscar Wilde's Philosophy of Art* (Charlottesville, V.A.: University Press of Virginia, 1997). Wilde believed that "engaging the art of other cultures together with that of one's own had the power to accomplish what neither abstract systems of ethics nor humanitarian sympathy could achieve: to make other nations a part of one's native heritage. 'One had ancestors in literature . . . as well as in one's own race'" (xvi).
77. Some critics employ the terms "rooted" or "vernacular cosmopolitanism" to draw attention to the dialectic between the local and global. See, for instance, Craig Calhoun, "The Class Consciousness of Frequent Travelers: Toward a Critique of Actually Existing Cosmopolitanism," *South Atlantic Quarterly* 101.4 (Fall 2002): 869–97, who, in making "a plea for the importance of the local and particular," writes,

    if cosmopolitan democracy is to be more than a good ethical orientation for those privileged to inhabit the frequent flyer lounges, it must

> put down roots in the solidarities that organize most people's sense of identity and location in the world. To appeal simply to liberal individualism—even with respect for diversity—is to disempower those who lack substantial personal or organization resources. (871, 893)

Charles L. Briggs, in "Genealogies of Race and Culture and the Failure of Vernacular Cosmopolitanisms: Rereading Franz Boas and W. E. B. Du Bois," *Public Culture* 17.1 (Winter 2005): 75–100, closely examines the writing of Boas and Du Bois to "theoriz[e] connections between cosmopolitanism and vernacularism more critically" and to "help challenge the neoconservative, neoliberal, and militaristic cosmopolitanisms that are defining the limits for imagination and action today" (78); and Domna C. Stanton, "Presidential Address 2005: On Rooted Cosmopolitanism," *PMLA* 121.3 (May 2006): 627–40, wants to avoid the "romantic" yet "well-intentioned efforts to define cosmopolitanism from the bottom up," when, for instance, James Clifford tries, "to find its hybrid forms among labor migrants and servants." Instead, Stanton writes, "It is more important, in my view, to recognize the specific situation of power/knowledge in which we are individually located and to engage in the forms of a rooted cosmopolitan praxis that privilege affords us" (637).

NOTES TO CHAPTER ONE

1. Journal entry (probably 1912), Box 60, Folder 1409, Jean Toomer Papers, James Weldon Johnson Collection, Yale Collection of American Literature, Beinecke Rare Book and Manuscript Library, Yale University (hereafter cited as Jean Toomer Papers).
2. The only essay explicitly about race that Toomer wrote and that was published during his life is "Race Problems and Modern Society," in *Problems of Civilization,* ed. Baker Brownell (New York: Van Nostrand, 1929), 67–111. A privately printed and circulated pamphlet, *A Fiction and Some Facts,* which Toomer wrote about his personal life, also focuses on the issue of race.
3. For the positive aspects of miscegenation and mixed race identity in Toomer's work, see George Hutchinson, "Jean Toomer and the 'New Negroes' of Washington," *American Literature* 63.4 (Dec. 1991): 683–92.
4. Michael Omi and Howard Winant, *Racial Formation in the United States: From the 1960s to the 1990s* (2nd edition; New York: Routledge, 1994), 55.
5. Ibid., 99. For additional reading about Toomer's active engagement with racial discourse in the United States, see Mary Battenfeld, "'Been Shapin Words T Fit M Soul': *Cane,* Language, and Social Change," *Callaloo* 25.4 (Fall 2002): 1238–49; Rudolph P. Byrd, "Jean Toomer and the Afro-American Literary Tradition," *Callaloo* 8.2 (Spring-Summer 1985): 310–19; Chester J. Fontenot, Jr., "Du Bois's 'Of the Coming of John,' Toomer's 'Kabnis,' and the Dilemma of Self-Representation," in *The Souls of Black Folk One Hundred Years Later,* ed. Dolan Hubbard (Columbia, M.O.: University of Missouri Press, 2003), 130–60; Mattew Prat Guterl, *The Color of Race in*

America, 1900–1940 (Cambridge, M.A.: Harvard University Press, 2001), introduction and chapter 4; Charles Harmon, "Cane, Race, and 'Neither/Norism,'" *Southern Literary Journal* 32:2 (2000): 90–101; Stephanie L. Hawkins, "Building the 'Blue' Race: Miscegenation, Mysticism, and the Language of Cognitive Evolution in Jean Toomer's 'The Blue Meridian,'" *Texas Studies in Literature and Language* 46.2 (Summer 2004): 149–80; Tace Hedrick, "Blood-Lines That Waver South: Hybridity, the 'South,' and American Bodies," *Southern Quarterly* 42.1 (Fall 2003): 39–52; George Hutchinson, "Jean Toomer and American Racial Discourse," *Texas Studies in American Literature and Language* 35.2 (Summer 1993): 226–50; Kathryne V. Lindberg, "Raising *Cane* on the Theoretical Plane: Jean Toomer's Racial Personae," *Cultural Difference and the Literary Text: Pluralism and the Limits of Authenticity in North American Literatures,* ed. Winfried Siemerling and Katrin Schewenk (Iowa City: University of Iowa Press, 1996), 49–74; Lizabeth A. Rand, "'I Am I': Jean Toomer's Vision beyond *Cane,*" *CLA Journal* 44.1 (Sept. 2000): 43–64; Jeff Webb, "Literature and Lynching: Identity in Jean Toomer's *Cane,*" *ELH* 67 (2000): 205–28; Mark Whalan, "'Taking Myself in Hand': Jean Toomer and Physical Culture," *Modernism/Modernity* 10.4 (Nov. 2003): 597–615; and Diana I. Williams, "Building the New Race: Jean Toomer's Eugenic Aesthetic," in *Jean Toomer and the Harlem Renaissance,* eds. Geneviève Fabre and Michel Feith (New Brunswick, N.J.: Rutgers University Press, 2001), 188–201. For more specific discussions of modernism and racial discourse, see Catherine Gunther Kodat, "To 'Flash White Light from Ebony': The Problem of Modernism in Jean Toomer's *Cane,*" *Twentieth Century Literature* 46.1 (Spring 2000): 1–19; and Werner Sollors, "Jean Toomer's *Cane:* Modernism and Race in Interwar America," in *Jean Toomer and the Harlem Renaissance,* 18–37. For an analysis of modernism and black masculinity, see Nathan Grant, *Masculinist Impulses: Toomer, Hurston, Black Writing, and Modernity* (Columbia, M.O.: University of Missouri Press, 2004). For a linking of queer theory to Toomer's racial disidentification and resistance to a discourse of naturalized racial identity, see Siobhan B. Somerville, *Queering the Color Line: Race and the Invention of Homosexuality in American Culture* (Durham: Duke University Press, 2000), chapter 5.

6. Barbara Christian, "The Race for Theory," in *Within the Circle: An Anthology of African American Literary Criticism from the Harlem Renaissance to the Present,* ed. Angelyn Mitchell (Durham, N.C.: Duke University Press, 1994), 352.
7. The Jean Toomer Papers are available in the James Weldon Johnson Collection at the Beinecke Rare Book and Manuscript Library at Yale University. See also various collections of Toomer's previously unpublished writing: John Chandler Griffin, ed., *The Uncollected Works of American Author Jean Toomer, 1894–1967*(Lewiston, N.Y.: E. Mellen Press, 2003); Robert B. Jones, ed., *Jean Toomer: Selected Essays and Literary Criticism* (Knoxville: University of Tennessee Press, 1996); Robert B. Jones and Margery Toomer Latimer, eds., *The Collected Poems of Jean Toomer* (Chapel Hill: University of North Carolina Press, 1988); Frederick L. Rusch, *A Jean*

Toomer Reader: Selected Unpublished Writings (New York: Oxford University Press, 1993); Darwin T. Turner, ed., *The Wayward and the Seeking: A Collection of Writings by Jean Toomer* (Washington, D.C.: Howard University Press, 1980); Mark Whalan, ed., *The Letters of Jean Toomer, 1919–1924* (Knoxville: University of Tennessee Press, 2006); and Charles Scruggs, "'My Chosen World': Jean Toomer's Articles in *The New York Call*," *Arizona Quarterly* 51.2 (Summer 1995): 103–26.

8. See George Hutchinson, *The Harlem Renaissance in Black and White* (Cambridge, M.A.: Belknap Press of Harvard University Press, 1995).
9. Jean Toomer Papers, Box 13, Folder 389.
10. Jean Toomer to *The Liberator,* 19 August 1922, Jean Toomer Papers, Box 4, Folder 145. Some versions include reference to his Spanish heritage, for instance, Jean Toomer, "The Crock of Problems," in *Jean Toomer: Selected Essays and Literary Criticism,* 56.
11. Toomer, "Crock of Problems," 58.
12. Ibid., 56.
13. Ibid., 58
14. Omi and Winant, *Racial Formation,* 92. For a counterargument and analysis of Toomer's association of membership in the "new race" with superiority and "in terms of the constructed boundaries it affirms" rather than resists, see Diana Williams, "Building the New Race: Jean Toomer's Eugenic Aesthetic," 189.
15. See Walter Benn Michaels, *Our America: Nativism, Modernism, and Pluralism* (Durham: Duke University Press, 1995): "Nativism, according to its most distinguished scholar, John Higham, can be defined as 'intense opposition to an internal minority on the grounds of its foreign (i.e. "un-American") connections,' opposition that, while it may 'vary widely' in target and intensity, ultimately expresses in each case 'the connecting, energizing force of modern nationalism'" (2). Also, see Mattew Prat Guterl, *The Color of Race in America, 1900–1940,* regarding "the increasing southernization of northeastern American racial discourse" (9).
16. George Hutchinson, "Identity in Motion: Placing *Cane,*" in *Jean Toomer and the Harlem Renaissance,* 53. For further discussion of the "acts of discursive violence that banish the forbidden terms and thus enable the social fictions by which we live," see George Hutchinson, "Jean Toomer and American Racial Discourse," *Texas Studies in American Literature and Language* 35.2 (Summer 1993): 226–50.
17. See Charles Scruggs and Lee Vandemarr, *Jean Toomer and the Terrors of American History* (Philadelphia: University of Pennsylvania Press, 1998), 20: Toomer's maternal grandfather, P. B. S. Pinchback, who raised him after his mother's death in 1908, had been a prominent Republican in Louisiana's Reconstruction politics and was elected lieutenant governor of the state in 1871. In 1893, Pinchback moved to Washington, D. C., where his money and political connections securely established him in that city's "mulatto elite" with its close ties to the Republican party and the federal administrative offices of the city. For an analysis of class in addition to racial consciousness regarding the mulatto elite of Washington, D.C., see Barbara Foley, "Jean

Toomer's Washington and the Politics of Class: From 'Blue Veins' to Seventh-Street Rebels," *Modern Fiction Studies* 42 (Summer 1996): 289–321.

18. Jean Toomer Papers, Box 51, Folder 1113.
19. Martha Nussbaum, "Patriotism and Cosmopolitanism," in *For Love of Country: Debating the Limits of Patriotism,* ed. Joshua Cohen (Boston: Beacon Press, 1996), 7.
20. Jean Toomer Papers, Box 51, Folder 1113.
21. Omi and Winant, *Racial Formation,* 54.
22. Ibid., 55.
23. Toomer, "Race Problems and Modern Society," in *Jean Toomer: Selected Essays and Literary Criticism,* 70.
24. See Geneviève Fabre and Michel Feith, "Tight-Lipped 'Oracle': Around and beyond *Cane,*" in *Jean Toomer and the Harlem Renaissance,* 3–4.
25. Michaels, *Our America,* 64.
26. Scruggs and Vandemarr, in *Jean Toomer and the Terrors of American History,* focus particularly on the gothic dimension or historical nightmare of race in Toomer's writing. See also Charles Scruggs, "The Reluctant Witness: What Jean Toomer Remembered from Winesburg, Ohio," *Studies in American Fiction* 28.1 (Spring 2000): 77–100, and "Jean Toomer and Kenneth Burke and the Persistence of the Past," *American Literary History* 13.1 (Spring 2001): 41–66.
27. Jean Toomer, *Cane,* ed. Darwin T. Turner, (1923; Norton critical edition, New York: W. W. Norton, 1988), 7, 9. Hereafter cited in the text.
28. John G. Mencke, *Mulattoes and Race Mixture: American Attitudes and Images, 1865–1918* (Ann Arbor: UMI Research Press, 1978), discusses how "a rash of books and pamphlets appeared," as an effect of a post-Reconstruction spread of "radical racism" in the South, "describing miscegenation as 'a crime' against God and man that 'will spread like a bubonic plague.'" Quoted in Scruggs and Vandemarr, *Jean Toomer and the Terrors of American History,* 26.
29. For further reading on representations of women in *Cane,* see Jessica Hays Baldanzi, "Stillborns, Orphans, and Self-Proclaimed Virgins: Packaging and Policing the Rural Women of *Cane,*" *Genders* 42 (2005). Online journal. http://www.genders.org/g42/g42_baldanzi.html; and Vera M. Kutzinski, "Unseasonal Flowers: Nature and History in Placido and Jean Toomer," *Yale Journal of Criticism* 3.2 (1990): 153–79. For more specific readings of the objectification of black female bodies and musical metaphors in *Cane,* see Katherine Boutry, "Black and Blue: The Female Body of Blues Writing in Jean Toomer, Toni Morrison, and Gayl Jones," in *Black Orpheus: Music in African American Fiction from the Harlem Renaissance to Toni Morrison,* ed. Saadi A. Simawe (New York: Garland, 2000), 91–118. For music in *Cane* as both a tool of resistance for women and a tool of entrapment for men, see Thomas Fahy, "The Enslaving Power of Folksong in Jean Toomer's *Cane,*" in *Literature and Music,* ed. Michael J. Meyer (Amsterdam: Rodopi, 2002), 47–63.
30. For further reading on representations of lynching in *Cane,* see Kimberly Banks, "'Like a Violin for the Wind to Play': Lyrical Approaches to

Lynching by Hughes, Du Bois, and Toomer," *African American Review* 38:3 (Fall 2004): 451–65; and Susan Edmunds, "The Race Question and the 'Question of the Home': Revisiting the Lynching Plot in Jean Toomer's *Cane*," *American Literature* 75.1 (Mar. 2003): 141–68.

31. Hutchinson, "Identity in Motion," 51.
32. For additional biographical information, see Cynthia Earl Kerman and Richard Eldridge, *The Lives of Jean Toomer: A Hunger for Wholeness* (Baton Rouge: Louisiana State University Press, 1987); Charles R. Larson, *Jean Toomer and Nella Larsen: Invisible Darkness* (Iowa City: University of Iowa Press, 1993); Nellie Y. McKay, *Jean Toomer, Artist: A Study of His Literary Life and Work, 1894–1936* (Chapel Hill: University of North Carolina Press, 1984); and Charles Scruggs and Lee Vandemarr, *Jean Toomer and the Terrors of American History* (Philadelphia: University of Pennsylvania Press, 1998).
33. See Scruggs and Vandemarr, *Jean Toomer and the Terrors of American History*, 9–10.
34. Quoted in the Norton Critical Edition of *Cane*, ed. Darwin T. Turner, 156.
35. Ibid., 151.
36. Many writers have discussed the mythic and/or nostalgic dimensions of Toomer's representations of the South, for example, William M. Ramsey, "Jean Toomer's Eternal South," *Southern Literary Journal* 36.1 (Fall 2003): 74–89. Some critics at least touch upon the tensions between the myth and historical testimony, such as Barbara E. Bowen, "Untroubled Voice: Call and Response in *Cane*," *Black American Literature Forum* 16:1 (Spring 1982): 12–18; David G. Nicholls, "Jean Toomer's *Cane*, Modernization, and the Spectral Folk," in *Modernism, Inc.: Body, Memory, Capital*, ed. Jani Scandura and Michael Thurston (New York: New York University Press, 2001), 151–70; Charles Scruggs, "The Mark of Cain and the Redemption of Art," *American Literature* 44 (May 1972): 276–91; and Alain Solard, "Myth and Narrative Fiction in *Cane*: 'Blood-Burning Moon,'" *Callaloo* 8 (Fall 1985): 551–62. Barbara Foley, in "'In the Land of Cotton': Economics and Violence in Jean Toomer's *Cane*," *African American Review* 32 (1998): 188–90, and in "Jean Toomer's Sparta," *American Literature* 67 (December 1995): 747–75, provides excellent readings of socio-economic realities and historical particularities, as well as the mythic realm, of the South—a tension that is embodied in the split characterization of Kabnis, the "spectatorial artist," and Lewis, the "engaged activist."
37. Karen Jackson Ford, in *Split-Gut Song: Jean Toomer and the Poetics of Modernity* (Tuscaloosa: University of Alabama Press, 2005), argues that *Cane* dramatizes the "failure" of "the modern black poet to transform the last echoes of the spirituals into a new poetry." This is most evident, she claims, in "the elegiac strains" of the book's poetry (3).
38. Hutchinson, "Identity in Motion," 54.
39. Ibid.
40. Jean Toomer to *The Liberator*, 19 August 1922, Jean Toomer Papers, Box 4, Folder 145.
41. Quoted in the Norton Critical Edition of *Cane*, ed. Darwin T. Turner, 160–61.

42. Quoted in Scruggs and Vandemarr, 10. For an analysis of the literary collaboration between Toomer and Frank, see Daniel Terris, "Waldo Frank, Jean Toomer, and the Critique of Racial Voyeurism," *Race and the Modern Artist,* ed. Heather Hathaway, Josef Jarab, and Jeffrey Melnick (Oxford: Oxford University Press, 2003), 92–114.
43. Jean Toomer to Boni & Liveright, 5 September 1923, Jean Toomer Papers, Box 1, Folder 16. For a discussion of small New York publishers, like Boni & Liveright, who both opened doors to and essentialized minority voices, see Michael Soto, "Jean Toomer and Horace Liveright; or a New Negro Gets 'Into the Swing of It,'" in *Jean Toomer and the Harlem Renaissance,* 162–87.
44. Jean Toomer to James Weldon Johnson, 11 July 1930, Jean Toomer Papers, Box 4, Folder 119. Quotes in the rest of this paragraph are taken from this letter.
45. Jean Toomer Papers, Box 51, Folder 1124.
46. Jean Toomer Papers, Box 51, Folder 1122.
47. Jean Toomer Papers, Box 51, Folder 1111.
48. James Baldwin, "Many Thousands Gone," in *Notes of a Native Son* (1955; Boston: Beacon Press, 1984), 24–25.
49. Jean Toomer Papers, Box 49, Folder 1045.
50. Jean Toomer Papers, Box 43, Folder 891.
51. Jean Toomer Papers, Box 51, Folder 1116.
52. Ross Posnock, *Color and Culture: Black Writers and the Making of the Modern Intellectual* (Cambridge, M.A.: Harvard University Press, 1998), 88.
53. Quoted in Amanda Anderson, "Cosmopolitanism, Universalism, and the Divided Legacies of Modernity," in *Cosmopolitics: Thinking and Feeling beyond the Nation,* eds. Pheng Cheah and Bruce Robbins (Minneapolis: University of Minnesota Press, 1998), 279.
54. Jean Toomer Papers, Box 51, Folder 1116.
55. This quote is taken from the draft version of "Race Problems and Modern Society," which differs from the published version. Jean Toomer Papers, Box 51, Folder 1120.
56. Toomer, "Race Problems and Modern Society," in *Jean Toomer: Selected Essays and Literary Criticism,* 67.
57. Ibid., 68
58. Ibid., 74.
59. Jean Toomer Papers, Box 39, Folder 816.
60. Toomer, "The Function of the Writer," in *Jean Toomer: Selected Essays and Literary Criticism,* 44, emphasis added.
61. Toomer, "Letter from America," in *Jean Toomer: Selected Essays and Literary Criticism,* 82.
62. Toomer, "The Questions of the *Cahiers de l'Etoile,*" in *Jean Toomer: Selected Essays and Literary Criticism,* 89.
63. A pamphlet (c. 1923), introducing "G. Gurdjieff's Institute for the Harmonious Development of Man," illustrates a concern for combining the methods of "European science" and "the ancient learning of the East" in order to "widen the horizon of human conception and, at the same

time, help to set right the processes of thought and consciousness" (Jean Toomer Papers, Box 68, Folder 1537). For in-depth analysis of Toomer's Gurdjieff work, see Jon Woodson, *To Make a New Race: Gurdjieff, Toomer, and the Harlem Renaissance* (Jackson: University Press of Mississippi, 1999); and Rudolph Byrd, *Jean Toomer's Years with Gurdjieff: Portrait of an Artist, 1923–1936* (Athens: University of Georgia Press, 1990).

64. Jean Toomer Papers, Box 51, Folder 1111.
65. Toomer, "Questions of the *Cahiers de l'Etoile,*" 89.
66. For additional discussions of spiritual incompleteness and narrative strategies of unification in *Cane,* see Joel B. Peckham, "Jean Toomer's Cane: Self as Montage and the Drive toward Integration," *American Literature* 72 (2000): 275–90; and Janet M. Whyde, "Mediating Forms: Narrating the Body in Jean Toomer's *Cane,*" *Southern Literary Journal* 26.1 (Fall 1993): 42–53.
67. For an analysis of machine technology, race and literary aesthetics in *Cane,* see Mark Whalan, "Jean Toomer, Race and Technology," *Journal of American Studies* 36 (Dec. 2002): 459–72.
68. Jean Toomer to Margaret Naumberg [n.d.], Jean Toomer Papers, Box 6, Folder 193.
69. Hutchinson, "Identity in Motion," 45. See also George Hutchinson, "The Whitman Legacy and the Harlem Renaissance," in *Walt Whitman: The Centennial Essays,* ed. Ed Folsom. (Iowa City: University of Iowa Press, 1994), 201–16, for a discussion of the religious, ecstatic, mystical, and linguistic influence of Walt Whitman in Toomer's writing, which combines the vernacular and slang with "elements of traditional 'high' culture" and "throws cultural hierarchies into question" (210).
70. Quoted in the Norton Critical Edition of *Cane,* ed. Darwin T. Turner, 174.
71. Ibid.
72. Quoted in Charles-Yves Grandjeat, "The Poetics of Passing in Jean Toomer's *Cane,*" in *Jean Toomer and the Harlem Renaissance,* 65.
73. Quoted in Shamoon Zamir, *Dark Voices: W. E. B. Du Bois and American Thought, 1888–1903* (Chicago: University of Chicago Press, 1995), 122.
74. Zamir, *Dark Voices,* 122.
75. Jean Toomer Papers, Box 43, Folder 890.
76. Ibid.
77. Ibid.
78. Jean Toomer Papers, Box 50, Folder 1099.
79. Jean Toomer Papers, Box 39, Folder 814.
80. Review by R. L. Duffus, *New York Times Book Review,* 13 September 1936, Psychology and Religion, Subject Files, Jean Toomer Papers, Box 70, Folder 1581.
81. Review by R. L. Duffus, *The New* Yorker [1936?], Psychology and Religion, Subject Files, Jean Toomer Papers, Box 70, Folder 1581.
82. *The New York Times,* 14 September 1936, Social History, Subject Files, Jean Toomer Papers, Box 70, Folder 1584.
83. Ibid.

84. Thomas Bender, *New York Intellect: A History of Intellectual Life in New York City, from 1750 to the Beginnings of Our Own Time* (New York: Knopf, 1987), 235.
85. Quoted in Bender, *New York Intellect,* 244.
86. Toomer, "Paul Rosenfeld in Port," in *Jean Toomer: Selected Essays and Literary Criticism,* 40.
87. Ibid., 41.
88. Toomer corresponded with Huxley in 1937:

    In point of fact I have felt moved towards you ever since the days (1923) when *Broom* magazine was in existence. I connected with it, and reviewed *On the Margin.* When *Point Counter Point* came out I felt strongly that we would inevitably meet, one of these days. But it is not as a writer that I now want this contact. It is as a human being, whose inner development has reached a stage which has basic points in common with your own; as one of the all too few western men who realize that the present plight of the human species is far more critical than the diagnosis furnished by those, however intelligent and earnest they may be, who are body-bound. And now something less serious. One of your characters in *Point Counter Point* turns the pages of the Encyclopedia Britannica and lights upon the name—P. B. S. Pinchback. This was odd enough. Well, P. B. S. Pinchback happened to have been my grandfather! So who can doubt that, however tenuous, there is some link between the man who put his finger on that name and the grandson of the man of that name? (Jean Toomer to Aldous Huxley, 22 November 1937, Jean Toomer Papers, Box 4, Folder 112)

    Toomer also likens himself to Huxley in a letter to the Macmillan publishers in order to bolster his manuscript's potential:

    And judging for one thing, by the appearance and the reception of Aldous Huxley's *Ends and Means,* I would say that the people with *human* consciousness are increasing not only in numbers but in earnestness and intelligent force. . . . If such an inner revolution towards the Human Good is in progress, there is every reason for believing that my works will be in demand, and increasingly so. (Jean Toomer to The Macmillan Company, 11 December 1937, Jean Toomer Papers, Box 5, Folder 170)
89. Henry Hazlitt, "Aldous Huxley's New Credo: In 'Ends and Means' He Fashions His Design for Living," *The New York Times Book Review,* 12 December 1937, Psychology and Religion, Subject Files, Jean Toomer Papers, Box 70, Folder 1581.
90. Bruce Clayton, *Forgotten Prophet: The Life of Randolph Bourne* (Baton Rouge: Louisiana State University Press, 1984), 262.
91. Ibid., 251.
92. Waldo Frank, *Our America* (New York: Boni & Liveright, 1919), 198–99.
93. Ibid., 199.
94. Ibid., 200.
95. Dewey quoted in Posnock, *Color and Culture,* 113.
96. Posnock, *Color and Culture,* 116.

97. Du Bois quoted in Posnock, 3.
98. Jean Toomer Papers, Box 60, Folder 1411.
99. Jean Toomer Papers, Box 49, Folder 1045.
100. Randolph Bourne, *War and the Intellectuals: Essays by Randolph S. Bourne 1915–1919*, ed. Carl Resek (New York: Harper Torchbooks, 1964), 108.
101. Posnock, *Color and Culture*, 128.
102. Ibid., 203.
103. Ibid., 206.
104. Jean Toomer Papers, Box 13, Folder 389.
105. Nussbaum, "Patriotism and Cosmopolitanism," 9.
106. Posnock, *Color and Culture*, 91–92.
107. Jean Toomer Papers, Box 13, Folder 389.
108. Linda M. G. Zerilli, "This Universalism Which Is Not One," *diacritics* 28.2 (1998): 3–20.
109. Ibid., 10, 8.
110. Ibid., 8.
111. Ibid., 15.
112. Jean Toomer Papers, Box 52, Folder 1166.

NOTES TO CHAPTER TWO

1. Jessie Redmon Fauset, *Plum Bun* (1929; Boston: Beacon Press, 1990), 337. Hereafter cited in the text.
2. For further discussion of Fauset's use of "the conventions of popular domestic fiction to represent the politics of gender, race, and class," see Susan Tomlinson, "'An Unwonted Coquetry': The Commercial Seductions of Jessie Fauset's *The Chinaberry Tree*," in *Middlebrow Moderns: Popular American Women Writers of the 1920s*, eds. Lisa Botshon and Meredith Goldsmith (Boston: Northeastern University Press, 2003), 227–43. Tomlinson writes about "the novel's hybridity as an antiromance romance novel that manipulates and even mutates the popular 'germ' in order to undermine and ultimately reinscribe it" (227–28). Deborah McDowell, in "The Neglected Dimension of Jessie Redmon Fauset," in *Conjuring Black Women, Fiction, and Literary Tradition*, eds. Marjorie Pryse and Hortense J. Spillers (Bloomington: Indiana University Press, 1985), 86–104, variously describes Fauset's adherence to the formal conventions of the novel of manners as "a self conscious artistic stratagem," a "protective mimicry," and "a kind of deflecting mask for her more challenging concerns" (87). More often, however, Fauset's use of the conventional marriage plot is read in less complex ways. See, for instance, Paula C. Barnes, in "Dorothy West: Harlem Renaissance Writer?" in *New Voices on the Harlem Renaissance: Essays on Race, Gender, and Literary Discourse*, eds. Australia Tarver and Paula C. Barnes (Madison, N.J.: Fairleigh Dickinson University Press, 2005), 99–124, who writes, "Although Fauset critiques the script of the sentimental novel, she appears to remain committed to it" (109); and Mary F. Sisney, in "The View from the Outside: Black Novels of Manners," in *The Critical Response to Gloria Naylor*, eds. Sharon Felton and Michelle

C. Loris (Westport, C.T.: Greenwood, 1997) 63–75, who claims that a "correct and proper" marriage brings order to the life of the Fauset heroine, who, thereafter, "finds her place in society. She belongs" (66).

3. For other critical approaches that focus on the central tensions and ambiguities of Fauset's work, see P. Gabrielle Foreman, "Looking Back from Zora, or Talking Out Both Sides My Mouth for Those Who Have Two Ears," *Black American Literature Forum* 24 (1990): 649–66; and Teresa Zackodnik, "Passing Transgressions and Authentic Identity in Jessie Fauset's *Plum Bun* and Nella Larsen's *Passing*," in *Literature and Racial Ambiguity*, eds. Teresa Hubel and Neil Brooks (Amsterdam: Rodopi, 2002), 45–69. Foreman considers the "tensions between different levels of textual meaning and interpretation which seem to contradict and pull away from each other" in order to analyze the ways in which both Hurston and Fauset "mediate their messages, their audience expectations, and their own ambivalence about representing race, gender, and power" (650, 653). Zackodnik shows how Fauset's novels "expose the tensions, ambiguities and interactions" between seeming oppositions such as communal and individualist politics and practice and essentialist and constructionist paradigms for approaching black identity (47).
4. Claudia Tate, *Psychoanalysis and Black Novels: Desire and the Protocols of Race* (New York: Oxford University Press, 1998), 10. However, Hiroko Sato, in "Under the Harlem Shadow: A Study of Jessie Fauset," in *Remembering the Harlem Renaissance*, ed. Cary D. Wintz (New York: Garland, 1996), 261–87, finds that Fauset combines the novel of manners of the Negro upper class with social protest at the expense of what LeRoi Jones calls an "investigation of the human soul" (80).
5. Angela Elizabeth Hubler, in "'From Home to Market': Private Emotion and Political Engagement in the Work of Emma Goldman, Jessie Fauset and Josephine Herbst," diss., Duke University, 1993, also questions the dominant opposition between public and private modalities and the associated categorical oppositions mental/emotional, male/female, universal/particular, as well at the literary boundaries structured by such oppositions in the narrative of modernism. Ann duCille, in "Blues Notes on Black Sexuality: Sex and the Texts of Jessie Fauset and Nella Larsen," *Journal of the History of Sexuality* 3.3 (Jan. 1993): 418–44, questions "the valorization of the vernacular" in black discourse and the denigration of "other cultural forms for their perceived adherence to and promotion of traditional (white) values" (421) and identifies a "double vision" at the heart of Fauset's work that critiques "both the pretensions of the black bourgeoisie and the primitivism assigned the transplanted urban masses" (422). In a related argument, Mary Hairston McManus, in "African-American Modernism in the Novels of Jessie Fauset and Nella Larsen," diss., University of Maryland, College Park, 1993, discovers themes that are mainstream modernist combined with strategies that are African American, such as "masking with the mulatta image" while exploring "broader arenas for female expression."
6. Tate, *Psychoanalysis and Black Novels*, 11–12.

7. See Carolyn Wedin Sylvander, *Jessie Redmon Fauset, Black American Writer* (Troy, N.Y.: Whitston, 1981) for an overview of the contemporaneous criticism of Fauset's novels. For bio-bibliographies of Fauset, see Janet L. Sims, "Jessie Redmon Fauset (1885–1961): A Selected Annotated Bibliography," *Black American Literature Forum* 14.4 (Winter 1980): 147–52; Emmanuel S. Nelson, "Jessie Redmon Fauset (1882–1961)," in *African American Authors, 1745–1945: A Bio-Bibliographical Critical Sourcebook*, ed. Emmanuel S. Nelson (Westport, C.T.: Greenwood, 2000), 155–60; and Rhonda Austin, "Jessie Redmon Fauset (1882–1961), in *American Women Writers, 1900–1945: A Bio-Bibliographical Critical Sourcebook*, ed. Laurie Champion (Westport, C.T.: Greenwood, 2000), 101–06. For a discussion of Fauset's work as a literary editor at *Crisis* in helping shape black literature of the 1920s, see Abby Arthur Johnson, "Literary Midwife: Jessie Redmon Fauset and the Harlem Renaissance," *Phylon* 39 (1978): 143–53.
8. Sharon L. Jones, *Rereading the Harlem Renaissance: Race, Class, and Gender in the Novels of Jessie Fauset, Zora Neale Hurston, and Dorothy West* (Westport, C.T.: Greenwood Press, 2002), 4. For examples of such critical devaluations, see Bernard Bell, *The Afro-American Novel and Its Traditions* (Amherst: University of Massachusetts Press, 1987); Robert Bone, *The Negro Novel in America* (1958; revised edition, New Haven: Yale University Press, 1965); and Nathan Huggins, *Harlem Renaissance* (New York: Oxford University Press, 1971).
9. Cheryl Wall, *Women of the Harlem Renaissance* (Bloomington: Indiana University Press, 1995), 84.
10. Hazel Carby, *Reconstructing Womanhood: The Emergence of the Afro-American Woman Novelist* (New York: Oxford University Press, 1995), 167.
11. Claudia Tate, *Psychoanalysis and Black Novels,* 11–12. For further discussion of female desire and sexual politics, see Ann duCille, *The Coupling Convention: Sex, Text, and Tradition in Black Women's Fiction* (New York: Oxford University Press, 1993).
12. Tate, *Psychoanalysis and Black Novels,* 10.
13. Jessie Redmon Fauset, *There Is Confusion* (1924; Boston: Northeastern University Press, 1989), 267. Hereafter cited in the text.
14. See Beth Ann McCoy, "'Do I Look Like This or This?': Race, Gender, Class, and Sexuality in the Novels of Jessie Fauset, Carl Van Vechten, Nella Larsen, and F. Scott Fitzgerald," diss., University of Delaware, 1995, for a reading of the "companion fantasies" of bourgeois and working class womanhood.
15. Jessie Redmon Fauset, *The Chinaberry Tree: A Novel of American Life & Selected Writings* (1931; Northeastern University Press, 1995), xxxi. Hereafter cited in the text.
16. For further discussion of the interplay of aestheticism and politics in Fauset's fiction, see Margaret D. Stetz, "Jessie Fauset's Fiction: Reconsidering Race and Revising Aestheticism," in *Literature and Racial Ambiguity,* eds. Teresa Hubel and Neil Brooks (Amsterdam: Rodopi, 2002), 253–70. In line with my own reading, Stetz identifies "fruitful contradictions held

in a kind of tension, rather than self-cancelling propositions" in Fauset's work (260).

17. See Mary Jane Lupton, in "Clothes and Closure in Three Novels by Black Women," *Black American Literature Forum* 20 (1986): 409–21, who suggests that Fauset offers a critical perspective of middle-class values and subverts the narrative structure of what she terms "the Cinderella line."
18. *Comedy: American Style* (1933; New York: G. K. Hall & Co., 1995), 9. Hereafter cited in the text.
19. Clearly Theresa's character problematizes the arguments several critics make regarding passing as simply a cause for celebration. See, for instance, Mary Condé, "Passing in the Fiction of Jessie Redmon Fauset and Nella Larsen," *Yearbook of English Studies* 24 (1994): 94–104; and Kathleen Anne Pfeiffer, "All the Difference: Race Passing and American Individualism," diss., Brandeis University, 1995. As always in Fauset's texts, one can find evidence to support such a reading, but passing as an expression of American individualism or a "seizing of rights" needs to be placed in the larger context of evidence that contradicts and complicates this view.
20. See Karen A. Chachere, "Visually White, Legally Black: Miscegenation, the Mulattos, and Passing in American Literature and Culture, 1965–1933,"diss., Illinois State University, 2004, who argues that miscegenation and passing in Fauset's fiction serve in a larger sense as indictments against claims of racial purity and white superiority, rather than cause for simple celebration.
21. Du Bois, *The Souls of Black Folk,* 11–12
22. Ibid., 42.
23. Waldo Frank, *Our America,* 146; Randolph Bourne, *War and the Intellectuals,* 108.
24. For further reading about Fauset's cosmopolitan worldview as expressed in her travel essays, see Erica L. Griffin, "The 'Invisible Woman' Abroad: Jessie Fauset's New Horizon," in *Recovered Writers/Recovered Texts,* ed. Dolan Hubbard (Knoxville: University of Tennessee Press, 1997) 75–89.

NOTES TO CHAPTER THREE

1. See Raymond Smith, "Langston Hughes: Evolution of the Poetic Person," in *Langston Hughes: Critical Perspectives Past and Present,* eds. Henry Louis Gates, Jr. and K. A. Appiah (New York: Amistad, 1993), 122; R. Baxter Miller, *The Art and Imagination of Langston Hughes* (Lexington, K.Y.: University Press of Kentucky, 1989), 4; and Monika Kaup, "'Our America' That Is Not One: Transnational Black Atlantic Disclosures in Nicolás Guillén and Langston Hughes," *Discourse* 22.3 (Fall 2000): 107.
2. For further discussion of Hughes's blues aesthetic, see David Chinitz, "Literacy and Authenticity: The Blues Poems of Langston Hughes," *Callaloo* 19.1 (1996): 177–192; Jane Olmsted, "Black Moves, White Ways, Every Body's Blues: Orphic Power in Langston Hughes's *The Ways of White Folks,*" in *Black Orpheus: Music in African American Fiction from the Harlem Renaissance to Toni Morrison,* ed. Saadi A. Simawe (New York:

Garland, 2000), 65–89; and Mariann Russell, "Langston Hughes and Melvin Tolson: Blues People," in *The Furious Flowering of African American Poetry,* ed. Joanne V. Gabbin (Charlottesville: University Press of Virginia, 1999), 38–46. For further discussion of Hughes's leftist politics and writing, see James Smethurst, "'Don't Say Goodbye to the Porkpie Hat': Langston Hughes, the Left, and the Black Arts Movement," *Callaloo* 25.4 (Fall 2002): 1225–36; and James Smethurst, "The Adventures of a Social Poet: Langston Hughes from the Popular Front," in *A Historical Guide to Langston Hughes,* ed. Steven C. Tracy (Oxford, England: Oxford University Press, 2004), 141–68.

3. For a discussion of Hughes's work as balancing politics and the aesthetics of popular art in particular, see Eric J. Sundquist, "Who Was Langston Hughes?" *Commentary* 102.6 (Dec. 1996): 55–59; and Jonathan Scott, "Advanced, Repressed, and Popular: Langston Hughes During the Cold War," *College Literature* 33.2 (Spring 2006): 30–51. For a more specific discussion of Hughes's negotiation of "multiracial social democracy" and "black cultural nationalist formations" in *Montage of a Dream Deferred,* see John Lowney, *History, Memory, and the Literary Left: Modern American Poetry, 1935–1968* (Iowa City: University of Iowa Press, 2006), chapter 4.
4. George Schuyler's "The Negro-Art Hokum" appeared 16 June 1926. Hughes's "The Negro Artist and the Racial Mountain" appeared 23 June 1926. Anticipating controversy, the editors of the *Nation* had solicited the essay from Hughes and planned to publish it the following week. It may not be a direct response given that fact that Hughes felt it necessary to write a letter to the editor, titled "American Art or Negro Art?" which appeared in the *Nation* two months later, 18 August 1926, directly addressing Schuyler's essay.
5. Langston Hughes, *The Collected Works of Langston Hughes: Volume 9: Essays on Art, Race, Politics, and World Affairs,* ed. Christopher C. De Santis (Columbia, M.O.: University of Missouri Press, 2002), 32–33. Hereafter cited in the text as *Essays.*
6. See Tish Dace, *Langston Hughes: The Contemporary Reviews* (Cambridge, England: Cambridge University Press, 1997).
7. Langston Hughes, *The Collected Works of Langston Hughes: Volume 1: The Poems: 1921–1940,* ed. Arnold Rampersad (Columbia, M.O.: University of Missouri Press, 2001), lines 1, 4, 7, 10, 14, 17. Unless otherwise noted, all poetry is from this volume and will be cited hereafter in the text by line number.
8. For further discussion of the effects Hughes's travels in Soviet Central Asia had on his ever-expanding vision of an African diaspora, see David C. Moore, "Local Color, Global 'Color': Langston Hughes, the Black Atlantic, and Soviet Central Asia, 1932," *Research in African Literatures* 27.4 (Winter 1996): 49–70; and David C. Moore, "Colored Dispatches from the Uzbek Border: Langston Hughes's Relevance, 1933–2002," *Callaloo* 25.4 (Fall 2002): 1115–35. For a discussion of Hughes's experiences in the Soviet Union in relation to his exploration of racial and sexual identities,

see Kate A. Baldwin, "The Russian Connection: Interracialism as Queer Alliance in Langston Hughes's *The Ways of White Folks*," *Modern Fiction Studies* 48.4 (Winter 2002): 795–824.

9. Langston Hughes, *Remember Me to Harlem: The Letters of Langston Hughes and Carl Van Vechten, 1925–1964*, ed. Emily Bernard (New York: Knopf, 2001), 121. Hereafter cited in the text as *Letters*.
10. Anthony Dawahare, "Langston Hughes's Radical Poetry and the 'End of Race,'" *MELUS* 23.2 (Fall 1998): 30.
11. Ibid., 21.
12. For a discussion of the tension between "the desire for acceptance in universal tradition and the desire to assert an African American vernacular," reflected in both Hughes's work and the editorial choices of Henry Louis Gates and Nellie McKay in the Norton Anthology of African American Literature, see Rebecca L. Walkowitz, "Shakespeare in Harlem: The Norton Anthology, 'Propaganda,' Langston Hughes," *Modern Language Quarterly* 60.4 (Dec. 1999): 495–519.
13. Dawahare, "Langston Hughes's Radical Poetry," 27.
14. Phillip M. Richards, in *Black Heart: The Moral Life of Recent African American Letters* (New York: Peter Lang, 2006), chapter 12, describes Hughes as a "bohemian black intellectual who nevertheless participates in a highly integrated artistic world and a similarly mixed Left" (184) and understands his "sense of ethnic identity as linked to a deep political commitment and consciousness" (183).
15. Elizabeth Davey, "Building a Black Audience in the 1930s: Langston Hughes, Poetry Readings, and the Golden Stair Press," in *Print Culture in a Diverse America*, eds. James P. Danky and Wayne A. Wiegand (Urbana: University of Illinois Press, 1998), 223.
16. Ibid., 124.
17. Quoted in Davey, 225.
18. For critical readings that stress Hughes's ability to negotiate modernist formal experiment and a grounding in folk culture, or Hughes "populist modernism," see Peter Brooker, "Modernism Deferred: Langston Hughes, Harlem and Jazz Montage," in *Locations of Literary Modernism: Region and Nation in British and American Modernist Poetry*, eds. Alex Davis and Lee M. Jenkins (Cambridge, England: Cambridge University Press, 2000), 231–47; Meta DuEwa Jones, "Listening to What the Ear Demands: Langston Hughes and His Critics," *Callaloo* 25.4 (Fall 2002): 1145–175; Steven A. Nardi, "'By the Pale Dull Pallor of an Old Gas Light': Technology and Vision in Langston Hughes's 'The Weary Blues,'" in *New Voices on the Harlem Renaissance: Essays on Race, Gender, and Literary Discourse*, eds. Australia Tarver and Paula C. Barnes (Madison, N.J.: Fairleigh Dickinson University Press, 2005), 253–68; Anita Patterson, "Jazz, Realism, and the Modernist Lyric: The Poetry of Langston Hughes," *Modern Language Quarterly* 61.4 (Dec. 2000): 651–82; Dalamu Ya Salaam, "Langston Hughes: A Supreme Poet," in *The Furious Flowering of African American Poetry*, ed. Joanne V. Gabbin (Charlottesville: University Press of Virginia, 1999), 17–24; and Steven C. Tracy, "Langston Hughes and Afro-American

Vernacular Music," in *A Historical Guide to Langston Hughes,* ed. Steven C. Tracy (Oxford, England: Oxford University Press, 2004), 85–118.

19. In April 1938, the International Workers Order printed 15, 000 copies of *A New Song* in pamphlet form, which sold for fifteen cents a copy.
20. Arnold Rampersad, *The Life of Langston Hughes: Volume I: 1902–1941: I, Too, Sing America* (2nd edition; New York: Oxford University Press, 2002), 290. See Elizabeth Schultz, "Natural and Unnatural Circumstances in Langston Hughes's *Not Without Laughter,*" *Callaloo* 25.4 (Fall 2002): 1177–187, for a nuanced reading of the "double-directed discourse" of the novel's representations of African American experience and nature as neither transcendental nor deterministic.
21. Rampersad, 290.
22. Langston Hughes, *The Ways of White Folks* (1934; New York: Knopf, 1979), 129. Hereafter cited in the text.
23. For a reading of the tragic mulatto theme in this text, see Arthur P. Davis, "The Tragic Mulatto Theme in Six Works of Langston Hughes," in *Interracialism: Black-White Intermarriage in American History, Literature, and Law,* ed. Werner Sollors (New York: Oxford University Press, 2000), 317–25.
24. For further discussion of resistance to stable identity formations, or "deferred subjectivity," see David Jarraway, *Going the Distance: Dissident Subjectivity in Modernist American Literature* (Baton Rouge: Louisiana State University Press, 2003), chapter 3. Building on Jarraway, Nicholas M. Evans, in "Wandering Aesthetic, Wandering Consciousness: Diasporic Impulses and 'Vagrant' Desires in Langston Hughes's Early Poetry," in *New Voices on the Harlem Renaissance: Essays on Race, Gender, and Literary Discourse,* eds. Australia Tarver and Paula C. Barnes (Madison, N.J.: Fairleigh Dickinson University Press, 2005), 151–93, writes of Hughes's "multiple, simultaneous affiliations" and his "ambivalent, 'wandering' aesthetic" as a way of both "actively defer[ring] racial, sexual and national selfhood" while "also indulg[ing] in strategic essentialism" (155). For further discussion of "this tension between the desire to fix and also the inclination to destabilize identity," see Juda Bennett, "Multiple Passings and the Double Death of Langston Hughes," *Biography* 23.4 (Fall 2000): 670–93.
25. Rampersad, 221.
26. Smith, 123.
27. Rampersad, 221.
28. For a different discussion of patronage in Hughes's career, see Michele Birnbaum, *Race, Work, and Desire in American Literature, 1860–1930* (Cambridge, England: Cambridge University Press, 2003), chapter 4. Birnbaum's focus is Hughes's working relationship with Carl Van Vechten and Amy Spingarn as both a function of the white patronage system and a subject for critical engagement in their art "rather than simply the condition for it" (100).
29. For further reading on other artists' relationships with Mrs. Mason, see Faith Berry, *Langston Hughes: Before and Beyond Harlem* (Westport, C.T.: Lawrence Hill, 1983), especially regarding Alain Locke and Zora Neale Hurston; and David Levering Lewis, *When Harlem Was in Vogue* (New

York: Knopf, 1981), regarding Locke, Hurston, Hughes, Aaron Douglass and Claude McKay.

30. Rampersad, 185.
31. Ibid., 184.
32. Quoted in Rampersad, 184.
33. Quoted in Rampersad, 185.
34. Langston Hughes, *The Big Sea: An Autobiography* (1940; New York: Hill and Wang, 1993), 327. Hereafter cited in the text as *Big Sea.*
35. Quoted in Rampersad, 200.
36. Quoted in Rampersad, 190.
37. For a psychoanalytic approach to Hughes's complex engagement with the ideology of primitivism as an antidote to repression in modern life and a rebellion against bourgeois values, see Rachel Comprone, *Poetry, Desire, and Fantasy in the Harlem Renaissance* (Lanham, M.D.: University Press of America, 2006), chapter 1.
38. H. Nigel Thomas, "Patronage and the Writing of Langston Hughes's *Not Without* Laughter: A Paradoxical Case," *CLA Journal* 42.1 (Sept. 1998): 63. Thomas's research was conducted at the Beinecke Library of Rare Books and Manuscripts, Yale University. All his references to correspondence between Hughes and Mrs. Mason and his information on the drafts, revisions and corrected galley proofs of Hughes's novel *Not without Laughter* (1930) are from the Langston Hughes Papers of the James Weldon Johnson Collection at Yale University.
39. Quoted in Rampersad, 172.
40. Quoted in Rampersad, 175.
41. Thomas, 69.
42. Quoted in Thomas. 54.
43. Quoted in Thomas, 53.
44. Quoted in Thomas, 53–54.
45. See Thomas, 58–59, where he produces evidence of this through the detailed work of piecing together correspondence, various manuscript versions of *Not without Laughter,* and historical and biographical details.
46. For additional commentary on "the strictly managed, though uneasy, modern subject," which Hughes produces in *The Big Sea* through efficiency and the subjection and disciplining of desire, see Lindon Barrett, "Subjectivity, Homoeroticism, and the Feminine in *The Big Sea,*" *Yale Journal of Criticism* 12.2 (1999): 383–397.
47. See David Chinitz, "Rejuvenation through Joy: Langston Hughes, Primitivism, and Jazz," *American Literary History* 9:1 (Spring 1997), 60–78, for a reading of this story as evidence of Hughes's struggle "to disengage ideas long fused in primitivist discourse" while "attempting to rescue elements of primitivism that he continued to find meaningful" (60).
48. For additional reading regarding Hughes's use of humor, particularly in his *Chicago Defender* columns, see John Lowe, "Newsprint Masks: The Comic Columns of Finley Peter Dunne, Alexander Posey, and Langston Hughes," in *Beyond the Binary: Reconstructing Cultural Identity in a Multicultural*

Context, ed. Timothy B. Powell (New Brunswick, N.J.: Rutgers University Press, 1999), 205–35.

49. Richard Wright, "Blueprint for Negro Writing," in *Within the Circle: An Anthology of African American Literary Criticism from the Harlem Renaissance to the Present,* ed. Angelyn Mitchell (Durham, N.C.: Duke University Press, 1994), 97, 100.
50. Ibid., 100.
51. Ibid., 105, 101
52. Ibid., 101.
53. Quoted in Abby Arthur Johnson and Ronald Maberry Johnson, *Propaganda and Aesthetics: The Literary Politics of Afro-American Magazines in the Twentieth Century* (Amherst: University of Massachusetts Press, 1979), 118.
54. The Common Council for American Unity (CCAU) was established in 1940, a reformation of the Foreign Language Information Services (FLIS), founded in 1918. Louis Adamic joined the FLIS Board of Trustees in 1934. In 1939, along with Read Lewis, director of FLIS since 1922, Adamic secured a grant from the Carnegie Corporation to form the CCAU and set up *Common Ground* as its publication. The CCAU was distinguished from other civic unity and race relations groups by its inclusivity, its recognition of cultural diversity and its opposition to a "melting pot" theory of American social relations. See William Beyer, "Langston Hughes and *Common Ground* in the 1940s," *American Studies in Scandinavia* 23.1 (1991): 29–31.
55. Johnson and Johnson, *Aesthetics and Propaganda,* 125.
56. Quoted in Johnson and Johnson, 128–29.
57. This title refers to two leading African-American periodicals: *Crisis,* vehicle for the NAACP, and *Opportunity,* vehicle for the National Urban League. Their prominence in *Common Ground*'s first issue underscores one of its primary editorial concerns to garner a readership across racial and ethnic lines from its very inception and to do so by promoting diversity as its strongest appeal for a common ground.
58. See Beyer, 30. Adamic had emigrated to the U. S. from Slovenia. His concern for the problems of immigrants led him to write a series of books in the late 1930s and early 1940s on U. S. cultural diversity. Its title, *A Nation of Nations,* is after Whitman's phrase, and its ideas are akin to Horace Kallen's "cultural pluralism."
59. *Common Ground* 1.1 (Autumn 1940): 65. Hereafter cited as *CG* in the notes.
60. Ibid., 66.
61. Beyer, 31.
62. "News Notes," *CG* 2.4 (Summer 1942), 105–06.
63. As revealed by a survey conducted by the magazine, *Common Ground*'s readership consisted predominantly of "old stock" and immigrant whites. In reaching a black audience in the 1940s, Hughes published in *Negro Digest, Opportunity, Negro Story, Crisis* and *Phylon*. In 1942, Hughes also began his popular weekly column in the *Chicago Defender.* See Beyer, 33.
64. Quoted in Beyer 32.
65. From *CG* 2.2 (Autumn 1941) and *CG* 2.3 (Spring 1942), respectively.

66. For a discussion of Hughes as the "first black male feminist writer of African American letters," see Joyce A. Joyce, "Hughes and Twentieth-Century Genderracial Issues," in *A Historical Guide to Langston Hughes,* ed. Steven C. Tracy (New York: Oxford University Press, 2004), 119–40.
67. From *CG* 3.2 (Winter 1943). Page numbers cited in the text. The other piece, "Democracy Was Not a Candidate," about a recent election in the South, is by Lillian Smith, co-editor of *South Today* and author of the novel *Strange Fruit.*
68. *CG* 4.2 (Winter 1944). Page numbers cited in the text. Beyer notes that this essay "provoked more comment from readers of *Common Ground* than any other piece it published," so much so that "Anderson herself took to the pages of *Common Ground* to chastise" the protestors for wanting to "ignor[e] the paradox of crusading for freedom overseas while denying it at home on the basis of color" (35).
69. *CG* 5.1 (Autumn 1944): 27–28.
70. *CG* 6.1 (Autumn 1945): 86–87.
71. *CG* 8.1 (Autumn 1947): 31–33. "Songs for Our Nation of Nation" includes four poems, "The Kids in School with Me," "We're All in the Telephone Book," "Friendly in a Friendly Way," and "Children's Song." *Street Scene* became a Broadway production with music by Kurt Weill, book by Elmer Rice, and lyrics by Langston Hughes. These excerpts, however, were not part of the final version of *Street Scene.* A note tells us that they were "show[n] visually rather than lyrically," "presenting by indirection [the] unity and friendship" of "the different nationalities in an American city."
72. *CG* 9.2 (Winter 1949): 21–27.
73. For more on the aesthetics of integration in magazines from 1940 to 1960, see Johnson and Johnson, 125–26.
74. Quoted in Johnson and Johnson, 148.
75. Ibid.
76. For further discussion of the role of pan-Africanism and diaspora in Hughes's writing, see Eddie Omotayo Asgill, "Langston Hughes and Africa," in *Of Dreams Deferred, Dead or Alive: African Perspectives on African-American Writers,* ed. Femi Ojo-Ade (Westport, C.T.: Greenwood, 1996), 43–52; Jeffery W. Westover, "Africa/America: Fragmentation and Diaspora in the Work of Langston Hughes," *Callaloo* 25.4 (Fall 2002): 1207–23; and Jeffery W. Westover, *The Colonial Moment: Discoveries and Settlements in Modern American Poetry* (DeKalb: Northern Illinois University Press, 2004), chapter 5. For further reading of Hughes as a diasporic modernist, who sees displacement as central to an understanding of cultural practice, see Isabel Soto, "Boundaries Transgressed: Modernism and Miscegenation in Langston Hughes's 'Red-Headed Baby,'" *Atlantic Studies* 3.1 (Apr. 2006): 97–110. And for the role of a black diasporic perspective in Hughes's ability to employ both "innovative modernist experiment and a powerful critique of modernism," see Seth Moglen, "Modernism in the Black Diaspora: Langston Hughes and the Broken Cubes of Picasso," *Callaloo* 25.4 (Fall 2002): 1189–205.
77. Alain Locke quoted in Johnson and Johnson, 151.

CHAPTER FOUR

1. Albert Murray, *Train Whistle Guitar* (1974; Boston: Northeastern University Press, 1989); Albert Murray, *The Spyglass Tree* (New York: Pantheon Books, 1991); Albert Murray, *The Seven League Boots: A Novel* (New York: Pantheon Books, 1995); Albert Murray, *The Magic Keys* (New York: Pantheon Books, 2005). Hereafter cited in the text as *TWG, ST, SLB,* and *MK,* respectively.
2. Albert Murray, *From the Briarpatch File: On Context, Procedure and American Identity* (New York: Pantheon Books, 2001), 155; Albert Murray, *The Hero and the Blues* (1973; New York: Vintage, 1995), 60. Hereafter cited in the text as *BP* and *HB,* respectively.
3. Albert Murray, *South to a Very Old Place* (1971; New York: Modern Library, 1995), 234. Hereafter cited in the text as *South.* See also Jacquelynne Jones Modeste, "The Blues and Jazz in Albert Murray's Fiction: A Study in the Tradition of Stylization," diss., College of William and Mary, 2005, for an analysis of the "the blues as a critical theory and as a literary model" in Murray's work. "Literature that uses the blues as an aesthetic guide," argues Modeste, "demonstrates variety of experience, human agency and an individual crafting of identity in relation to group identity" (vii).
4. Henry Louis Gates, Jr., *The Signifying Monkey: A Theory of Afro-American Literary Criticism* (New York: Oxford University Press, 1988), xxiv.
5. Ibid., xxvi-xxvii.
6. Claudia Tate, *Psychoanalysis and Black Novels: Desire and the Protocols of Race* (New York: Oxford University Press, 1998), 4.
7. Jessie Redmon Fauset, *The Chinaberry Tree: A Novel of American Life & Selected Writings* (1931; Boston: Northeastern University Press, 1995), 9, 17.
8. W. E. B. Du Bois, "The Talented Tenth," in *Writings* (New York: Library of America, 1996), 847.
9. Ibid.
10. For a bio-bibliographical source on Murray, see Roy Kay, "Albert Murray (1916-)," in *Contemporary African American Novelists: A Bio-Bibliographical Critical Sourcebook,* ed. Emmanuel S. Nelson (Westport, C.T.: Greenwood, 1999), 355–59. For a review of Murray's work and interview with the author, see Tony Scherman, "The Omni-American," *American Heritage* 47.5 (Sept. 1996): 68–77.
11. Cornel West and Henry Louis Gates, Jr., *The Future of the Race* (New York: Knopf, 1996), 78, 57–58.
12. Ibid., 78.
13. Du Bois, "The Revelation of Saint Orgne the Damned," in *Writings,* 1048.
14. I would also argue that "Of the Passing of the First Born" (upon which West briefly touches), "Of the Sorrow Songs," and especially "Of the Coming of John" (and to some extent "Of Alexander Crummell") grapple with the tragic and absurd elements of modern existence, underscoring the significance of the more subjective and expressive forms of these pieces than others in *Souls* and further suggesting Du Bois's acute sense of rhetorical strategy and textual congruity.

15. Du Bois, "Talented Tenth," 847.
16. Du Bois, "Careers Open to College-Bred Negroes," in *Writings,* 840.
17. For further discussion of Burke's notion of "equipment for living," see Roberta S. Maguire, "From the Blues to Jazz: Lewis Nordan's Fiction as 'Equipment for Living,'" *Southern Quarterly* 41.3 (Spring 2003): 7–19.
18. Du Bois, "Careers," 827.
19. Kelly Miller, *Radicals and Conservatives: And Other Essays on the Negro in America* (1908; New York: Schocken, 1968), 277–78.
20. Albert Murray, *The Blue Devils of Nada: A Contemporary American Approach to Aesthetic Statement* (New York: Pantheon Books, 1996), 220–21. Hereafter cited in the text as *BDN.*
21. West and Gates, *Future of the Race,* 64–65.
22. Ibid., 68–69.
23. Ibid., 78.
24. Ibid., 77.
25. Ibid., 77–78.
26. For further discussion of Scooter, the first person narrator of *Train Whistle Guitar,* as "the literary equivalent of an Ellington orchestration of a . . . down home saying. . . . *I live in a land menaced by dragons and even Grand Dragons, and that's why I have to be nimble . . . and must either find or forge my own magic sword and be heroic or nobody,*" see "Regional Particulars and Universal Statement in Southern Writing," a talk Murray gave at a symposium on "Southern distinctiveness" on 16 April 1983, at the University of Alabama in Tuscaloosa (reprinted in *Callaloo* 38 [Winter 1989], 3–6). For a different interpretation of *Train Whistle Guitar* as an attempt to deny history, see Wolfgang Karrer, "Nostalgia, Amnesia, and Grandmothers: The Uses of Memory in Albert Murray, Sabine Ulibarri, Paula Gunn Allen, and Alice Walker," in *Memory, Narrative, and Identity: New Essays in Ethnic American Literatures,* eds. Amritjit Singh, Joseph T. Skerrett, Jr. and Robert E. Hogan (Boston: Northeastern University Press, 1994), 128–44. Reading *Train Whistle Guitar* as "a multicultural memoir in fictionalized form" (130), Karrer argues that "Murray ritualizes not only the events he recalls but also the very process of recall itself" (132). It is in Scooter's substitution of "ritualized recall for going home" that "Gasoline Point is saved from time like a fly in amber"; in other words, "as the structure of the apprenticeship or initiation story emphasizes the change in the individual, it often tends to blot out the changes in the community within which the initiation takes place" (133). Ultimately, Karrer argues that the "outside world of change, the urban ghettos of the 1970s, are obliterated in *Train Whistle Guitar.* But at the same time they are omnipresent in the affirmation of the past idyll in Gasoline Point" (142).
27. Albert Murray, *Stomping the Blues* (1976; New York: Da Capo Press, 1987), 20. Hereafter cited in the text as *SB.*
28. "Academic Lead Sheet" is based upon an address Murray gave on January 20, 1978, at the Howard University Honors Convocation.
29. Ralph Ellison, *Invisible Man* (1952; New York: Vintage International, 1995), 8.

30. In an early essay, "Something Different, Something More," in *Anger and Beyond: The Negro Writer in the United States,* ed. Herbert Hill (New York: Harper & Row, 1966), 112–137 (reprinted in Albert Murray, *The Omni-Americans: New Perspectives on Black Experience and American Culture* [New York: Outerbridge & Dienstfrey, 1970]), Murray praises Ellison's *Invisible Man* for achieving what U. S. Negro music achieves and for "representing the very spirit of American life" (137). This discussion of the importance of "a U.S. Negro tradition" follows directly his discussion of "the philosophical relevance of the blues tradition for modern life" (134) and is, in Murray's view, the antidote to *Négritude* and the Black Arts movements, which "confuse tradition (or cultural inheritance) with racial inheritance (or racial mysticism)" (123), as well as the protest fiction which James Baldwin claims to deplore but then produces because he is, according to Murray, too focused on "the material *plight* of Harlem" and not focused enough on "a U. S. Negro tradition" (119).
31. For further reading of Murray on Duke Ellington, see Albert Murray, "Ellington Hits 100," *Nation* 268.7 (Feb. 22, 1999): 23–26, 28–29; and Albert Murray, "The Vernacular Imperative: Duke Ellington's Place in the National Pantheon," *Callaloo* 14.4 (Fall 1991): 771–75.
32. Albert Murray, *The Omni-Americans: New Perspectives on Black Experience and American Culture* (New York: Outerbridge & Dienstfrey, 1970), 44. Hereafter cited in the text as *OA*.
33. Quoted in Ross Posnock, *Color and Culture: Black Writers and the Making of the Modern Intellectual* (Cambridge, M.A.: Harvard University Press, 1998), 265.
34. Albert Murray, *Conversations with Albert Murray,* ed. Roberta S. Maguire (Jackson: University Press of Mississippi, 1997), 59. Hereafter cited in the text as *Conversations*.
35. Ralph Ellison, *Going to the Territory* (New York: Vintage International, 1986), 242, my italics.
36. Ibid., 56, my italics.
37. Ibid., 242.
38. Walter Pater, *Selected Writings of Walter* Pater, ed. Harold Bloom (1868; New York: Columbia University Press, 1974), 61.
39. Du Bois, *Writings,* 1060.
40. Ibid., 1061.
41. For further reading of Murray on Faulkner, see Albert Murray, "Me and Old Uncle Billy and the American Mythosphere," in *Faulkner at 100: Retrospect and Prospect,* eds. Donald M. Kartiganer and Ann J. Abadie (Jackson: University Press of Mississippi, 2000), 238–49.
42. See also Barbara A. Baker, "Turning Impossibility into Possibility: Teaching Ellison, Murray, and the Blues at Tuskegee," in *White Scholars/African American Texts,* ed. Lisa A. Long (New Brunswick, N.J.: Rutgers University Press, 2005), 68–77. As a white scholar teaching black texts at a black college, Baker focuses on her concern with "understanding our shared culture and the interconnectedness of blackness and whiteness" through Ellison's and Murray's texts (75). In addition, she argues that Murray

and Ellison sought "to formulate an aesthetic framework that fitted African American contribution into a global and modern perspective" (71), "forg[ing] a theory that shows that blackness is fundamental to the most uniquely American contributions to the art of the world" (72).

43. Ellison, *Going to the Territory,* 128.
44. Ibid., 139.
45. T. S. Eliot, "Tradition and the Individual Talent," in *The Norton Anthology of English Literature: Volume 2,* eds. M. H. Abrams and Stephen Greenblatt (7th edition; New York: W. W. Norton & Co., 2000), 2397.
46. Carolyn M. Jones, "Race and Intimacy: Albert Murray's *South to a Very Old Place,*" *Critical Survey* 12.1 (2000): 111–31. Through Murray's use of the blues idiom and Homi Bhabha's concept of "a structure of liminality," Jones discusses how "the 'I' in the blues is communal as well as individual." Her larger concerns have to do with the tension-filled intimacy between black and white Americans in "Murray's interrogation of the blue steel edge of our 'kinship and aginship,' the 'familiar difference and similar otherness.'"
47. Posnock, 88.
48. Du Bois, *Writings,* 1050.
49. W. E. B. Du Bois, *The Souls of Black Folk* (1903; New York: Penguin, 1989), 90.
50. Quoted in Posnock, 114.
51. For further discussion, see Warren Carson, "Albert Murray: Literary Reconstruction of the Vernacular Community," *African American Review* 27.2 (Summer 1993): 287–95, who argues that "the force that has driven Murray is the desire to reconstruct a black Southern community that challenges on all fronts the degrading and pathological portrayals that had become the stock of liberal white and reactionary black writers and critics" (295). For a discussion of how Murray's going against the grain of a one-dimensional portrait of black life centered on suffering and rage has led to "Murray's virtual anonymity as a mainstream black intellectual," see Sanford Pinsker, "Albert Murray: The Black Intellectuals' Maverick Patriarch," *Virginia Quarterly Review* 72.4 (Autumn 1996): 678–84.
52. See Constance Rourke, *American Humor: A Study of the National Character* (New York: Harcourt, Brace and Company, 1931) and *The Roots of American Culture, and Other Essays* (New York: Harcourt, Brace & World, 1942).
53. For a discussion of "the heroic tradition in African American culture" as represented in the work of fellow artists, collaborators and friends, Albert Murray, Romare Bearden and Ralph Ellison, see Horace A. Porter, *Jazz Country: Ralph Ellison in America* (Iowa City: University of Iowa Press, 2001), chapter 3, pp. 49–51 and 61–71. Murray himself represents this artistic fellowship in his most recent novel, *The Magic Keys,* when, in New York, Scooter visits art museums, galleries, and the studio of his friend Roland Beasley (Romare Bearden) and becomes reacquainted with an upper classman from his college days, Taft Edison (Ralph Ellison), who "read[s] parts of his manuscript to [Scooter]. Because he had decided that being two

book-loving down-home boys he and I had a lot to talk about, especially about the literary possibilities of the down-home idiom. Something beyond the same old overworked sociopolitical clichés about race and injustice that had long since become so usual that they were also the expected and tolerated and indulged" (56). For further reading on the collaborative work between Bearden and Murray, see the transcript of a conversation, edited by Myron Schwartzman, "A Bearden-Murray Interplay: One Last Time," *Callaloo* 36 (Summer1988): 410–15. Also of interest are the excerpts from a conversation among Alvin Ailey, James Baldwin, Romare Bearden and Albert Murray, edited by Nelson E. Breen, "To Hear Another Language," *Callaloo* 40 (Summer 1989): 431–52, particularly the first part about gaining perspective on the American experience while living and working in Paris in the 1950s.

54. Quoted in Posnock, 90.
55. Posnock, 107.
56. For further discussion of Murray's critical approach to racial discourse in the United States and his influence on fellow writer Walker Percy, see Roberta S. Maguire, "Walker Percy and Albert Murray: The Story of Two 'Part Anglo-Saxon Alabamians,'" *Southern Quarterly* 41.1 (Fall 2002): 10–28.
57. Posnock, 103–04.
58. Ibid., 40–41.
59. Ralph Ellison, *Shadow and Act* (1953; New York: Vintage International, 1995), 271.
60. Ibid., 215.
61. Ellison, Going to the Territory, 111.
62. Henry Louis Gates, Jr., "King of Cats," *The New Yorker* (Apr. 8, 1996): 76.
63. Ellison, *Going to the Territory,* 111.
64. Ibid., 69.
65. Ibid., 72–73.
66. Scooter's book project with Royal Highness closely resembles *Good Morning Blues: The Autobiography of Count Basie,* as told to Albert Murray (New York: Random House, 1985).
67. W. E. B. Du Bois, *Against Racism: Unpublished Essays, Papers, Addresses, 1887–1961,* ed. Herbert Aptheker (Amherst: University of Massachusetts Press, 1985), 242.
68. See Ross Posnock on William James's problem with Hegelianism's "virtual frenzy of 'reconciliation'" in *Color and Culture,* 121.
69. Tate, *Psychoanalysis and Black Novels,* 14, 4.
70. Ibid., 11–12.
71. Ibid., 11.
72. Du Bois, *Writings,* 822.

Selected Bibliography

PRIMARY SOURCES

Adorno, Theodor. "The Essay as Form." *The Adorno Reader.* Malden, M.A.: Blackwell, 2002. 3–23.

Arendt, Hannah. *Lectures on Kant's Political Philosophy.* Chicago: University of Chicago Press, 1982.

———. "Truth and Politics." *Between Past and Future: Eight Exercises in Political Thought.* New York: Penguin, 1993. 227–95.

Baldwin, James. *Notes of a Native Son.* 1955. Boston: Beacon Press, 1984.

Bourne, Randolph. *War and the Intellectuals: Essays by Randolph S. Bourne 1915–1919.* Ed. Carl Resek. New York: Harper Torchbooks, 1964.

Brooks, Van Wyck. "The Critics and Young America." *Criticism in America: Its Function and Status.* New York: Harcourt, Brace, 1924. 116–51.

Common Ground 1.1—9.5 (Autumn 1940—Autumn 1949).

Du Bois, W. E. B. *Against Racism: Unpublished Essays, Papers, Addresses, 1887–1961.* Ed. Herbert Aptheker. Amherst: University of Massachusetts Press, 1985.

———. *The Souls of Black Folk.* 1903. New York: Penguin, 1989.

———. *Writings.* New York: Library of America, 1996.

Eliot, T. S. "Tradition and the Individual Talent." *The Norton Anthology of English Literature: Volume 2.* Ed. M. H. Abrams and Stephen Greenblatt. 7th ed. New York: W. W. Norton & Co., 2000. 2395–2401.

Ellison, Ralph. *Going to the Territory.* New York: Vintage International, 1986.

———. *Invisible Man.* 1952. New York: Vintage International, 1995.

———. *Shadow and Act.* 1953. New York: Vintage International, 1995.

———. *Trading Twelves: The Selected Letters of Ralph Ellison and Albert Murray.* Ed. Albert Murray and John F. Callahan. New York: Modern Library, 2000.

Emerson, Ralph Waldo. *Selections from Ralph Waldo Emerson: An Organic Anthology.* Ed. Stephen E. Whicher. Boston: Houghton Mifflin, 1957.

Fauset, Jessie Redmon. *The Chinaberry Tree: A Novel of American Life & Selected Writings.* 1931. Boston: Northeastern University Press, 1995.

———. *Comedy: American Style.* 1933. New York: G. K. Hall, 1995.

———. *Plum Bun: A Novel Without a Moral.* 1929. Boston: Beacon Press, 1990.

———. *There Is Confusion.* 1924. Boston: Northeastern University Press, 1989.

Frank, Waldo. *Our America.* New York: Boni & Liveright, 1919.

Hughes, Langston. *The Big Sea: An Autobiography.* 1940. New York: Hill and Wang, 1993.

———. *The Collected Works of Langston Hughes: Volume 1: The Poems: 1921–1940.* Ed. Arnold Rampersad. Columbia, M.O.: University of Missouri Press, 2001.

———. *The Collected Works of Langston Hughes: Volume 9: Essays on Art, Race, Politics, and World Affairs.* Ed. Christopher C. De Santis. Columbia, M.O.: University of Missouri Press, 2002.

———. *Remember Me to Harlem: The Letters of Langston Hughes and Carl Van Vechten, 1925–1964.* Ed. Emily Bernard. New York: Knopf, 2001.

———. *The Ways of White Folks.* 1934. New York: Knopf, 1979.

Kallen, Horace M. *Culture and Democracy in the United States: Studies in the Group Psychology of the American People.* New York: Boni and Liveright, 1924.

Miller, Kelly. *Radicals and Conservatives: And Other Essays on the Negro in America.* 1908. New York: Schocken, 1968.

Murray, Albert. *The Blues Devils of Nada: A Contemporary American Approach to Aesthetic Statement.* New York: Pantheon, 1996.

———. *Conversations with Albert Murray.* Ed. Roberta S. Maguire. Jackson: University Press of Mississippi, 1997.

———. "Ellington Hits 100." *Nation* 268.7 (Feb. 22, 1999): 23–26, 28–29.

———. *From the BriarPatch File: On Context, Procedure, and American Identity.* New York: Pantheon, 2001.

———. *Good Morning Blues: The Autobiography of Count Basie,* as told to Albert Murray. New York: Random House, 1985.

———. *The Hero and the Blues.* 1973. New York: Vintage, 1995.

———. *The Magic Keys.* New York: Pantheon Books, 2005.

———. "Me and Old Uncle Billy and the American Mythosphere." *Faulkner at 100: Retrospect and Prospect.* Eds. Donald M. Kartiganer and Ann J. Abadie. Jackson: University Press of Mississippi, 2000. 238–49.

———. *The Omni-Americans: New Perspectives on Black Experience and American Culture.* New York: Outerbridge & Dienstfrey, 1970.

———. "Regional Particulars and Universal Statement in Southern Writing." *Callaloo* 38 (Winter 1989): 3–6.

———. *The Seven League Boots: A Novel.* New York: Pantheon, 1995.

———. "Something Different, Something More." *Anger and Beyond: The Negro Writer in the United States.* Ed. Herbert Hill. New York: Harper & Row, 1966. 112–137.

———. *South to a Very Old Place.* 1971. New York: Modern Library, 1995.

———. *The Spyglass Tree.* New York: Pantheon, 1991.

———. *Stomping the Blues.* 1976. New York: Da Capo Press, 1987.

———. *Train Whistle Guitar.* 1974. Boston: Northeastern University Press, 1989.

———. "The Vernacular Imperative: Duke Ellington's Place in the National Pantheon." *Callaloo* 14.4 (Fall 1991): 771–75.

Pater, Walter. "Conclusion to *The Renaissance.*" 1868. *Selected Writings of Walter Pater.* Ed. Harold Bloom. New York: Columbia University Press, 1974. 58–62.

Rourke, Constance. *American Humor: A Study of the National Character.* New York: Harcourt, Brace and Company, 1931.

———. *The Roots of American Culture, and Other Essays.* New York: Harcourt, Brace & World, 1942.

Spingarn, J. E. "Criticism in the United States." *Criticism in America: Its Function and Status.* New York: Harcourt, Brace, 1924. 287–308.

Stein, Gertrude. *Three Lives.* 1909. New York: Penguin, 1990.

Toomer, Jean. *Cane: A Norton Critical Edition.* 1923. Ed. Darwin T. Turner. New York: Norton, 1988.

———. *A Jean Toomer Reader: Selected Unpublished Writings.* Ed. Frederick L. Rusch. New York: Oxford University Press, 1993.

———. *Jean Toomer: Selected Essays and Literary Criticism.* Ed. Robert B. Jones. Knoxville, T.N.: University of Tennessee Press, 1996.

———. *The Letters of Jean Toomer, 1919–1924.* Ed. Mark Whalan. Knoxville, T.N.: University of Tennessee Press, 2006.

———. Jean Toomer Papers. James Weldon Johnson Collection. Beinecke Rare Book and Manuscript Library, Yale University.

———. *The Wayward and the Seeking: A Collection of Writings by Jean Toomer.* Ed. Darwin T. Turner. Washington, D.C.: Howard University Press, 1980.

Wright, Richard. "Blueprint for Negro Writing." *Within the Circle: An Anthology of African American Literary Criticism from the Harlem Renaissance to the Present.* Ed. Angelyn Mitchell. Durham, N.C.: Duke University Press, 1994. 97–106.

SECONDARY SOURCES

Abrahams, Edward. *The Lyrical Left: Randolph Bourne, Alfred Stieglitz and the Origins of Cultural Radicalism in America.* Charlottesville: University Press of Virginia, 1986.

Allen, Carol. *Black Women Intellectuals: Strategies of Nation, Family, and Neighborhood in the Works of Pauline Hopkins, Jessie Fauset, and Marita Bonner.* New York: Garland, 1998.

Anderson, Amanda. "Cosmopolitanism, Universalism, and the Divided Legacies of Modernity." *Cosmopolitics: Thinking and Feeling beyond the Nation.* Eds. Pheng Cheah and Bruce Robbins. Minneapolis: University of Minnesota Press, 1998. 265–89.

———. *The Powers of Distance: Cosmopolitanism and the Cultivation of Detachment.* Princeton, N.J.: Princeton University Press, 2001.

———. *The Way We Argue Now: A Study in the Cultures of Theory.* Princeton, N.J.: Princeton University Press, 2006.

Appiah, Kwame Anthony. "The Case for Contamination." *The New York Times Magazine.* January 1, 2006. 30–37, 52. http://www.nytimes.com/2006/01/01/magazine/01cosmopolitan.html.

———. *Cosmopolitanism: Ethics in a World of Strangers.* New York: W. W. Norton & Co., 2006.

———. *The Ethics of Identity.* Princeton, N.J.: Princeton University Press, 2005.

Archibugi, Daniele, ed. *Debating Cosmopolitics.* New York: Verso, 2003.

Asgill, Eddie Omotayo. “Langston Hughes and Africa.” *Of Dreams Deferred, Dead or Alive: African Perspectives on African-American Writers.* Ed. Femi Ojo-Ade. Westport, C.T.: Greenwood, 1996. 43–52.

Austin, Rhonda. “Jessie Redmon Fauset (1882–1961).” *American Women Writers, 1900–1945: A Bio-Bibliographical Critical Sourcebook.* Ed. Laurie Champion. Westport, C.N.: Greenwood, 2000. 101–06.

Baker, Barbara A. “Turning Impossibility into Possibility: Teaching Ellison, Murray, and the Blues at Tuskegee.” *White Scholars/African American Texts.* Ed. Lisa A. Long. New Brunswick, N.J.: Rutgers University Press, 2005. 68–77.

Baker, Houston A., Jr. *Modernism and the Harlem Renaissance.* Chicago: University of Chicago Press, 1987.

Baldanzi, Jessica Hays. “Stillborns, Orphans, and Self-Proclaimed Virgins: Packaging and Policing the Rural Women of *Cane.*” *Genders* 42 (2005). 39 para. Online journal. http://www.genders.org/g42/g42_baldanzi.html

Baldwin, Kate A. “The Russian Connection: Interracialism as Queer Alliance in Langston Hughes's *The Ways of White Folks.*” *Modern Fiction Studies* 48.4 (Winter 2002): 795–824.

Banks, Kimberly. “‘Like a Violin for the Wind to Play’: Lyrical Approaches to Lynching by Hughes, Du Bois, and Toomer.” *African American Review* 38:3 (Fall 2004): 451–65.

Barnes, Paula C. “Dorothy West: Harlem Renaissance Writer?” *New Voices on the Harlem Renaissance: Essays on Race, Gender, and Literary Discourse.* Eds. Australia Tarver and Paula C. Barnes. Madison, N.J.: Fairleigh Dickinson University Press, 2005. 99–124.

Barrett, Lindon. “Subjectivity, Homoeroticism, and the Feminine in *The Big Sea.*” *Yale Journal of Criticism* 12.2 (1999): 383–397.

Batker, Carol J. *Reforming Fictions: Native, African, and Jewish American Women's Literature and Journalism in the Progressive Era.* New York: Columbia University Press, 2000.

Battenfeld, Mary. “‘Been Shapin Words T Fit M Soul’: *Cane,* Language, and Social Change.” *Callaloo* 25.4 (Fall 2002): 1238–49.

Baucom, Ian. *Specters of the Atlantic: Finance Capital, Slavery, and the Philosophy of History.* Durham, N.C.: Duke University Press, 2005.

Beck, Ulrich. “The Cosmopolitan Society and Its Enemies.” *Theory, Culture & Society* 19.1–2 (Feb.-Apr. 2002): 17–44.

Bell, Bernard. *The Afro-American Novel and Its Traditions.* Amherst: University of Massachusetts Press, 1987.

Bender, Thomas. “The Boundaries and Constituencies of History.” *American Literary History* 18.2 (Summer 2006): 267–82.

———. *New York Intellect: A History of Intellectual Life in New York City, from 1750 to the Beginnings of Our Own Time.* New York: Knopf, 1987.

Benhabib, Seyla. *Another Cosmopolitanism,* with commentaries by Jeremy Waldron, Bonnie Honig, and Will Kymlicka. Ed. Robert Post. New York: Oxford University Press, 2006.

———. *Situating the Self: Gender, Community and Postmodernism in Contemporary Ethics,* New York: Routledge, 1992.

Bennett, Juda. "Multiple Passings and the Double Death of Langston Hughes." *Biography* 23.4 (Fall 2000): 670–93.

Berman, Jessica. *Modernist Fiction, Cosmopolitanism, and the Politics of Community.* Cambridge, England: Cambridge University Press, 2001.

Berry, Faith. *Langston Hughes: Before and Beyond Harlem.* Westport, C.N.: Lawrence Hill, 1983.

Beyer, William. "Langston Hughes and *Common Ground* in the 1940s." *American Studies in Scandinavia* 23.1 (1991): 29–42.

Birnbaum, Michele. *Race, Work, and Desire in American Literature, 1860–1930.* Cambridge, England: Cambridge University Press, 2003.

Bone, Robert. *The Negro Novel in America.* Revised edition. New Haven: Yale University Press, 1965.

Boutry, Katherine. "Black and Blue: The Female Body of Blues Writing in Jean Toomer, Toni Morrison, and Gayl Jones." *Black Orpheus: Music in African American Fiction from the Harlem Renaissance to Toni Morrison.* Ed. Saadi A. Simawe. New York: Garland, 2000. 91–118.

Bowen, Barbara E. "Untroubled Voice: Call and Response in *Cane.*" *Black American Literature Forum*16:1 (Spring 1982): 12–18.

Boyne, Roy. "Cosmopolis and Risk: A Conversation with Ulrich Beck." *Theory, Culture & Society* 18.4 (Aug. 2001): 47–63.

Breckenridge, Carol A., Sheldon Pollack, Homi K. Bhabha, and Dipesh Chakrabarty, eds. "Cosmopolitanisms." *Public Culture* 12.3 (Fall 2000): 578–786 (Special issue).

Breen, Nelson E., ed. "To Hear Another Language." *Callaloo* 40 (Summer 1989): 431–52.

Brennan, Timothy. *At Home in the World: Cosmopolitanism Now.* Cambridge, M.A.: Harvard University Press, 1997.

———. "Cosmo-Theory." *South Atlantic Quarterly* 100.3 (Summer 2001): 659–91.

———. *Wars of Position: The Cultural Politics of Left and Right.* New York: Columbia University Press, 2006.

Briggs, Charles L. "Genealogies of Race and Culture and the Failure of Vernacular Cosmopolitanisms: Rereading Franz Boas and W. E. B. Du Bois." *Public Culture* 17.1 (Winter 2005): 75–100.

Brock, Gillian and Harry Brighouse, eds. *The Political Philosophy of Cosmopolitanism.* Cambridge, England: Cambridge University Press, 2005.

Bronner, Stephen Eric. *Reclaiming the Enlightenment: Toward a Politics of Radical Engagement.* New York: Columbia University Press, 2004.

Brooker, Peter. "Modernism Deferred: Langston Hughes, Harlem and Jazz Montage." *Locations of Literary Modernism: Region and Nation in British and American Modernist Poetry.* Eds. Alex Davis and Lee M. Jenkins. Cambridge, England: Cambridge University Press, 2000. 231–47.

Brown, Julia Prewitt. *Cosmopolitan Criticism: Oscar Wilde's Philosophy of Art.* Charlottesville, V.A.: University Press of Virginia, 1997.

Butler, Judith. *Bodies That Matter: On the Discursive Limits of "Sex."* New York: Routledge, 1993.

Byrd, Rudolph P. "Jean Toomer and the Afro-American Literary Tradition." *Callaloo* 8.2 (Spring-Summer 1985): 310–19.

———. *Jean Toomer's Years with Gurdjieff: A Portrait of an Artist, 1923–1936.* Athens: University of Georgia Press, 1990.

Calhoun, Craig. "The Class Consciousness of Frequent Travelers: Toward a Critique of Actually Existing Cosmopolitanism." *South Atlantic Quarterly* 101.4 (Fall 2002): 869–97.

Calloway, Licia Morrow. *Black Family (Dys)Function in Novels by Jessie Fauset, Nella Larsen, & Fannie Hurst.* New York: Peter Lang, 2003.

Carby, Hazel. *Reconstructing Womanhood: The Emergence of the Afro-American Woman Novelist.* New York: Oxford University Press, 1995.

Carson, Warren. "Albert Murray: Literary Reconstruction of the Vernacular Community." *African American Review* 27.2 (Summer 1993): 287–95.

Chachere, Karen A. "Visually White, Legally Black: Miscegenation, the Mulatto, and Passing in American Literature and Culture, 1865–1933." Ph.D. diss., Illinois State University, 2004.

Charters, Ann. Introduction. *Three Lives.* By Gertrude Stein. New York: Penguin, 1990. vii-xx.

Chay, Deborah Grace. "Black Feminist Criticism and the Politics of Reading Jessie Fauset." Ph.D. diss., Duke University, 1993.

Cheah, Pheng. *Inhuman Conditions: On Cosmopolitanism and Human Rights.* Cambridge, M.A.: Harvard University Press, 2006.

———. *Spectral Nationality: Passages of Freedom from Kant to Postcolonial Literatures of Liberation.* New York: Columbia University Press, 2003.

Chinitz, David. "Literacy and Authenticity: The Blues Poems of Langston Hughes." *Callaloo* 19.1 (1996): 177–192.

———. "Rejuvenation through Joy: Langston Hughes, Primitivism, and Jazz." *American Literary History* 9:1 (Spring 1997), 60–78.

Christian, Barbara. "The Race for Theory." *Within the Circle: An Anthology of African American Literary Criticism from the Harlem Renaissance to the Present.* Ed. Angelyn Mitchell. Durham, N.C.: Duke University Press, 1994. 348–59.

Clayton, Bruce. *Forgotten Prophet: The Life of Randolph Bourne.* Baton Rouge: Louisiana State University Press, 1984.

Comprone, Raphael. *Poetry, Desire, and Fantasy in the Harlem Renaissance.* Lanham, M.D.: University Press of America, 2006.

Condé, Mary. "Passing in the Fiction of Jessie Redmon Fauset and Nella Larsen." *Yearbook of English Studies* 24 (1994): 94–104.

Dace, Tish. *Langston Hughes: The Contemporary Reviews.* Cambridge, England.: Cambridge University Press, 1997.

Davey, Elizabeth. "Building a Black Audience in the 1930s: Langston Hughes, Poetry Readings, and the Golden Stair Press." *Print Culture in a Diverse America.* Eds. James P. Danky and Wayne A. Wiegand. Urbana: University of Illinois Press, 1998. 223–43.

Davis, Arthur P. "The Tragic Mulatto Theme in Six Works of Langston Hughes." *Interracialism: Black-White Intermarriage in American History, Literature, and Law.* Ed. Werner Sollors. New York: Oxford University Press, 2000. 317–25.

Dawahare, Anthony. "Langston Hughes's Radical Poetry and the 'End of Race.'" *MELUS* 23.3 (Fall 1998): 21–41.

Dharwadker, Vinay, ed. *Cosmopolitan Geographies: New Locations in Literature and Culture.* New York: Routledge, 2001.

duCille, Ann. "Blues Notes on Black Sexuality: Sex and the Texts of Jessie Fauset and Nella Larsen." *Journal of the History of Sexuality* 3.3 (Jan. 1993): 418–44.

———. *The Coupling Convention: Sex, Text, and Tradition in Black Women's Fiction.* New York: Oxford University Press, 1993.

Duck, Leigh Anne. *The Nation's Region: Southern Modernism, Segregation, and U.S. Nationalism.* Athens: University of Georgia Press, 2006.

Edmunds, Susan. "The Race Question and the 'Question of the Home': Revisiting the Lynching Plot in Jean Toomer's *Cane.*" *American Literature* 75.1 (Mar. 2003): 141–68.

Egar, Emmanuel Adame. *The Poetics of Rage: Wole Soyinka, Jean Toomer, and Claude McKay.* Lanham, M.D.: University Press of America, 2005.

Evans, Nicholas M. "Wandering Aesthetic, Wandering Consciousness: Diasporic Impulses and 'Vagrant' Desires in Langston Hughes's Early Poetry." *New Voices on the Harlem Renaissance: Essays on Race, Gender, and Literary Discourse.* Eds. Australia Tarver and Paula C. Barnes. Madison, N.J.: Fairleigh Dickinson University Press, 2005. 151–93.

Fabre, Geneviève and Michel Feith, eds. *Jean Toomer and the Harlem Renaissance.* New Brunswick, N. J.: Rutgers University Press, 2001.

———. "Tight-Lipped 'Oracle': Around and beyond *Cane.*" Fabre and Feith 3–14.

Fahy, Thomas. "The Enslaving Power of Folksong in Jean Toomer's *Cane.*" *Literature and Music.* Ed. Michael J. Meyer. Amsterdam: Rodopi, 2002. 47–63.

Featherstone, Mike, ed. "Cosmopolis." *Theory, Culture & Society* 19.1–2 (Feb.-Apr. 2002): 1–253 (Special issue).

Feher, Michel. "The Schisms of '67: On Certain Restructurings of the American Left, from the Civil Rights Movement to the Multiculturalist Constellation." *Blacks and Jews: Alliances and Arguments.* Ed. Paul Berman. New York: Delacorte, 1994. 263–85.

Finseth, Ian. "Evolution, Cosmopolitanism, and Emerson's Antislavery Politics." *American Literature* 77.4 (Dec. 2005): 728–60.

Fojas, Camilla. *Cosmopolitanism in the Americas.* West Lafayette, I.N.: Purdue University Press, 2005.

Foley, Barbara. "'In the Land of Cotton': Economics and Violence in Jean Toomer's *Cane.*" *African American Review* 32 (1998): 188–90.

———. "Jean Toomer's Sparta." *American Literature* 67 (December 1995): 747–75.

———. "Jean Toomer's Washington and the Politics of Class: From 'Blue Veins' to Seventh-Street Rebels." *Modern Fiction Studies* 42 (Summer 1996): 289–321.

Fontenot, Chester J., Jr. "Du Bois's 'Of the Coming of John,' Toomer's 'Kabnis,' and the Dilemma of Self-Representation." *The Souls of Black Folk One Hundred Years Later.* Ed. Dolan Hubbard. Columbia, M.O.: University of Missouri Press, 2003. 130–60.

Ford, Karen Jackson. *Split-Gut Song: Jean Toomer and the Poetics of Modernity.* Tuscaloosa, A.L.: University of Alabama Press, 2005.

Foreman, P. Gabrielle. "Looking Back from Zora, or Talking Out Both Sides My Mouth for Those Who Have Two Ears." *Black American Literature Forum* 24 (1990): 649–66.

Fritzsche, Peter. "Global History and Bounded Subjects: A Response to Thomas Bender." *American Literary History* 18:2 (Summer 2006): 283–87.

Gates, Henry Louis, Jr. "King of Cats." *New Yorker* (Apr. 8, 1996): 70–76, 78–81.

———. *The Signifying Monkey: A Theory of Afro-American Literary Criticism.* New York: Oxford University Press, 1988.

Gibson, Donald B. Introduction. *The Souls of Black Folk.* By W. E. B. Du Bois. New York: Penguin, 1989. vii-xxxv.

Gikandi, Simon. "Race and Cosmopolitanism." *American Literary History* 14.3 (Fall 2002): 593–615.

Gilroy, Paul. *Against Race: Imagining Political Culture beyond the Color Line.* Cambridge, M.A.: Belknap Press of Harvard University Press, 2000.

———. *The Black Atlantic: Modernity and Double Consciousness.* Cambridge, M.A.: Harvard University Press, 1993.

———. *Postcolonial Melancholia.* New York: Columbia University Press, 2005.

Gossett, Thomas F. *Race: The History of an Idea in America.* Dallas: Southern Methodist University Press, 1963.

Grandjeat, Charles-Yves. "The Poetics of Passing in Jean Toomer's *Cane.*" Fabre and Feith 58–66.

Grant, Nathan. *Masculinist Impulses: Toomer, Hurston, Black Writing, and Modernity.* Columbia, M.O.: University of Missouri Press, 2004.

Griffin, Erica L. "The 'Invisible Woman' Abroad: Jessie Fauset's New Horizon." *Recovered Writers/Recovered Texts.* Ed. Dolan Hubbard. Knoxville: University of Tennessee Press, 1997. 75–89.

Guterl, Mattew Prat. *The Color of Race in America, 1900–1940.* Cambridge, M.A.: Harvard University Press, 2001.

Harmon, Charles. "*Cane,* Race, and 'Neither/Norism.'" *Southern Literary Journal* 32:2 (2000): 90–101.

Harper, Phillip Brian. *Framing the Margins: The Social Logic of Postmodern Culture.* New York: Oxford University Press, 1994.

Hawkins, Stephanie L. "Building the 'Blue' Race: Miscegenation, Mysticism, and the Language of Cognitive Evolution in Jean Toomer's 'The Blue Meridian.'" *Texas Studies in Literature and Language* 46.2 (Summer 2004): 149–80.

Hedrick, Tace. "Blood-Lines That Waver South: Hybridity, the 'South,' and American Bodies." *Southern Quarterly* 42.1 (Fall 2003): 39–52.

Hollinger, David A. *Cosmopolitanism and Solidarity: Studies in Ethnoracial, Religious, and Professional Affiliation in the United States.* Madison, W.I.: University of Wisconsin Press, 2006.

———. *In the American Province: Studies in the History and Historiography of Ideas.* Bloomington: Indiana University Press, 1985.

———. *Postethnic America: Beyond Multiculturalism.* New York: BasicBooks, 1995.

Hubler, Angela Elizabeth. "'From Home to Market': Private Emotion and Political Engagement in the Work of Emma Goldman, Jessie Fauset and Josephine Herbst." Ph.D.diss., Duke University, 1993.

Huggins, Nathan Irvin. *Harlem Renaissance.* New York: Oxford University Press, 1971.

Hutchinson, George. *The Harlem Renaissance in Black and White.* Cambridge, M.A.: Belknap Press of Harvard University Press, 1995.

———. "Identity in Motion: Placing *Cane*." Fabre and Feith 40–54.

———. "Jean Toomer and American Racial Discourse." *Texas Studies in American Literature and Language* 35.2 (Summer 1993): 226–50.

———. "Jean Toomer and the 'New Negroes' of Washington." *American Literature* 63.4 (Dec. 1991): 683–92.

———. "The Whitman Legacy and the Harlem Renaissance." *Walt Whitman: The Centennial Essays*. Ed. Ed Folsom. Iowa City: University of Iowa Press, 1994. 201–16.

Jarraway, David. *Going the Distance: Dissident Subjectivity in Modernist American Literature*. Baton Rouge: Louisiana State University Press, 2003.

Johnson, Abby Arthur. "Literary Midwife: Jessie Redmon Fauset and the Harlem Renaissance." *Phylon* 39 (1978): 143–53.

Johnson, Abby Arthur and Ronald Maberry Johnson. *Propaganda and Aesthetics: The Literary Politics of Afro-American Magazines in the Twentieth Century*. Amherst: University of Massachusetts Press, 1979.

Jones, Carolyn M. "Race and Intimacy: Albert Murray's *South to a Very Old Place*." *Critical Survey* 12.1 (2000): 111–31.

Jones, Meta DuEwa. "Listening to What the Ear Demands: Langston Hughes and His Critics." *Callaloo* 25.4 (Fall 2002): 1145–175.

Jones, Robert B. *Jean Toomer and the Prison-House of Thought: A Phenomenology of the Spirit*. Amherst: University of Massachusetts Press, 1993.

Jones, Sharon L. *Rereading the Harlem Renaissance: Race, Class, and Gender in the Fiction of Jessie Fauset, Zora Neale Hurston, and Dorothy West*. Westport, C.T.: Greenwood, 2002.

Joyce, Joyce A. "Hughes and Twentieth-Century Genderracial Issues." *A Historical Guide to Langston Hughes*. Ed. Steven C. Tracy. New York: Oxford University Press, 2004. 119–40.

Karrer, Wolfgang. "Nostalgia, Amnesia, and Grandmothers: The Uses of Memory in Albert Murray, Sabine Ulibarri, Paula Gunn Allen, and Alice Walker." *Memory, Narrative, and Identity: New Essays in Ethnic American Literatures*. Eds. Amritjit Singh, Joseph T. Skerrett, Jr., and Robert E. Hogan. Boston: Northeastern University Press, 1994. 128–44.

Kaup, Monika. "'Our America' That Is Not One: Transnational Black Atlantic Disclosures in Nicolás Guillén and Langston Hughes." *Discourse* 22.3 (Fall 2000): 87–113.

Kay, Roy. "Albert Murray (1916-)." *Contemporary African American Novelists: A Bio-Bibliographical Critical Sourcebook*. Ed. Emmanuel S. Nelson. Westport, C.T.: Greenwood, 1999. 355–59.

Kerman, Cynthia Earl, and Richard Eldridge. *The Lives of Jean Toomer: A Hunger for Wholeness*. Baton Rouge: Louisiana State University Press, 1987.

Kodat, Catherine Gunther. "To 'Flash White Light from Ebony': The Problem of Modernism in Jean Toomer's *Cane*." *Twentieth Century Literature* 46.1 (Spring 2000): 1–19.

Kuenz, Jane. "The Face of America: Performing Race and Nation in Jessie Fauset's *There Is Confusion*." *The Yale Journal of Criticism* 12.1 (1999) 89–111.

Kutzinski, Vera M. "Unseasonal Flowers: Nature and History in Placido and Jean Toomer." *Yale Journal of Criticism* 3.2 (1990): 153–79.

Lamothe, Daphne. "*Cane:* Jean Toomer's Gothic Black Modernism." *The Gothic Other: Racial and Social Constructions in the Literary Imagination.* Eds. Ruth Bienstock Anolik and Douglas L. Howard. Jefferson, N.C.: McFarland, 2004. 54–71.

Larson, Charles R. *Jean Toomer and Nella Larsen: Invisible Darkness.* Iowa City: University of Iowa Press, 1993.

Levison, Susan. "Performance and the 'Strange Place' of Jessie Redmon Fauset's *There Is Confusion.*" *Modern Fiction Studies* 46.4 (Winter 2000) 825–48.

Lewis, David Levering. *When Harlem Was in Vogue.* New York: Knopf, 1981.

Lindberg, Kathryne V., "Raising *Cane* on the Theoretical Plane: Jean Toomer's Racial Personae." *Cultural Difference and the Literary Text: Pluralism and the Limits of Authenticity in North American Literatures.* Eds. Winfried Siemerling and Katrin Schewenk. Iowa City: University of Iowa Press, 1996. 49–74.

Lott, Eric. *The Disappearing Liberal Intellectual.* New York: Basic Books, 2006.

Lowe, John. "Newsprint Masks: The Comic Columns of Finley Peter Dunne, Alexander Posey, and Langston Hughes." *Beyond the Binary: Reconstructing Cultural Identity in a Multicultural Context.* Ed. Timothy B. Powell. New Brunswick, N.J.: Rutgers University Press, 1999. 205–35.

Lowney, John. *History, Memory, and the Literary Left: Modern American Poetry, 1935–1968.* Iowa City: University of Iowa Press, 2006.

Lupton, Mary Jane. "Clothes and Closure in Three Novels by Black Women." *Black American Literature Forum* 20 (1986): 409–21.

Lutz, Tom. "The Cosmopolitan Midland." *American Periodicals* 15.1 (2005): 74–85.

———. *Cosmopolitan Vistas: American Regionalism and Literary Value.* Ithaca, NY: Cornell University Press, 2004.

Maguire, Roberta S. "From the Blues to Jazz: Lewis Nordan's Fiction as 'Equipment for Living.'" *Southern Quarterly* 41.3 (Spring 2003): 7–19.

———. "Walker Percy and Albert Murray: The Story of Two 'Part Anglo-Saxon Alabamians.'" *Southern Quarterly* 41.1 (Fall 2002): 10–28.

McCaskill, Barbara. "The Folklore of the Coasts in Black Women's Fiction of the Harlem Renaissance." *College Language Association Journal* 39.3 (Mar. 1996): 273–301.

McCoy, Beth Ann. "'Do I Look Like This or This?': Race, Gender, Class, and Sexuality in the Novels of Jessie Fauset, Carl van Vechten, Nella Larsen, and F. Scott Fitzgerald." Ph.D. diss., University of Delaware, 1995.

McDowell, Deborah E. "The Neglected Dimension of Jessie Redmon Fauset." *Conjuring Black Women, Fiction, and Literary Tradition.* Eds. Marjorie Pryse and Hortense J. Spillers. Bloomington: Indiana University Press, 1985. 86–104.

McKay, Nellie Y. *Jean Toomer, Artist: A Study of His Literary Life and Work, 1894–1936.* Chapel Hill: University of North Carolina Press, 1984.

McLendon, Jacquelyn Y. *The Politics of Color in the Fiction of Jessie Fauset and Nella Larsen.* Charlottesville: University Press of Virginia, 1995.

McManus, Mary Hairston. "African-American Modernism in the Novels of Jessie Fauset and Nella Larsen." Ph.D. diss., University of Maryland, College Park, 1993.

Michaels, Walter Benn. *Our America: Nativism, Modernism, and Pluralism.* Durham: Duke University Press, 1995.

Miller, Nina. "Femininity, Publicity, and the Class Division of Cultural Labor: Jessie Redmon Fauset's *There Is Confusion*." *African American Review* 30 (1996): 205–20.

Miller, R. Baxter. *The Art and Imagination of Langston Hughes*. Lexington, K.Y.: University Press of Kentucky, 1989.

———. "'For a Moment I Wondered': Theory and Symbolic Form in the Autobiographies of Langston Hughes." *The Langston Hughes Review* 3.2 (1984): 1–6.

Mitchell, Angelyn, ed. *Within the Circle: An Anthology of African American Literary Criticism from the Harlem Renaissance to the Present*. Durham, NC: Duke University Press, 1994.

Modeste, Jacquelynne Jones. "The Blues and Jazz in Albert Murray's Fiction: A Study in the Tradition of Stylization." Ph.D. diss., College of William and Mary, 2005.

Moglen, Seth. "Modernism in the Black Diaspora: Langston Hughes and the Broken Cubes of Picasso." *Callaloo* 25.4 (Fall 2002): 1189–205.

Moore, David Chioni. "Colored Dispatches from the Uzbek Border: Langston Hughes' Relevance, 1933–2002." *Callaloo* 25.4 (Fall 2002): 1115–135.

———. "Local Color, Global 'Color': Langston Hughes, the Black Atlantic, and Soviet Central Asia, 1932." *Research in African Literatures* 27.4 (Winter 1996): 49–70.

Moore, Sharon Lynn. "'I Can Never Be That Wretched, Diffident, Submissive Girl Again': (Un)Veiling the Black, Feminist, Modernist Aesthetic of Jessie Redmon Fauset." Ph.D. diss., University of Georgia, 1999.

Nardi, Steven A. "'By the Pale Dull Pallor of an Old Gas Light': Technology and Vision in Langston Hughes's 'The Weary Blues.'" *New Voices on the Harlem Renaissance: Essays on Race, Gender, and Literary Discourse*. Eds. Australia Tarver and Paula C. Barnes. Madison, N.J.: Fairleigh Dickinson University Press, 2005. 253–68.

Nelson, Casey Blake. *Beloved Community: The Cultural Criticism of Randolph Bourne, Van Wyck Brooks, Waldo Frank, & Lewis Mumford*. Chapel Hill, N.C.: University of North Carolina Press, 1990.

Nelson, Emmanuel S. "Jessie Redmon Fauset (1882–1961)." *African American Authors, 1745–1945: A Bio-Bibliographical Critical Sourcebook*. Ed. Emmanuel S. Nelson. Westport, C.T.: Greenwood, 2000. 155–60.

Nero, Charles I. "Re/Membering Langston: Homophobic Textuality and Arnold Rampersad's *Life of Langston Hughes*." *Queer Representations: Reading Lives, Reading Cultures*. Ed. Martin Duberman. New York: New York University Press, 1997. 188–96.

Nicholls, David G. "Jean Toomer's *Cane*, Modernization, and the Spectral Folk." *Modernism, Inc.: Body, Memory, Capital*. Eds. Jani Scandura and Michael Thurston. New York: New York University Press, 2001. 151–70.

North, Michael. *The Dialect of Modernism: Race, Language, and Twentieth-Century Literature*. New York: Oxford University Press, 1994.

Nussbaum, Martha. "Patriotism and Cosmopolitanism." *For Love of Country: Debating the Limits of Patriotism*. Ed. Joshua Cohen. Boston: Beacon, 1996. 3–15.

O'Brien, C. C. "Cosmopolitanism in Georgia Douglas Johnson's Anti-Lynching Literature." *African American Review* 38.4 (Winter 2004): 571–87.

O'Daniel, Therman B., ed. *Jean Toomer: A Critical Evaluation*. Washington D.C.: Howard University Press, 1988.

Olmsted, Jane. "Black Moves, White Ways, Every Body's Blues: Orphic Power in Langston Hughes's *The Ways of White Folks*." *Black Orpheus: Music in African American Fiction from the Harlem Renaissance to Toni Morrison*. Ed. Saadi A. Simawe. New York: Garland, 2000. 65–89.

Omi, Michael and Howard Winant. *Racial Formation in the United States: From the 1960s to the 1990s*. 2nd ed. New York: Routledge, 1994.

Patterson, Anita. "Jazz, Realism, and the Modernist Lyric: The Poetry of Langston Hughes." *Modern Language Quarterly* 61.4 (Dec. 2000): 651–82.

Peckham, Joel B. "Jean Toomer's Cane: Self as Montage and the Drive toward Integration." *American Literature* 72 (2000): 275–90.

Pereira, Malin. *Rita Dove's Cosmopolitanism*. Urbana: University of Illinois Press, 2003.

Pfeiffer, Kathleen Anne. "All the Difference: Race Passing and American Individualism." Ph.D. diss., Brandeis University, 1995.

———. "The Limits of Identity in Jessie Fauset's *Plum Bun*." *Legacy* 18.1 (2001) 79–93.

Pinsker, Sanford. "Albert Murray: The Black Intellectuals' Maverick Patriarch." *Virginia Quarterly Review* 72.4 (Autumn 1996): 678–84.

Porter, Horace A. *Jazz Country: Ralph Ellison in America*. Iowa City: University of Iowa Press, 2001.

Posnock, Ross. *Color and Culture: Black Writers and the Making of the Modern Intellectual*. Cambridge, M.A.: Harvard University Press, 1998.

———. "The Dream of Deracination: The Uses of Cosmopolitanism." *American Literary History* 12.4 (Winter 2000): 802–18.

Pratt, Mary Louise. "Modernity and Periphery: Towards a Global and Relational Analysis." *Beyond Dichotomies: Histories, Identities, Cultures, and the Challenge of Globalization*. Ed. Elisabeth Mudimbe-boyi. Albany: State University of New York Press, 2002. 21–48.

Rampersad, Arnold. "The Legacy of Black Intellectuals." *Raritan* 18.4 (Spring 1999): 116–22.

———. *The Life of Langston Hughes: Volume I: 1902–1941: I, Too, Sing America*. 2nd edition. New York: Oxford University Press, 2002.

Ramsey, William M. "Jean Toomer's Eternal South." *Southern Literary Journal* 36.1 (Fall 2003): 74–89.

Rand, Lizabeth A. "'I Am I': Jean Toomer's Vision beyond *Cane*." *CLA Journal* 44.1 (Sept. 2000): 43–64.

Richards, Phillip M. *Black Heart: The Moral Life of Recent African American Letters*. New York: Peter Lang, 2006.

Robotham, Don. "Cosmopolitanism and Planetary Humanism: The Strategic Universalism of Paul Gilroy." *South Atlantic Quarterly* 104.3 (Summer 2005): 561–82.

Rowe, John Carlos. "Henry James in a New Century." *A Companion to American Fiction, 1865–1914*. Eds. Robert Paul Lamb and G. R. Thompson. Malden, M.A.: Blackwell, 2005. 518–35.

Rueschmann, Eva. "Sister Bonds: Intersections of Family and Race in Jessie Redmon Fauset's *Plum Bun* and Dorothy West's *The Living Is Easy*." *The Significance of*

Sibling Relationships in Literature. Eds. JoAnna Stephens Mink and Janet Doubler Ward. Bowling Green, O.H.: Popular Press, 1992. 120–31.

Russell, Mariann. "Langston Hughes and Melvin Tolson: Blues People." *The Furious Flowering of African American Poetry*. Ed. Joanne V. Gabbin. Charlottesville: University Press of Virginia, 1999. 38–46.

Salaam, Kalamu Ya. "Langston Hughes: A Supreme Poet." *The Furious Flowering of African American Poetry*. Ed. Joanne V. Gabbin. Charlottesville: University Press of Virginia, 1999. 17–24.

Sato, Hiroko. "Under the Harlem Shadow: A Study of Jessie Fauset." *Remembering the Harlem Renaissance*. Ed. Cary D. Wintz. New York: Garland, 1996. 261–87.

Scherman, Tony. "The Omni-American." *American Heritage* 47.5 (Sept. 1996): 68–77.

Schor, Naomi. "French Feminism Is a Universalism." *Differences* 7:1 (Spring 1995): 13–47.

Schultz, Elizabeth. "Natural and Unnatural Circumstances in Langston Hughes' *Not without Laughter*." *Callaloo* 25.4 (Fall 2002): 1177–187.

Schwartzman, Myron. "A Bearden-Murray Interplay: One Last Time." *Callaloo* 36 (Summer 1988): 410–15.

Scott, Jonathan. "Advanced, Repressed, and Popular: Langston Hughes During the Cold War." *College Literature* 3.2 (Spring 2006): 30–51.

Scruggs, Charles. "Jean Toomer and Kenneth Burke and the Persistence of the Past." *American Literary History* 13.1 (Spring 2001): 41–66.

———. "The Mark of Cain and the Redemption of Art." *American Literature* 44 (May 1972): 276–91.

———. "'My Chosen World': Jean Toomer's Articles in *The New York Call*." *Arizona Quarterly* 51.2 (Summer 1995): 103–26.

———. "The Reluctant Witness: What Jean Toomer Remembered from Winesburg, Ohio." *Studies in American Fiction* 28.1 (Spring 2000): 77–100.

Scruggs, Charles and Lee Vandemarr. *Jean Toomer and the Terrors of American History*. Philadelphia: University of Pennsylvania Press, 1998.

Siebers, Tobin. "The Ethics of Anti-Ethnocentrism." *Michigan Quarterly Review* 32 (Winter 1993): 41–70.

Sims, Janet L. "Jessie Redmon Fauset (1885–1961): A Selected Annotated Bibliography." *Black American Literature Forum* 14.4 (Winter 1980): 147–52.

Sisney, Mary F. "The View from the Outside: Black Novels of Manners." *The Critical Response to Gloria Naylor*. Ed. Sharon Felton and Michelle C. Loris. Westport, C.T.: Greenwood, 1997. 63–75.

Smethurst, James. "The Adventures of a Social Poet: Langston Hughes from the Popular Front." *A Historical Guide to Langston Hughes*. Ed. Steven C. Tracy. New York: Oxford University Press, 2004. 141–68.

———. "'Don't Say Goodbye to the Porkpie Hat': Langston Hughes, the Left, and the Black Arts Movement." *Callaloo* 25.4 (Fall 2002): 1225–236.

Smith, Raymond. "Langston Hughes: Evolution of the Poetic Persona." *Langston Hughes: Critical Perspectives Past and Present*. Eds. Henry Louis Gates, Jr. and K. A. Appiah. New York: Amistad, 1993. 120–34.

Solard, Alain. "Myth and Narrative Fiction in *Cane:* 'Blood-Burning Moon.'" *Callaloo* 8 (Fall 1985): 551–62

Sollors, Werner. *Beyond Ethnicity: Consent and Descent in American Culture.* New York: Oxford University Press, 1986.

———. "Jean Toomer's *Cane:* Modernism and Race in Interwar America." *Jean Toomer and the Harlem Renaissance.* Eds. Geneviève Fabre and Michel Feith. New Brunswick, N.J.: Rutgers University Press, 2001. 18–37.

———. *Neither Black nor White yet Both: Thematic Explorations of Interracial Literature.* New York: Oxford University Press, 1997.

Somerville, Siobhan B. *Queering the Color Line: Race and the Invention of Homosexuality in American Culture.* Durham: Duke University Press, 2000.

Soto, Isabel. "Boundaries Transgressed: Modernism and Miscegenation in Langston Hughes's 'Red-Headed Baby.'" *Atlantic Studies* 3.1 (Apr. 2006): 97–110.

Soto, Michael. "Jean Toomer and Horace Liveright; or a New Negro Gets 'into the Swing of It.'" *Jean Toomer and the Harlem Renaissance.* Ed. Geneviève Fabre and Michel Feith. New Brunswick, N.J.: Rutgers University Press, 2001. 162–87.

Stanton, Domna C. "Presidential Address 2005: On Rooted Cosmopolitanism." *PMLA* 121.3 (May 2006): 627–40.

Sten, Christopher. "Melville's Cosmopolitanism: A Map for Living in a (Post-) Colonialist World." *Melville 'Among the Nations.'* Eds. Sanford E. Marovitz and A. C. Christodoulou. Kent, O.H.: Kent State University Press, 2001. 38–48.

Stetz, Margaret D. "Jessie Fauset's Fiction: Reconsidering Race and Revising Aestheticism." *Literature and Racial Ambiguity.* Eds. Teresa Hubel and Neil Brooks. Amsterdam: Rodopi, 2002. 253–70.

Sundquist, Eric J. "Who Was Langston Hughes?" *Commentary* 102.6 (Dec. 1996): 55–59.

Sylvander, Carolyn Wedin. *Jessie Redmon Fauset, Black American Writer.* Troy, N.Y.: Whitston, 1981.

Tate, Claudia. *Psychoanalysis and Black Novels: Desire and the Protocols of Race.* New York: Oxford University Press, 1998.

Terris, Daniel. "Waldo Frank, Jean Toomer, and the Critique of Racial Voyeurism." *Race and the Modern Artist.* Eds. Heather Hathaway, Josef Jarab, and Jeffrey Melnick. Oxford: Oxford University Press, 2003. 92–114.

Thomas, H. Nigel. "Patronage and the Writing of Langston Hughes's *Not Without Laughter:* A Paradoxical Case." *CLA Journal* 42.1 (Sept. 1998): 48–70.

Todorov, Tzvetan. *On Human Diversity: Nationalism, Racism, and Exoticism in French Thought.* Trans. Catherine Porter. Cambridge, M.A.: Harvard University Press, 1993.

Tomlinson, Susan. "'An Unwonted Coquetry': The Commercial Seductions of Jessie Fauset's *The Chinaberry Tree.*" *Middlebrow Moderns: Popular American Women Writers of the 1920s.* Eds. Lisa Botshon and Meredith Goldsmith. Boston: Northeastern University Press, 2003. 227–43.

———. "Vision to Visionary: The New Negro Woman as Cultural Worker in Jessie Redmon Fauset's *Plum Bun.*" *Legacy* 19.1 (2002): 90–97.

Tracy, Steven C. "Langston Hughes and Afro-American Vernacular Music." *A Historical Guide to Langston Hughes.* Ed. Steven C. Tracy. Oxford, England: Oxford University Press, 2004. 85–118.

Turner, Bryan S. "Cosmopolitan Virtue, Globalization and Patriotism." *Theory, Culture & Society* 19:1–2 (Feb.-Apr. 2002): 45–63.

Turner, Darwin T. *In a Minor Chord: Three Afro-American Writers and Their Search for Identity.* Carbondale: Southern Illinois University Press, 1971.

Venn, Couze. "Altered States: Post-Enlightenment Cosmopolitanism and Transmodern Socialities." *Theory, Culture & Society* 19:1–2 (Feb-Apr. 2002): 65–80.

Waldron, Jeremy. "Minority Cultures and the Cosmopolitan Alternative." *The Rights of Minority Cultures.* Ed. Will Kymlicka. New York: Oxford University Press, 1995.

Walkowitz, Rebecca L. *Cosmopolitan Style: Modernism Beyond the Nation.* New York: Columbia University Press, 2006.

———. "Shakespeare in Harlem: The Norton Anthology, 'Propaganda,' Langston Hughes." *Modern Language Quarterly* 60.4 (Dec. 1999): 495–519.

Wall, Cheryl A. *Women of the Harlem Renaissance.* Bloomington: Indiana University Press, 1995.

Webb, Jeff. "Literature and Lynching: Identity in Jean Toomer's *Cane.*" *ELH* 67 (2000): 205–28.

West, Cornel. *Keeping Faith: Philosophy and Race in America.* New York: Routledge, 1993.

West, Cornel and Henry Louis Gates, Jr. *The Future of the Race.* New York: Knopf, 1996.

Westover, Jeffrey W. "Africa/America: Fragmentation and Diaspora in the Work of Langston Hughes." *Callaloo* 25.4 (Fall 2002): 1207–23.

———. *The Colonial Moment: Discoveries and Settlements in Modern American Poetry.* DeKalb: Northern Illinois University Press, 2004.

Whalan, Mark. "Jean Toomer, Race and Technology." *Journal of American Studies* 36 (Dec. 2002): 459–72.

———. "'Taking Myself in Hand': Jean Toomer and Physical Culture." *Modernism/Modernity* 10.4 (Nov. 2003): 597–615.

Whyde, Janet M. "Mediating Forms: Narrating the Body in Jean Toomer's *Cane.*" *Southern Literary Journal* 26.1 (Fall 1993): 42–53.

Williams, Diana I. "Building the New Race: Jean Toomer's Eugenic Aesthetic." *Jean Toomer and the Harlem Renaissance.* Ed. Geneviève Fabre and Michel Feith. New Brunswick, N.J.: Rutgers University Press, 2001. 188–201.

Williamson, Joel. *Miscegenation and Mulattoes in the United States.* New York: Free Press, 1980.

Woodson, Jon. *To Make a New Race: Gurdjieff, Toomer, and the Harlem Renaissance.* Jackson, M.S.: University Press of Mississippi, 1999.

Zackodnik, Teresa. "Passing Transgressions and Authentic Identity in Jessie Fauset's *Plum Bun* and Nella Larsen's *Passing.*" *Literature and Racial Ambiguity.* Eds. Teresa Hubel and Neil Brooks. Amsterdam: Rodopi, 2002. 45–69.

Zamir, Shamoon. *Dark Voices: W. E. B. Du Bois and American Thought, 1888–1903.* Chicago: University of Chicago Press, 1995.

Zerilli, Linda M. G. "This Universalism Which Is Not One." *diacritics* 28.2 (1998): 3–20.

Index

I

J

K

L

M

N

For Product Safety Concerns and Information please contact our EU representative GPSR@taylorandfrancis.com Taylor & Francis Verlag GmbH, Kaufingerstraße 24, 80331 München, Germany

Printed and bound by CPI Group (UK) Ltd, Croydon, CR0 4YY

08/06/2025

01897001-0013